An Introduction to the *Use* of the *Rapier*

William E. Wilson

Art of Defence

Introduction to the *Use* of the *Rapier*

Published by

Chivalry Bookshelf

http://www.chivalrybookshelf.com

(866)-268-1495

ISBN: 1-891-448-18-8

SUBJECTS

Fencing | Martial Arts | History--Italy

Wilson, William E. (1956 -)

Design by Brian R. Price

Printed in China

Publisher: *Chivalry Bookshelf*, Union City, CA.

Table of Contents

Chapter I -- Introduction........1
Chapter II -- Of Honor & Honorable Quarrels........7
Judicial Combats........8
Private Duels........11
Dueling Culture........12
Chapter III -- The Ring of Steel........19
Defining the Rapier........19
The Medieval Sword........21
The Tuck........24
The Sidesword........24
The Rapier........25
Chapter IV -- Mystery of the Sidesword........40
Chapter V -- The True Fight - Learning the Rapier........53
Stances & Foot Movement........54
The Guards........64
Basic Defense........72
Preparing for Combat........83
Attacks with the Single Rapier........85
Chapter VI -- Fighting Double........133
Rapier & Dagger........133
Rapier & Cloak........140
Rapier & Buckler........143
Case of Rapiers........145
Chapter VII - Further Study........151
Armoring........151
Teaching Historical Fencing........152
Appendix A -- Sample Lesson Plan........155
Appendix B -- An Article on the Rapier........158
Appendix C -- Suppliers........160

Glossary........161
Bibliography........162
Index........165

)pposite: A duel engraving by P. Jazet,
'rom *L'Art du Duel*, 1895

This work is dedicated to my Lady, for without her I would not have the inspiration to complete such a task.

I would like to thank the following people for their inspiration and help in this endeavor:

Rhys Wilson, Tieg Wilson, Gary Chelak, Roger Siggs, Gary McClellan, Margo Folsom, Richard Rouse, Giovanni Rapisardi, Patri Pugliese, Jared Kirby, Maitre Adam Crown, Maestro Andrea Lupo-Sinclair, Maestro Ramon Martinez, Maestra Jeanette Acosta-Martinez, Master Paul Macdonald, Greg Mele and Brian Price.

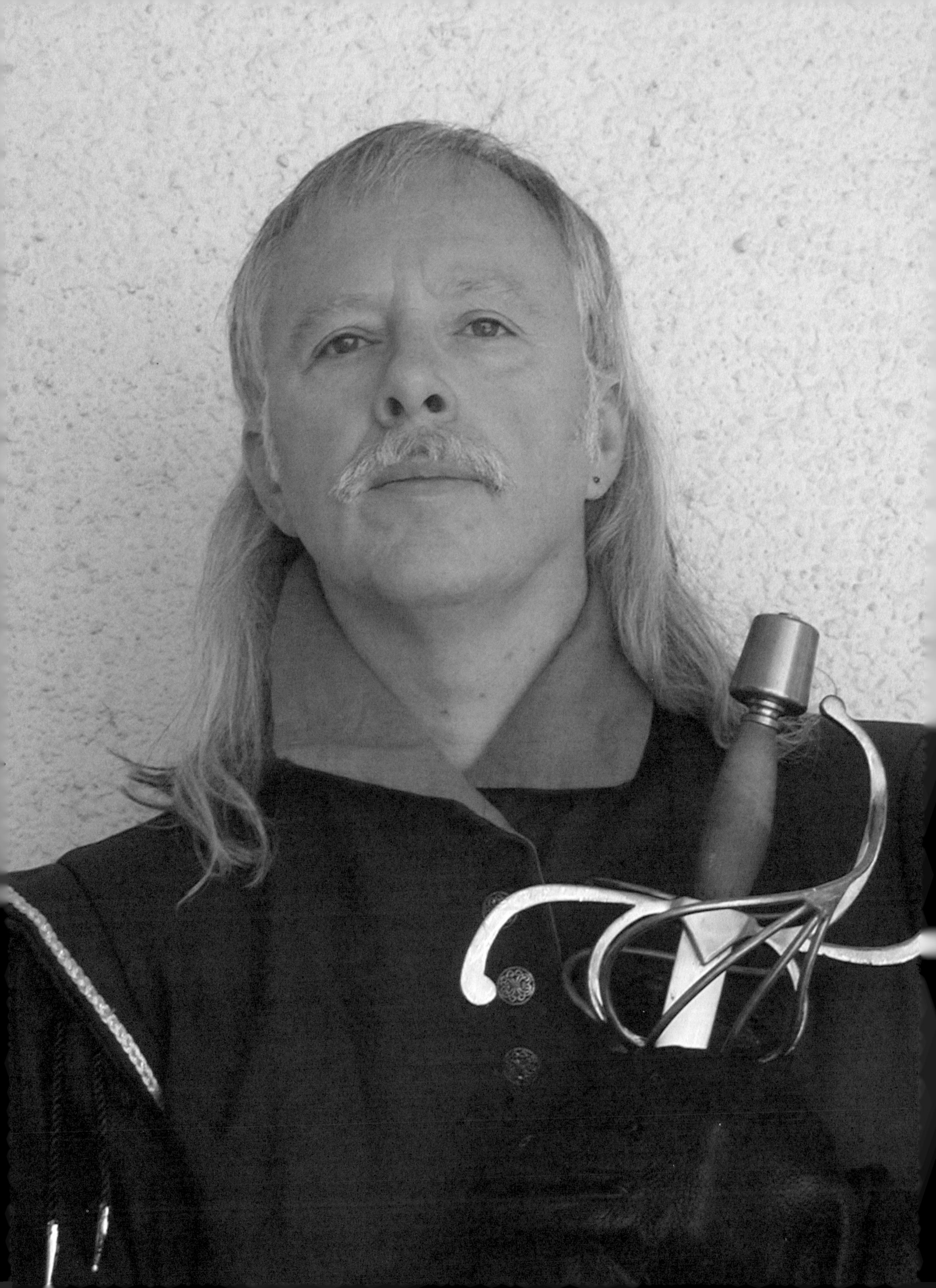

William E. Wilson is the President of the Tattershall School of Defence and is the advisor and coach for the fencing club at Northern Arizona University. Mr. Wilson is on the Board of Directors for the Association of Historical Fencing and is also on the advisory board for Swordplay Symposium International (SSI).

At the Academy for European Medieval Martial Arts (AEMMA) Workshop held in Toronto during October 2000 Mr. Wilson was accepted as a Master of Arms candidate by the International Master of Arms Federation (IMAF). On the 31st of January 2002 he was admitted as an Acknowledged Instructor in Italian Rapier and Sidesword by the IMAF.

Mr. Wilson began his study of fencing under Master Bella from Canada and Mr. Silverberg in Buffalo, New York in 1974. He has since received instruction from other Masters and instructors including Dr. Rita Ashcroft of Northern Arizona University.

In the Society for Creative Anachronism (SCA) he is known as Barwn Master Gwylym ab Owain, OL, OP and is the premier member of the Order of the White Scarf in Atenveldt, the highest award for fencing in the Kingdom.

Mr. Wilson works as an applied anthropologist at Northern Arizona University. In the Western martial arts community he teaches at various seminars and has been instrumental in providing historical fencing information on the World Wide Web, including the translation of a number of texts from the original Italian.

Mr. Wilson specializes in teaching beginners classical fencing foil, epee and saber. He teaches beginning and advanced students the art of defence with rapier and sidesword. He also teaches beginning longsword and backsword.

Tattershall
School of Defence

The Tattershall School of Defense (TSD) is a nonprofit corporation founded tomeet the needs of the historically-oriented fencing community.

The TSD exists to teach, preserve and support the art of historical fencing (from the 15th, 16th and 17th centuries) as well as the classical period. In order to accomplish this, the TSD plans to organize seminars, lectures, workshops and similar programs, and to disseminate knowledge and basic factual material to its membership.

Members and instructors of the Tattershall School are also encouraged to help and support other institutions such as the AHF and SSI.

The TSD strives to raise public awareness by hosting exhibitions and demonstrations.

Along with the teaching of the mechanical aspects of historical fencing, The Tatershall School will promote the study of philosophical and social aspects of the historical and classical fencing eras.

Contact the school through its website:

http://www.chivalrybookshelf.com/tattershall/go.html

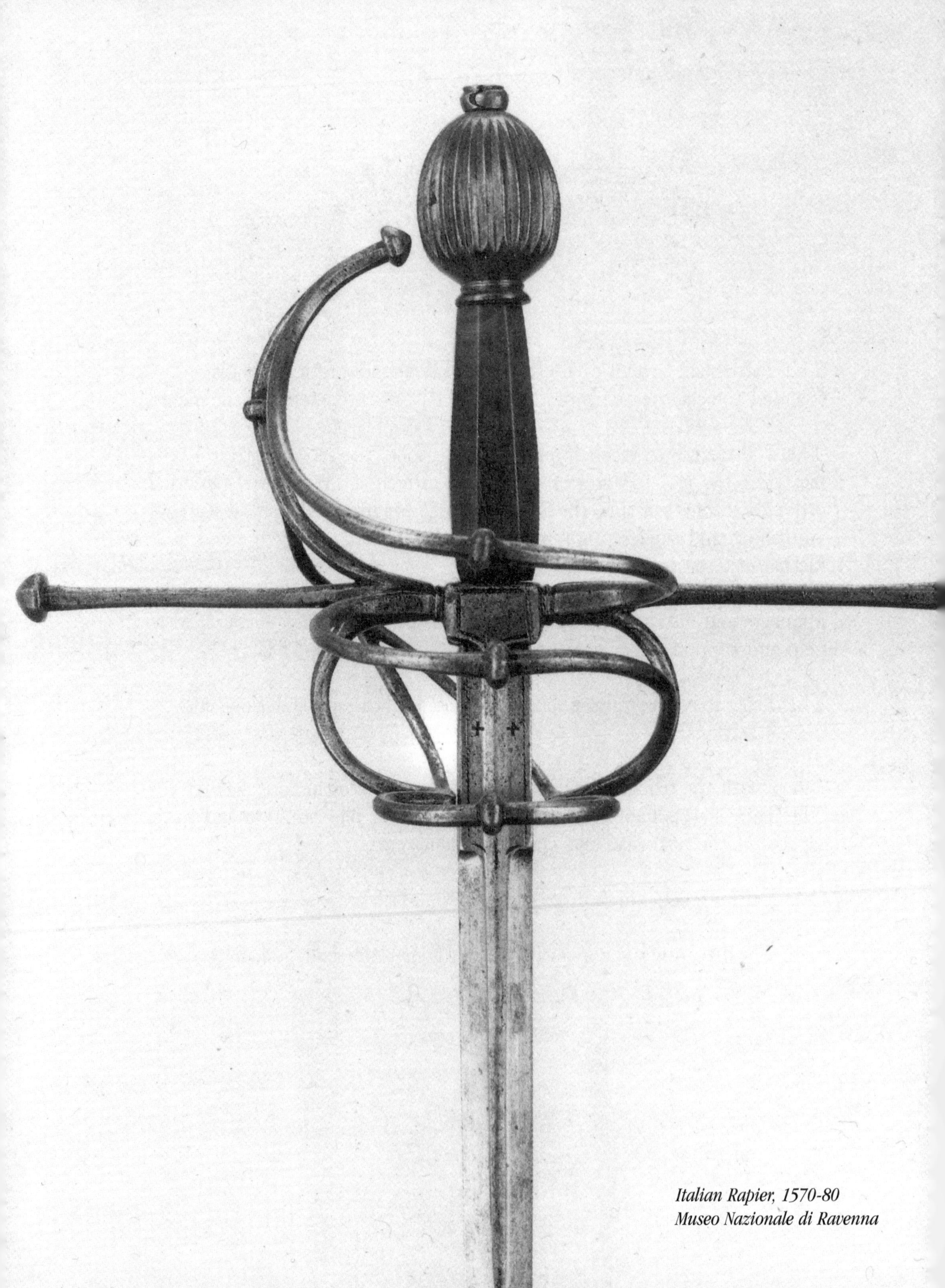

Italian Rapier, 1570-80
Museo Nazionale di Ravenna

Introduction

"A *Discourse* most necessarie for all Gentlemen that have in regarde their *honours* touching the giving and receiving of the *Lie*, whereupon the *Duello* & the *Combats* in divers sortes doth insue and many other inconveniences, for lack only of the true knowledge of *honor*, and the contrarie: and the right understanding of wordes, which heere is plainly set downe, beginning thus..."[1]

Vincentio Saviolo, 1595

This book offers historical fencing students a practical approach to fighting in an early 17th c. Italian style with the rapier. The Italian gentleman of the 16th and 17th centuries relied upon his sword not only for the defense of his reputation and honor, but for his very life. He might be called upon to use his sword in a variety of contexts: to defend himself on the road or in the street, as a willing participant or engaged bystander in a brawl, or if he found himself involved in a public or private duel.

In all cases, his knowledge of fencing—"de-fence"— provided the critical tools upon which his life depended. The study of arms was thus as much a serious affair for civilians as it was for military men. Those possessing the advantage of technique, earned through arduous practice in the salle d'armes under the tutelage of a renowned master, commanded a significant advantage not only upon the field or in the close, but in social contexts as well. A man skilled with edge and point was one not to be trifled with; he was a man whose security was enhanced by an art that sought to refine and develop swordsmanship into an almost mystical "perfect," unbeatable style.

Most students who come to the study of the sword do so through modern fencing; however, modern fencing is not rapier fencing and to fight with the rapier you must study it in context. Modern fencing weapons are lightweight sports equipment that simply do not and cannot approximate the rapier. Further, the rules of modern fencing are designed so that only a light touch with the sword is required to score a point. Rapiers were made to kill people, plain and simple. The Art of Fencing with a rapier is the study of the Science of Fencing not only for sport, but to be victorious in a duel. You must study not only its form (i.e. the sword itself) but also the historical techniques to fully appreciate the mechanics of the weapon and its use.

This manual focuses on the use of the Renaissance civilian sword that English speakers call the *rapier*. Yet it is crucially important to know that combat with the rapier did not arise full-blown out of obscurity, but flowed from the teachings and traditions of centuries of fencing masters. As the rising middle class found its niche in Renaissance society the use of the sword to settle personal disputes rose, and masters developed and taught systems of fencing that could be specifically employed in civilian combat. For this same reason, this book also seeks to briefly explain the social and philosophical context out of which this lethal art was born. Just as you cannot study rapier fencing without understanding the rapier, you cannot understand the rapier itself without understanding the history and philosophy of both the duel and sword combat of the Renaissance. To better clarify this, I will also provide a brief discussion of the evolution of the rapier and the duel to illustrate how the sword and the method of its use developed and changed over time.

The civilian Art of Defence (fencing)[2] arose during the decline in the use of heavy armour and weapons at the close of the Middle Ages. Egerton Castle's monumental *Schools and Masters of Fence* (1885) promoted a philosophy that the knight or noble warrior was an unschooled combatant who relied solely on strength to win the day.[3]

> " – two very distinct schools of fighting existed side by side with very little in common. One was that of the noble warrior who cultivated his battering power in the lists and tournaments and the accuracy of his eye by tilting at the ring or quintain, but who otherwise learned little of what would avail him were he deprived of his protecting armor. Indeed, the chivalrous science had anything but a retarding effect on the science of fence."

Castle went on to note that without the benefit of armor, ruffians and middle class gentlemen relied more on their strength and agility than skill to win the day. Over time, while noblemen practiced at the barriers, keeping alive the use of sword, lance and heavy armor, the burgesses and artisans of the rising middle class — who also owned weapons, albeit of a less "noble" kind — learned their skill from traveling masters. With the onset of the Age of Enlightenment and the newfound independence of many towns and cities, schools of defense were founded where those possessing the pluck, skill and money could take schooling in the Art of Fence. Castle argued that this Art was born of whole cloth in the 16th century, and then steadily evolved and refined itself over the next three centuries.

Castle's views were consistent with those of his fellows, and remained the foundation for the accepted "history" of fencing to the present day.[4] Modern scholarship[5] has brought to light an entire tradition of fencing manuals from the late Middle Ages, detailing both armored and civilian combat.[6] The Art of Fence of the Renaissance was certainly a refinement and new development in the history of personal combat, but it did not develop on its own, rather evolving from a long line of masters dating back centuries.[7]

In *The Martial Arts of Renaissance Europe,* Sydney Anglo details the foundation of fencing schools as well as fencing masters throughout Europe. He notes that in 1220 Walter de Strewton was charged with murder and ordered to take part in a trial by combat. After he was released on bail he took lessons in combat and later won the trial. Anglo notes, "throughout the Middle Ages and the Renaissance masters of arms enjoyed an equivocal position in European society. Their skills were recognized and utilized, but the kind of reckless violence engendered in many pupils by their teaching earned them an unsavory reputation."[8]

One proof of the abundance of fencing schools lies in the laws on the books prohibiting said schools or in the foundation of fencing academies. The following is a partial list:

- 1285 – London – fencing instruction prohibited on pain of imprisonment
- 1386 – Heidelberg – Students forbidden to attend schools of arms
- 1415 – Heidelberg – Above prohibition repeated by the Rector
- 1496 – London – Playing at sword and buckler illegal without royal license
- 1554 – Paris – Ordinance prohibits masters of fence
- 1572 – London – Humphrey Gilbert proposes an academy for London which would have a dispensation from the "Statute of Rogues"
- 1575 – Paris – 1554 ordinance repeated[9]

Even with these prohibitions, fencing schools still flourished throughout Europe. Germany saw the first "licensed" fighting-fraternity, when Frederick III granted a royal charter to the masters of Nuremberg on 10 August 1487. This charter legitimized the Marxbrüder ("Brotherhood of St. Mark") who promoted and taught fencing with a wide variety of weapons, and may have existed over a century earlier.[10] Records of a process of "licensing" fencing masters in France and Spain also date from roughly the same period.[11] In 1540 the King of England signed a bill to establish a commission to investigate fencing masters. At the same time, a royal charter had been given to the London Masters of Defence to teach fencing.[12]

By the 16th century, fencing masters were publicly teaching students the Art of Defence. Achille Marozzo in his *Arte dell'Armi* states:

> "I also advise you that as you start teaching someone, you should not begin with something difficult, since that would seem too hard to them; doing so would turn them away and would cause them to not learn as eagerly as those who start with something more gradual. Anyway, I will expand your mind later. Now, I want to start with the first part of said third assault. However, I wish to give you a lesson about teaching.
>
> "Please note that if you wish to teach, I advise you not to teach all the painstaking details of the third assault in public, in order to avoid others trying to copy it. In other words, you should make sure that others do not see your principles. Also, you should avoid this for another reason. If you teach them such play and close techniques, you cannot step to the next level since there is a difference between wide and close play. Besides, a beginner would be confused by all the half-swording techniques. Therefore, they would not be satisfied, but would always expect you to move on to something better, not appreciating the good instruction you are giving. It is for these reasons that you should

start with other things. That is, teach them the fundamental things; once they have learned the said fundamentals, I want you to give them the principles of this third assault. In this manner, you will make them happy. Please know that I exhort you to teach these things so that you do not forget them; also, sometimes you will have to re-read this book so that you will not forget. Do as the proverb says: he who pays well learns well, and he who pays poorly learns poorly. Therefore, teach well those who pay well, because you will conscientiously repay them. It is a great sin of the soul not to teach well those who pay their debt to their teacher. This is equally true for the rich and for the poor, since a 'ducato '[14] is worth to a poor man what two are worth to a rich one."[15]

Producing a fencing manual targeted at a larger audience became a real possibility with the advent of the printing press. By the end of the 16th c. numerous masters had published manuals on the use of the sword and other weapons; more will be given on these masters in the appendices.

With the rise of civilian combats, fundamental changes in fighting strategy were formulated. Focus became solely upon the sword, used with small side arms such as the dagger or buckler, or used alone. The use of the point, already prominent in late medieval swordsmanship, became the dominant form of attack. Thus, the use of the rapier became the primary weapon used to settle personal disputes.[16]

The earliest and most famous schools[17] of rapier fencing (after which all other schools were patterned) came from Spain and Italy. Hieronimo de Caranza and his student Don Luys Pacheco de Narvaez founded the Spanish School in the late 16th century, which lasted for centuries and is today taught by Maestro Ramon Martinez.[18] In Italy, Nepo Bardi founded a school in Bolgna in 1413, producing such renowned masters as Antonio Manciolino, Achille Marozzo and Giovanni Dall'Agocchie.[19] While the Italians believed that simplification led to the perfection of Fence, the Spanish moved towards making fencing what many call a "mysterious science."[20] Spanish masters were required to know geometry and natural philosophy.[21] Castle noted "as the title leads one to anticipate, there is as much of the author's ethical and theological theories in this celebrated work as of swordsmanship proper."[22]

Writers such as Castle did not believe that the early masters taught a codified method of fencing, instead teaching "tricks" they had learned throughout their lives. In my reading and study of early manuals written by masters such as Fiore dei Liberi, Achille Marozzo, Giovanni Dall'Agocchie and others, I cannot agree. Fiore dei Liberi's early 15th c. treatise on combat encompasses a complete, internally consistent, system that ranges from unarmed,

Hear followeth an indenture of covenants made between the four anciant maisters of the noble science of Defense Withinthe Citye of London

This Indenture made the last daye of October In the Therd yeare of the raigne of our soveraigne Lorde Kinge Edward the sixte by the grace of God &cetera Betweene Willyam Hunt on thone partye, R. G. on the second partie and W. B. on the therd partie beinge anciente maisters of the noble science of Defence With in the citie of London WITNESETH that the sayde parties [have] Covenented condiscended and agreed to gether in manner and forme followinge That is to saye every of the same parties covenanteth and grantith, to and With the other parties, that neither of saide parties shall from henceforth set forth any of their schollers prizes without the consent and agrement of all saide parties AND allso that none of their schollers shall play his provosts prize within vij years after his schollers prize ALLSO the saide parties do likewyese covenaunte and graunt everye of them with the other that none of them shall permitt or suffer anny of their saide schollers after [he hath] playd his Provosts prize, to playe their maisters prize within five yeares after their Provosts prize MOREOVER the same parties ar consented and agreed together That everye of them shall kepe one Boxe Whearin he shall put for every scholler that he hath (or from hence forth shall have) ijd towards the mayntenance of necessaries beloninge to the saide science And every of them shall kepe a Juste and true boke of the monye in the sayde boxes severally And every of the same parties shall bringe att two sundry tymes in the yeare, all the money in theire severall boxes gatherd, To soch a place as the maister...[13]

--Sloan MS. 2530, Henry VIII
--1590

to unarmored and armored combat with the arming sword, longsword and polearms.[23] Marozzo, Manciolino and others also taught codified systems and by the time of Camillo Agrippa (circa 1550) a "scientific" approach to fencing was beginning to be established.[24] Quantitative and geometric analysis was applied to practically every endeavor and all aspects of life, but their impact upon fencing manuals and the study of fencing seems to have been particularly powerful.

Achille Marozzo (early 16th c.) is the first Italian writer of note on the art of civilian combat with the sword.[25] His manual was published in five known editions from 1536 to 1615. Following Marozzo, Camillo Agrippa, Giacomo di Grassi, and others of the time taught more practical applications of fence and focused less on philosophy. The masters of this period (from the mid 16th century to the start of the 17th century) also began to emphasize the thrust as the prevalent mode of attack for civilian combat.[26] Prior to this cuts and thrusts were used equally.[27]

Vigianni was another late 16th century master, who professed the thrust superior to the cut. He simplified Marozzo's guards and terminology, and minutely classified many thrusts. He is also attributed with introducing the lunge.

During this period the Germans were also considered great fencing masters. They favored the old longsword and the dusak,[28] continuing the martial tradition traced to Johannes Liechtenauer in the late 14th century. The Germans imported the early cut-and-thrust rapier, and then native masters adapted it to their own sensibilities as detailed in Joachim Meyer's massive 1570 fencing manual.[29]

Outside of Germany, until the 16th century, Italian and Spanish masters were the principle fencing instructors. As the use of the rapier spread from Spain and Italy across Europe, Italian masters moved to England, the Low Countries, and France to teach. The French initially sought out Italian masters, as did the English. Henry Sainct Didier is the first known published French author on the Art of Defence (see bibliography). It was generations before the French were considered leaders in the art of fencing. Rocco Bonetti and Vincentio Saviolo were the first known rapier masters teaching in England. Saviolo even published the first fencing manual in English.[30] Giacomo di Grassi's fencing manual was also translated from the original Italian and published in English.[31] "Teachers, the majority Italian, found pupils everywhere."[32] The predominant position of the Italian masters during this period was due in part, perhaps, to not only the quality of the Italian method itself, but that of their fencing books, combined with the popularity of all things "Italianate" in the Renaissance.

By the late 1600's, rapier fencing had established a firm foundation. Many schools existed in Europe and England and masters such as Rocco Bonetti, Vincentio Saviolo, Salvatore Fabris, and Ridolfo Capo Ferro taught in schools and privately.

An illustration of rapier and cloak from Giacomo di Grassi's 1594 His True Art of Defence, *a popular text translated into English from an earlier 1570 Italian manual. Di Grassi's text is straightforward and comprehensible, intended for those who knew little of the art and who perhaps were trying to learn swordsmanship without the aid of a fencing master--no mean task. Yet as di Grassi himself states, victory in a sword-fight is not about what you know, but about what you can do in the heat of combat.*

[1]Vincentio Saviolo. *His Practice.* Book II p 79.

[2]The term *fencing* comes from the word *defence*. Other countries called it various things, *fechten* in Germany and *scherma/schermire* in Italy, for example.

[3]Egerton Castle. *Schools and Masters of Fence.* p 18.

[4]For example, Arthur Wise's highly influential, and lavishly illustrated *Art and History of Personal Combat*, in which he bases his entire position on medieval swordsmanship on Castle, despite including analysis and plates of early 16th century texts that are clearly a continuance of an established tradition, not a new one.

[5]See Sydney Anglo, *The Martial Arts of Renaissance Europe*, (Yale, 2000), Mark Rector, *Medieval Combat* (Greenhill, 2000) and Christian Tobler, *Secrets of Medieval Swordsmanship: Sigmund Ringeck's Commentaries on Liechtenauer's Verse* (Chivalry Bookshelf, 2002).

[6]The full corpus of surviving pre-rapier works is still yet to be determined, but is easily at least two dozen texts. The earliest known fencing treatise is Royal Armouries MS. I.33, depicting German sword and buckler fencing, c.1295 AD. The earliest surviving Italian manuscript is the *Fior di Battaglia* of Fiore dei Liberi da Premariacco (1409). This latter manuscript provides a systematic study of armed and unarmed combat on foot and horseback, and both in and out of armour, little in keeping with Castle's theories.

[7]For example, the use of binds and beats are clearly detailed and defined in Royal Armouries MS. I.33, while the classification of cuts and the basic "Renaissance" footwork of the pass, advance, slope, and compass pace had already been detailed by dei Liberi.

[8]Sydney Anglo. *The Martial Arts of Renaissance Europe.* p 7.

[9]Ibid., Chapter 1.

[10]Ibid., p 9.

[11]Ibid., pp 9 – 11.

[12]Ibid., p 8.

[13]In the original manuscript the *indenture* stops here and seems to be missing a page as a new matter begins on the next page.

[14]A unit of currency from the time period that the book was written.

[15]Achille Marozzo. *Arte dell'Armi.* Chapter 13.

[16]See Kiernan, *Duel in European History*.

[17]That is, national styles.

[18]Maestro Martinez has reconstructed the style from primary source material, and teaches it in New York City and in seminars around the world. For more information, see www.martinez-destreza.com.

[19]Luigi Barbasetti. *Art of the Foil.* p 220.

[20]In reality, the Spanish school is only "mysterious," in the sense that it was aimed at a well-educated student, educated in geometry, so as to be able to understand the system's precise foot and blade work.

[21]Arthur Wise. *The Art and History of Personal Combat.* p 48-51.

[22]Castle. p 97

[23]Fiore dei Liberi, *Fior di Battaglia* (1409)

[24]Sydney Anglo. *Martial Arts of Renaissance Europe.* p 25.

[25]There are earlier manuscripts such as those by Fiore dei Liberi and Filipo Vadi, but they were written for the military class and not for civilians. Also, it is accepted that Manciolino's book on fencing predated Marozzo's. Carl Thimm and Luigi Barbasetti both give an initial publication date of 1517, which Sydney Anglo attributes to a bibliographical error in Thimm's work. Certainly, no such addition has ever been cited elsewhere, and Marozzo's work seems to be contemporary with, not precursor to, Manciolino's.

[26]Achille Marozzo, *Arte dell'Armi.* 1536

[27]There is a long-standing myth of fencing history that prior to the rapier masters, the thrust had been all but ignored since the end of the Roman era. It should be noted, however, that military combat masters such as Liberi, Vadi and others taught the use of the point. In 1409, dei Liberi referred to the thrust as being particularly *"cruel and mortal,"* (*Fior di Battaglia*, 22r) and many of his longsword plays, both in and out of armour, end with the thrust. Filippo Vadi, who closely modeled his work after Fiore's, also esteemed the thrust, *"The thrust in the middle with deceit and sorrow/often clears our sky."* (*Arte gladiatoria dimicandi,* Cap. 5), and advised keeping the point on-line, and making sure that all parries finished with the point in-line with the adversary's breast or face (Cap. 16). A century later, Vadi's advice that the sword should be a "point with two edges," (*Arte gladiatoria dimicandi,* Cap.5) was being repeated, nearly verbatim by di Grassi and Saviolo. However, these early masters clearly felt that the thrust was simply one more element of the swordsman's repetoire, not it's pinnacle. After first extolling its virtues, Vadi is then quite explicit that over-reliance upon the thrust is exceptionally dangerous (Arte gladiatoria dimicandi, Cap. 5). In my study of Marozzo and Manciolino, whose sidesword teachings are the clear predecessors to the rapier I would estimate that between 50 and 80 percent of attacks are by the cut, whereas in the early 17th century, Fabris shows (through his exercises) that over 90 percent of his attacks are thrusts.

[28]The *dusack* was a wooden, "single-edged" weapon, rather like both a flax knife, and a falchion, and was about the length of a man's arm. German fencers used it as a training weapon for all single-handed swords.

[29]Meyer, Joachim, *Gründtliche Bechreibung der Freyen Ritterlichen unnd Adelichen kunst des Fechtens*, Strasbourg, 1570. This work was reprinted in 1600, and as late as 1663.

[30]Vincentio Saviolo. *His Practice.* 1594.

[31]Giacomo di Grassi. *Ragione di Adoprar sicuramente l'Arme.* 1570. *His True Art of Defense.* 1594.

[32]V. G. Kiernan. *The Duel in European History.* p 64.

Frontispiece from Vulson's
Vray Theatre d'Honneur et de Chevalerie

"The reason as I take it, is because that amongst *Knights*, *Captains*, and valiant *Soldiers*, the RAPIER is it which sheweth who are men of armes and of *honor*, and which obtaineth right for those which are wronged: and for this reason it is made with two edges and one point, and being the weapon which ordinarily Noble men, Knights, Gentlemen and Soldiers wear by their side, as being more proper and fit to be worn then other weapons: therefore this is it which must first be learned, especially being so usual to be worn and taught."[1]

—V. Saviolo, c. 1595

While a man of the early 17th century might be caught upon the road or in the city street by either bandits or cutpurses, the formal duel best captures the essence of the Italian fencing masters practice; a curious fact, given that each of them thought it important enough to add injunctions against dueling in their various treatises. But the reality of the time was that the duel—especially in France—was one of the most important places where the Art of Defence would be put to the test, a place where a man's honor and life might both depend upon the hours of drill, instruction, bouting and experience he had added to his natural talents, and his sheer determination to live.

To study the rapier in context we need to examine this curious aspect of Renaissance swordsmanship because use of the sword was far more than a set of techniques; it was integrally bound with a man's sense of sovereignty, his sense of honor. How he applied the techniques laid out by the fencing master would include instructions concerning when and why the skills were to be employed.

Because France was especially important in the history of the duel, it is emphasized in this chapter, but the experience of England and Italy must also be mentioned, as both the Italian masters and the dueling culture that surrounded the Art of Defence in the 16th and 17th centuries infected these places as well.[2]

Owing to problems of modern connotation, we will start with my definition of the word "duel," since I have been unable to find one that is satisfactory:

> "A planned encounter between two or more individuals with equal numbers on each side, resulting in combat where both parties are equally armed; the purpose of which is to settle a point of honor between the parties involved. The duel was strictly organized and the rules of the duel agreed upon before the onset of the combat itself."

Duels were much different than brawls, private battles, jousts or tournaments and took one of two forms: judicial and extra-judicial. The judicial duel was the descendant of the trial by combat of the Middle Ages, which in turn goes back to the Dark Ages. These types of duels were presided over by a sovereign and were formal affairs held in special locales. The masters of the 16th and early 17th centuries were preparing people for the duel or for deadly combat. Saviolo wrote:

> "L. But I praye you of freendship tell me, if a man were to goe into the feelde with some freend of his whome hee would bee loth to kill, should not these mandrittaes be good to wound him, and not put him in danger of his life,

I praye you therefore tell mee your opinion, and how a man in respect of his honour were to use and order himselfe, put the case he would not kill his freend, but would willingly save and keepe him from harme.

"V. I will speake mine opinion of these things which concerne a mans life and honour, and firste I would wish every one which is challenged into the feeld, to consider that he which challengeth him, dooth not require to fight with him as a freend, but as an enemye, and that he is not to thinke any otherwise of his minde but as full of rancor and malice towards him: wherefore when you with weapons in his hand that will neede fight with you, although hee were your freend or kinseman, take him for an enemye, and trust him not, how great a freend or how nigh of kin soever he be, for the inconvenience that may grow therby, is seene in many histories both ancient and moderne."[3]

Judicial Combat

Judicial duels extend back to the Germanic tribes of late Antiquity as an alternative to trial by ordeal, and continued as a common form of settling legal disputes well into the Renaissance.[4]

The general requirements for the design of the field, and the role of the seconds, were largely consistent throughout Europe. The field was an open area, typically a courtyard or open field where there was enough room to hold the combat and also allow for the judges and spectators. Judicial duels were announced and well attended. Each combatant would have a *grandfather* who would be the spokesperson and one or more seconds. The grandfathers would come to the terms of the combat (the grandfathers or seconds helped the primaries decide which weapons were to be used, if any armor were to be worn, time of the combat, etc.) and they would also check for hidden weapons, armor and amulets of protection.[5] The seconds would either fight on the side of, or for, the parties involved. They were also there as both witness and moral support. The duel would typically end when one party had been injured, one or both had been killed, or when the sun had set. At times the Crown would call an early end to the duel without even the spilling of blood.

By the turn of the 14th century, efforts were already being made to curtail trial by combat. King Philip IV (the Fair) issued an edict that outlined four qualifications that must be met to allow a judicial duel:

1. The charge applied to suspicion of a capital crime, such as murder, rape, treason, etc.;
2. The accused have the responsibility to present themselves in court;
3. Minor charges such as theft or robbery were not acceptable for trial by battle;
4. The accuser(s) must present full charges in public court.

Although these general rules were followed, in reality judicial combat remained an accepted legal alternative for both high and

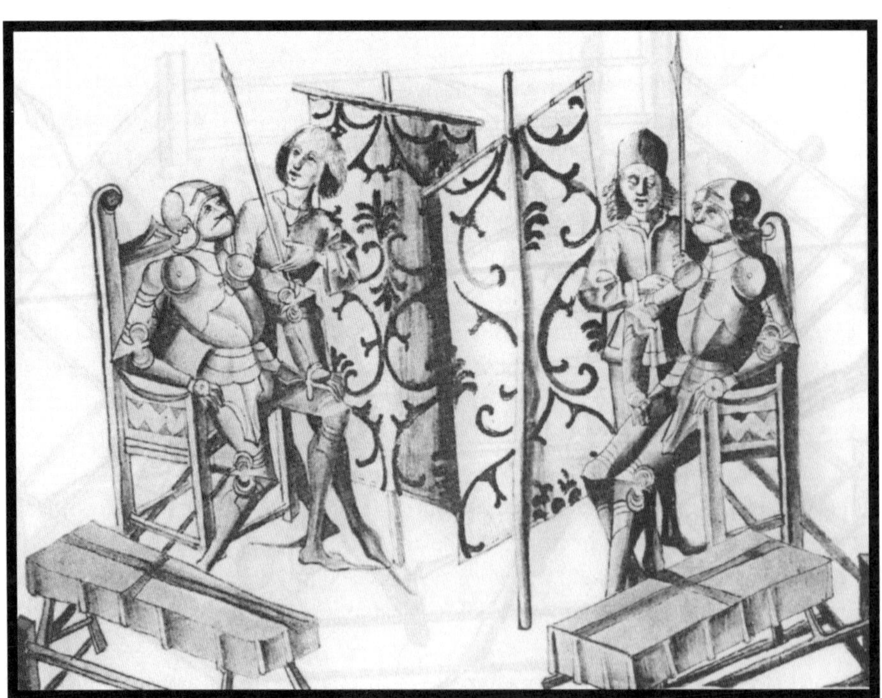

Plate from Hans Talhoffer's 1467 Fechtbuch, depicting a judicual duel. Plate courtesy Greenhill Books.

low crimes throughout Europe. Grounds for trial by combat were usually either civil land and property disputes or criminal cases of treason or felony, each with its own method of execution.[6] A civil judicial duel was entered into as a part of due process in a legal hearing. If a claim was made against another's property, the accuser would offer decision by Assize (a legal inquest), or by battle, either through his or her own person,[7] or that of a champion. If trial by battle was chosen, the court set a date, and the parties were released to prepare for the event.

Civil duels occurred on foot. In the case of the nobility, the duel could be fought in full harness with sword, spear and dagger; the same three weapons first assigned to judicial combats in the law codes of the sixth century.

For commoners, combat was fought with specialized weapons and clothing, specifically called out in the legal codes.

> "...ffirst by the order of the lawe both the parties must at their own charge be armed wthoute any yron or long armoure, their heades bare and bare handed and bare footed, everyone of them having a Baston horned at ech ende of one length. And euie of them must haue a Targett or Sheeld wth iiij corns wthoute any other armoure wherewth th'one may grete thither."[8]

This special dueling equipment was oddly similar throughout Europe,[9] and methods of fighting with these weapons and their variants are discussed at length in surviving medieval German fencing manuscripts.[10]

Criminal cases, particularly between nobles, with their complex familial alliances, were an even graver affair, and a great deal of effort was made to prevent the dispute from coming to arms. In criminal cases it remained the responsibility of the injured party to call out the opponent, in essentially the same process laid out by Philip in 1303. Prior to the 1600s the call or challenge was made by throwing a glove, dagger or favor at the feet of the opponent, combined with an offer of single combat in the lists.[11] After the challenge was given, the Crown (or if the two contenders shared a common overlord, such as a Count or Duke, this would often suffice) would be petitioned for a field, thereby requesting that the dispute be settled by force of arms. The 14th century historian/biographer Jean Froissart details a famous French trial by combat that took place in 1386:[12]

> "About this period, there was much conversation in France respecting a duel which was to be fought, for life or death, at Paris. It had been thus ordered by the parliament of Paris, where the cause, which had lasted a year, had been tried, between a squire called James le Gris and John de Carogne, both of them of the household of Peter, count d'Alençon, and esteemed by him; but more particularly James le Gris, whom he loved above all others, and placed his whole confidence in him. As this duel made so great a noise, many from distant parts, on hearing of it, came to Paris to be spectators. I will relate the cause, as I was then informed.
>
> "It chanced that Sir John de Carogne took it into his head he should gain glory if he undertook a voyage to the Holy Land, having long had an inclination to go thither.
>
> "He took leave of his lord, the count d'Alençon, and of his wife, who was then a young and handsome lady, and left her in his castle, called Argenteil, on the borders of Perche, and began his journey towards the sea-side. The lady remained, with her household, in this castle, living in the most decent manner.
>
> "Now it happened (this is the matter of quarrel) that the devil, by divers and perverse temptations, entered the body of James le Gris, and induced him to commit a crime, for which he afterwards paid. He cast his thoughts on the lady of sir John de Carogne, whom he knew to be residing with her attendants, at the castle of Argenteil.
>
> "One day, therefore, he set out, mounted on the finest horse of the count, and arrived, full gallop, at Argenteil, where he dismounted. The servants made a handsome entertainment for him, because they knew he was a particular friend, and attached to the same lord as their master; and the lady, thinking him no ill, received him with pleasure, led him to her apartment, and shewed him many of her works. James, fully intent to accomplish his wickedness, begged of her to conduct him to the dungeon, for that his visit was partly to examine it. The lady instantly complied, and led him thither; for, as she had the utmost confidence in his honour, she was not accompanied by valet or chambermaid. As soon as they had entered the dungeon, James le Gris fastened the door unnoticed by the lady, who was before him, thinking it might have been the work of the wind, as he gave her to understand. When they were thus alone, James embraced her, and she discovered what his intentions were: the lady was much astonished, and would willingly have escaped had she been able, but the door was fastened; and James, who was a strong man, held her tight in his arms, and flung her down on the floor, and had his will of her."

Sir John returns and his wife tells him of James le Gris' assault. The knight appeals to his overlord, the Count d'Alencon for the right to challenge le Gris to single combat. An inquest is held, and Lady Corogne gives here testimony in front of the squire. He in turn denies the charges, claiming that witness would place him at home in bed that evening, and as that meant he would have ridden nearly seventy miles in one day her charges were impossible. The count tells Lady Corogne she must have dreamt the entire assault, and orders her to not further defame the squire further. But Sir John de Corogne has other ideas.

The knight, being a man of courage, and believing what his wife has told him, will not submit to this, but goes to Paris and appeals to parliament. The parliament summoned James le Gris, who replies, and gives pledges to obey whatever judgment the parliament should give.

> "The cause lasted upwards of a year, and they could not any way compromise it, for the knight was positive, from his wife's information, of the fact, and declared, that since it was now so public, he would pursue it until death. The count d'Alençon, for this, conceived a great hatred against the knight, and would have had him put to death, had he not placed himself under the safeguard of the parliament. It was long pleaded, and the parliament at last, because they could not produce other evidence than herself against James le Gris, judged it should be decided in the tilt-yard, by a duel for life or death. The knight, the squire, and the lady, were instantly put under arrest until the day of this mortal combat, which, by order of parliament, was fixed for the ensuing Monday, in the year 1387; at which time the king of France and his barons were at Sluys, intending to invade England. The king, on hearing of this duel, declared he would be present at it. The dukes of Berry, Burgundy, Bourbon, and the constable of France, being also desirous of seeing it, agreed it was proper he should be there. The king, in consequence, sent orders to Paris to prolong the day of the duel, for that he would be present. This order was punctually obeyed, and the king and his lords departed for France.
>
> "... When the king of France was returned to Paris, lists were made for the champions in the place of St. Catherine, behind the Temple; and the lords had erected on one side scaffolds, the better to see the sight. The crowd of people was wonderful. The two champions entered the lists armed at all points, and each was seated in a chair opposite the other; the count de St. Pol directed sir John de Carogne, and the retainers of the count d'Alençon James le Gris. On the knight entering the field, he went to his lady, who was covered with black and seated on a chair, and said,-. "Lady, from your accusation, and in your quarrel, am I thus adventuring my life to combat James le Gris: you knew whether my cause be loyal and true." "My lord," she replied "it is so; and you may fight securely, for your cause is good." ...
>
> "The two champions were then advanced, and placed opposite to each other; when they mounted their horses, and made a handsome appearance, for they were both expert men at arms. They ran their first course without hurt to either. After the tilting, they dismounted, and made ready to continue the fight. They behaved with courage; but sir John de Carogne was, at the first onset, wounded in the thigh, which alarmed all his friends: notwithstanding this, he fought so desperately that he struck down his adversary, and, thrusting his sword through the body, caused instant death; when he demanded of the spectators if he had done his duty: they replied that he had. The body of James le Gris was delivered to the hangman, who dragged it to Montfaucon, and there hanged it. Sir John de Carogne approached the king and fell on his knees: the king made him rise, and ordered one thousand francs to be paid him that very day: he also retained him of his household, with a pension of two hundred livres a-year, which he received as long as he lived."

This detailed account shows the formality of the judicial duel, and the complexity required to gain a grant of combat; purposefully delayed so that all attempts could be made to reconcile the parties. It thus also serves as an excellent counterpoint to the private duel of the 16th century. For although Philip IV's rules were still being cited as the basic qualifications for judicial combat in early 17th century texts of honor,[13] in reality the judicial combat had effectively died two generations earlier, in the Jarnac-Chastaigneraye duel of 1547. This duel was the last fully regular case of a judicial duel in French history. [14]

The End of the Judicial Duel

Francois de Vivonne, Lord of Chastaigneraye was a favored courtier of both Francis I and Henri II, famed for his beauty, stature, dexterity, generosity, and skill at arms. Guy de Chabot, eldest son of the Lord Jarnac was also a favorite at Francis court, but was not well loved by his son Henri.

Chestaigneraye repeated a rumor to King Francis that de Chabot had had an illicit affair with his one of his in-laws. Francis, not altogether believing the story, made a joke of it at court, thus further embarrassing Jarnac. Jarnac, knowing the source of the rumor, then publicly declared that whoever made such a claim was a crass liar. This "giving the lie," prompted Chestaigneraye to demand satisfaction and ask Francis for the right to a list. Francis refused and declared the matter settled.

This might have been the end of it, had Francis not died shortly thereafter, and Chestaigneraye brought the case up again with the newly crowned Henri II. Since neither man would change his position, and since it was impossible to verify either's claims with an investigation, Henri agreed, giving the men a month to prepare themselves. While Chestaigneraye, confident in his wrestling and fencing, simply enjoyed life, Jarnac hired an Italian fencing master named Caizo to train him in sword and buckler fighting.

The two men met in the lists on July 10, 1547, at St. Germain-en-Laye, with King Henri presiding as judge. Still confident, Chestaigneraye had set up a huge marquee and ordered a celebratory banquet to be prepared, to which he had invited the king. Each man appeared at the lists with their seconds and their retainers, and donned their arms and armor: a mail shirt, gauntlets, a steel helmet, a buckler, a sword, a dagger, and a boot-knife. Each swears their case upon the gospels and after again refusing to back down battle is joined.

In the fighting, Chestaigneraye seemed to overpower Jarnac, but using a technique that Caizo had taught him, Jarnac slipped his point behind Chestaigneraye's knee, and using the false edge of the sword, cut Chastaigneraye's hamstrings to the bone. Unable to stand, Chestaigneraye fell to the ground and Jarnac demanded that he acknowledge Jarnac's innocence. Chestaigneraye refused, and Jarnac turned to King Henri, saying that if the King would consider the matter finished, he would spare the man's life. Only after multiple requests did Henri agree to save his favorite's life, but he still made no move to pass judgment on the duel. Chestaigneraye's servants bandaged his wounds, but humiliated, he tore off the bandages and allowed himself to bleed to death.

Francois Billacois' *The Duel* devotes an entire chapter to this duel.[15] He believes that in supporting Chastaigneraye, Henri, lost face upon his defeat by Jarnac. With his adversary's death, Jarnac was declared the victor, but in so abdicating his authority as judge, Henri established a de facto belief that the outcome of the duel itself legitimized the actions of the victorious party. This duel is accepted as the last judicial duel in France, and the turning point in history to focus on the private duel.[16]

Private Duels

Following the death of Chastaigneraye, Henri II vowed to never again grant a list to any claimant. The result was an end to judicial combats in France, but not to the end of dueling. Denied royal sponsorship, men began to simply arrange to meet in a quiet field, forest glade, or rented hall, and settle the affair between themselves and their seconds. The extra-judicial duel, an unsanctioned, private affair, was a criminal offense, held in contempt of the law; yet it is this type of duel that most think of.

Private duels were held without any legal sanction or justification, other than the "injured" party's sense of honor or perceived injury. Times just before the outbreak of war, or just after its cessation seemed to have been most conducive to dueling. But what prompted men to duel? Except for duels for fun, Billacois isolated five primary causes for duels:

1. Duels fought over women,
2. Duels fought by men belonging to rival clans or factions,
3. Duels fought over public office,
4. Duels following differences or legal cases concerning family or seigniorial inheritances,
5. Duels of rivalry over precedence or honorific distinctions.[17]

Since private duels were unannounced, they did not draw crowds, as would a judicial duel. The practice of throwing down a gauntlet was gradually abandoned in favor of an oral challenge, either in front of witnesses or by a *cartel* (a written challenge). Typically the duel did not result from one isolated incident, but as the culmination of the quarrels between two individuals or groups. Without the legal formalities of the judicial combat, or its audience of witnesses, duels became an increasingly chaotic affair. Defendants would attempt to conceal mail shirts under their clothes for added defense, hire assassins to waylay the challenger on his way to the duel, or use poison.[18] To counter these aberrations, duelists found it increasingly important to bring seconds with them to the duel. Previously, the role of the second had been to try and reconcile the parties to each other, and while this remained part of their role, as the "seconds" really became thirds, fourths and fifths, it became customary for seconds to enter combat as well.[19]

The most famous, and one of the most disastrous, duels of fighting seconds was fought during the reign of Henri III. Henri surrounded himself with a circle of young, pretty, and promiscuous roustabouts that were known as His Majesty's Mignons. Of this inner circle, Henri's favorite was Quélus, son of the Governor of Rovergne. Quélus was particularly jealous of Sieur d'Entragues. Further complicating the issue was that d'Entragues was a favorite of the Duke of Guise, whose own family saw themselves as rivals to the royal House of Valois.[20] Thus their rivalry also became a convenient way for King and Duke to contest with one another.

Both Quélus and d'Entragues favored the same woman. Seeing d'Entragues coming out of her apartments at court one evening, Quélus taunted him that he was but one in a long line of the lady's lovers, and not the first. D'Entragues called him a liar, and Quélus demanded satisfaction. Each chose two other Mignons to be their seconds: Riberac and Schomberg for d'Entragues, and Maugiron and Livarot for Quélus. The seconds' role was to try and reconcile the two men, and failing that, to make sure that no treachery was committed.

The six men met just before dawn the following Sunday morning, near the ramparts of the Porte Saint-Antoine. Accounts vary as to exactly what happened, but most agree that d' Entragues and his seconds were amenable to a reconciliation, but Quélus' second, Maugiron would hear nothing of it, and taunted and insulted Riberac until he was honor-bound to defend his own name. With no recourse left, the duel broke out between all six men. Quélus complained that d'Entragues had brought a dagger to the duel, whereas he had only a sword, but d'Entragues would not throw it away, chiding him, 'The more fool you for leaving yours at home.'[21]

Shortly after the start of the duel by the principals, Riberac and Maugiron began to fight. Seeing all four of their companions fighting, Schomberg and Livarot came to the odd conclusion that their own honor would be besmirched if they did not join in. Within a few moments Maugiron was dead and Riberac was mortally wounded. Schomberg cut off half of Livarot's cheek, but Livarot ran him through, killing him on the spot. With the advantage of his dagger, d'Entragues stabbed Quélus multiple times, with only a scratch on his arm.

Of the two victorious seconds, Riberac died the next day of his wounds. Livarot, horribly disfigured, was no longer of interest to the King. He was killed in a duel over a woman two years later.[22] As for the principals, d'Entragues made his escape from France (and the King's vengeance), while Quélus died a month later from his wounds.[23]

Henri III, devastated by the loss of so many of his favorites, forbade all dueling upon penalty of death. But he also erected marble effigies and monuments to the slain Mignons, and was unable to conceal his grief. This only made the fame of *Les duelles des mignons* spread, and turned the dead men into celebrities. Edict or not, the duel now was not only perceived as a way to maintain face, it had become a fad.

Dueling Culture

The outgrowth of the chivalric sciences (dating back to the 1300s in Italy) grew in preponderance until 1560. Giovanni da Legnano, Giracomo Muzio and others wrote voluminous works on dueling,[24] injunctions against such, and honor.[25] The attempts of these tracts was to set a proper tone and character to the duel, the so-called *Code Duello* much in the same way that Philip IV's rules had tried to moderate judicial combat. The Catholic Church also tried to control the rising "epidemic" of private duels, threatening excommunication for those individuals taking part in duels, stating that anyone killed in a duel could not be buried in hallowed ground.[26] In practice this normally was not enforced, but throughout the 1600's the voice of the Church against duels increased. Despite the edicts against dueling, during the reign of Henri IV of France (1589 – 1607) no fewer than four thousand men were killed in "affairs of honor."[27]

Fencing masters had begun to adopt the same concerns, and addressed both judicial combat, and increasingly, the private duel, in their treatises. In his *De Arte Gladiatoria Dimicandi* (1482) Filipo Vadi warns against those who cause quarrels and seek to settle them with the sword.[28] Achille Marozzo wrote, "One who is provoked to defend one's honor has a just cause to combat."[29] The entirety of Book II of Saviolo's *His Practice* is devoted to the discussion of honor. "All injuries are reduced to two kindes and are either by wordes or deedes. In the first, he that offereth the injurie ought to be the challenger: in the later he that is injured: Caius sayeth to Seius that he is a traitor: unto which Seius aunswereth by giving the lie: whereuppon ensueth, that the charge of combat falleth on Caius, because hee is to maintain what he said, and therefore to challenge Seius. Now when an injurie is offered by deede, then do they proceed in this manner. Caius striketh Seius, giving him a box on the ear, or some other waie hurteth him . . . whereby Seius is forced to challenge Caius. . ."[30]

In *The Sixteenth Century Italian Duel* Frederick Bryson writes:

> "The duel was regarded as illogical, in the first place, because the instruments of proof were arms, which signify only violence. To "conquer with arms in hand" had no connection, for example, with the question whether one was an adulterer or a traitor. Violence is proper to wild beasts, and in the ability to use it they are superior to men…On the other hand, men can protect themselves by erecting walls and by enacting laws. All these facts show that man was intended to settle his differences not by fighting but by reason."[31]

Yet for all of their decrying the duel, the simple truth is that with each new generation of fencing master, their work shifted further and further to first civilian swordsmanship with matched weapons, then to the sword and it's adjunct weapons, and finally to the sword alone, or its use with the other accepted weapons of daily "fashion" – the cloak and dagger. The fencing master of the early 1600s was clearly preparing his pupil for the duel first, and street defense, second.

The dueling temperament and philosophy also differed between the countries of England, Italy, France and Spain. During the late 16th and early 17th centuries the most favored teachers and texts were from Italy. The French took to the use of the rapier very quickly, while in England there were movements to keep the rapier out of the country. George Silver, a prominent English gentleman and fencer, berated the Italian teachers and their "dangerous" practices, believing that all English swordsmen should follow and adhere to good English traditions.

> "Paradoxes of defense, wherein is proved the true grounds of fight to be in the short ancient weapons, and that the short sword hath advantage of the long sword or long rapier. And the weakness and imperfection of the rapier-fights displayed. Together with an admonition to the noble, ancient, victorious, valiant, and most brave nation of Englishmen, to beware of false teachers of defence, and how they forsake their own natural fights: with a brief commendation of the noble science or exercising of arms.

> "The reason which moved me to adventure so great a task, is the desire I have to bring the truth to light, which hath long time lain hidden in the cause of contempt, while we like degenerate sons, have forsaken our forefather's virtues with their weapons, and have lusted like men sick of a strange ague, after the strange vices and devices of Italian, French and Spanish Fencers, little remembering, that these apish toys could not free Rome from Brennius sack, nor France from King Henrie the Fifth his conquest."[32]

Silver taught the use of the short sword,[33] not the rapier. Despite his invective, the Italian schools flourished, the most famous of which was Bonetti's school at Blackfriars in London, which opened in 1576. The English did not exhibit the fervor for the judicial duel of the French. "In England, where Puritanism, capitalism, free enterprise and freedom of thought were important in a society which was otherwise very hierarchical, only isolated and more or less anti-social individuals felt the need to fight duels."[34]

Looking at Shakespeare one may see in many of his plays the thoughts of the time on dueling and things Italian.[35]

Spain's dueling culture was outwardly similar to England's, in that few resorted to the duel, although history shows that the judicial duel was a legal enterprise in Spain for many years.[36] While it would seem that with the Spanish values and thoughts on honor, and the prominence of their fencing tradition, the duel would have found its Elysian Fields, historical documents do not back this up. In fact, the word *duello* and its normal forms do not occur very often in legal documents of the time.

The duel in Spain was legal only when a field was granted by royal decree. Although the granting of a field was a relatively easy accomplishment, the duel was still not commonly resorted to as it was in France or Italy. Those that took part in illegal duels were subject to stiff penalties such as banishment or execution. The need for dueling may also have been abated by the abundance of other blood sports such as cane fighting, animal fights and bullfighting. One other note is that that it was common practice to simply hire an assassin to perform a murder over slights taken, rather than further risking honor, or injury, in a duel:

> "Murder is quite normal in this country on several grounds which are even authorized by custom . . . These things can only be avenged by killing. They say the reason is that after such insults it would not be just to risk one's life in single combat with equal arms, where the offended party might die at the hand of the aggressor; and they will wait twenty years for vengeance if they cannot carry it out before then." [37]

So dueling in Spain did not take on the dimensions that it did in other countries.

Dueling as a practice had its climax towards the end of the 1500's and then small resurgences during the early and mid-1600's. Oddly, afterwards, the dueling craze was looked back on as a golden era:

> "A generation later. . . recall that golden age when the duel was 'more practiced in Italy than anywhere else in Europe' and when renowned closed fields welcomed any man with an affair of honor to settle; but 'today' the duel is no longer practiced in this way. "[38]

It appears that the decline in the use of the duel, judicial or extra-judicial, occurs at about the same time that there was a shift philosophically from *scienza cavalleresca* (chivalric science) to the use of the *pareri*, which were opinions or discussions on points of honor.

> "gentlemen both great and small make declamations about duels and denounce present-day softness, but if they are offered the opportunity for a duel, they dodge it with some subtlety taken from chivalric science, a science which they have turned into a state secret. "[39]

Even though they gave to the other countries of Europe their masters of fence and general codes of honor the Italians did not resort to dueling in murderous proportions. It was the French who "recklessly engaged in duels" and who we may look to when we study or think of dueling in general. Billacois believes that the French practiced dueling because of their national character.

"… we have to conclude that after the third quarter of the sixteenth century 'only the French' – as a contemporary put it – 'recklessly engaged in duels,' or at least engaged in them with an ardour which had no equivalent elsewhere. The accounts given by foreigners are the best proof of this. We must therefore take as a pertinent observation and not as boasting the affirmation by French authors that their compatriots surpassed their Italian masters and that the duel, which was brought back from Naples by Charles VIII's army, found its most favorable territory in France – as already witnessed by the character of the ancient Gauls. For it was not enough to state that dueling was a chiefly French phenomenon. This fact was justified and interpreted with all sorts of arguments which we can classify as natural and supernatural.

"According to the supernatural arguments, the French aptitude, and indeed vocation, for single combat was beyond all rational explanation, except perhaps for that of the astrologers. It had been announced, and therefore imposed, by the most ancient and venerable prophecies, ranging from the vision which King Chilperic had at the dawn of French history to one of David's psalms or Nebuchadnezzar's dreams in the Holy Writ itself. So the French were duellists because of a mysterious and divine decision.

"According to the natural arguments, the arguments of the 'naturalists', the French were 'full of blood', their complexion was 'generous' and 'heat' was the basis of the 'Gallic temperament'. So the French were duelists because of their national character."[40]

And now, as a final question: Who should learn the right and proper use of the rapier? To quote Saviolo:

> "The reason as I take it, is because that amongst Knights, Captains, and valiant Soldiers, the Rapier is it which sheweth who are men of armes and of honor, and which obtaineth right for those which are wronged: and for this reason it is made with two edges and one point, and being the weapon which ordinarily Noble men, Knights, Gentlemen and Soldiers wear by their side, as being more proper and fit to be worn then other weapons: therefore this is it which must first be learned, especially being so usual to be worn and taught."[41]

Another part of the mindset of the time lies in the backdrop of the religious beliefs of the period. Throughout Europe during the 15th through the early 17th centuries the prevalent religion of the time was Catholicism. Chapter 1 of Marozzo's *Arte dell'Armi* nicely displays the religious character of the Renaissance fencing master.

> "To the Great and Glorious God omnipotent, and the Mother Saintly Virgin Mary, and of Saint Sebastiano and Saint Roco and the Knight Saint Georgio and of all the others Known as Saints of God, in this book will I give more things to you of the art of fencing, for you should reduce to memory all that you have learned from me: and this I write in case you did not exercise such mysteries, then you should remember. And in this way have I written in this book a little of my intentions, but you, and those people that have learned well from me, and also with great hard work will be able to do it: they will be vanquished who have not exercised as you have; nevertheless advise you in this, some have no stamina to read it and take part in practical exercising with the sword in hand; but with a little hard work you can do this with imagination. The practical principles of playing and honor I give to you for your comfort so you do not make such a mystery of this art: for this is of great danger: but in order to say to you if fortune allows me to give this art to you, that you may know this, that of doing it: and therefore I will show you the way to teach your students, and foremost in the name of God, that you put the sword in hand and tell them what you want from them in this instruction of arms. Again in the name of God, and the Mother, and of Saint Georgio you will put the sword in hand, and you will show what it means."[42]

Marozzo goes on to say in chapter six:

> "Still I say to you, that when you will want to begin, you will say it to them in this way: here my children and brothers: I want you to swear on this sword which is the cross of God, to do nothing counter to your Master and not to teach any other person that which you have learned without my license: Do this before starting."[43]

Whatever the reality of how these skills went on to be used in the streets or fields, these two examples typify the mind set of the time period. Fencing, as an art and science, was a gift from, and thus dedicated back to, God, paradoxical as that may seem today. Secondly, the seriousness of the skills imparted by the master was further instilled by the need to swear an oath of secrecy and loyalty on the Cross to the master giving you instruction.

The Italian Duello
Act III from William Shakespeare's Romeo & Juliet

SCENE I. A public place.

Enter MERCUTIO, BENVOLIO, Page, and Servants

BENVOLIO
I pray thee, good Mercutio, let's retire: The day is hot, the Capulets abroad, And, if we meet, we shall not scape a brawl; For now, these hot days, is the mad blood stirring.

MERCUTIO
Thou art like one of those fellows that when he enters the confines of a tavern claps me his sword upon the table and says 'God send me no need of thee!' and by the operation of the second cup draws it on the drawer, when indeed there is no need.

BENVOLIO
Am I like such a fellow?

MERCUTIO
Come, come, thou art as hot a Jack in thy mood as any in Italy, and as soon moved to be moody, and as soon moody to be moved.

BENVOLIO
And what to?

MERCUTIO
Nay, an there were two such, we should have none shortly, for one would kill the other. Thou! why, thou wilt quarrel with a man that hath a hair more, or a hair less, in his beard, than thou hast: thou wilt quarrel with a man for cracking nuts, having no other reason but because thou hast hazel eyes: what eye but such an eye would spy out such a quarrel? Thy head is as fun of quarrels as an egg is full of meat, and yet thy head hath been beaten as addle as an egg for quarrelling: thou hast quarrelled with a man for coughing in the street, because he hath wakened thy dog that hath lain asleep in the sun: didst thou not fall out with a tailor for wearing his new doublet before Easter? with another, for tying his new shoes with old riband? and yet thou wilt tutor me from quarrelling!

BENVOLIO
An I were so apt to quarrel as thou art, any man should buy the fee-simple of my life for an hour and a quarter.

MERCUTIO
The fee-simple! O simple!

BENVOLIO
By my head, here come the Capulets.

MERCUTIO
By my heel, I care not.

Enter TYBALT and others

TYBALT
Follow me close, for I will speak to them. Gentlemen, good den: a word with one of you.

MERCUTIO
And but one word with one of us? couple it with something; make it a word and a blow.

TYBALT
You shall find me apt enough to that, sir, an you will give me occasion.

MERCUTIO
Could you not take some occasion without giving?

TYBALT
Mercutio, thou consort'st with Romeo,—

MERCUTIO
Consort! what, dost thou make us minstrels? an thou make minstrels of us, look to hear nothing but discords: here's my fiddlestick; here's that shall make you dance. 'Zounds, consort!

BENVOLIO
We talk here in the public haunt of men: Either withdraw unto some private place, And reason coldly of your grievances, Or else depart; here all eyes gaze on us.

MERCUTIO
Men's eyes were made to look, and let them gaze; I will not budge for no man's pleasure, I.

Enter ROMEO

TYBALT
Well, peace be with you, sir: here comes my man.

MERCUTIO
But I'll be hanged, sir, if he wear your livery: Marry, go before to field, he'll be your follower; Your worship in that sense may call him 'man.'

TYBALT
Romeo, the hate I bear thee can afford No better term than this,—thou art a villain.

ROMEO
Tybalt, the reason that I have to love thee Doth much excuse the appertaining rage. To such a greeting: villain am I none; therefore farewell; I see thou know'st me not.

TYBALT
Boy, this shall not excuse the injuries that thou hast done me; therefore turn and draw.

ROMEO
I do protest, I never injured thee, but love thee better than thou canst devise,
Till thou shalt know the reason of my love:
And so, good Capulet,—which name I tender As dearly as my own,—be satisfied.

MERCUTIO
O calm, dishonourable, vile submission! Alla stoccata carries it away. *Draws* Tybalt, you rat-catcher, will you walk?

TYBALT
What wouldst thou have with me?

MERCUTIO
Good king of cats, nothing but one of your nine lives; that I mean to make bold withal, and as you shall use me hereafter, drybeat the rest of the eight. Will you pluck your sword out of his pitcher by the ears? make haste, lest mine be about your ears ere it be out.

TYBALT
I am for you. *Drawing*

ROMEO
Gentle Mercutio, put thy rapier up.

MERCUTIO
Come, sir, your passado. *They fight*

ROMEO
Draw, Benvolio; beat down their weapons. Gentlemen, for shame, forbear this outrage! Tybalt, Mercutio, the prince expressly hath Forbidden bandying in Verona streets: Hold, Tybalt! good Mercutio!

TYBALT under ROMEO's arm stabs MERCUTIO, and flies with his followers

MERCUTIO
I am hurt. A plague o' both your houses! I am sped. Is he gone, and hath nothing?

BENVOLIO
What, art thou hurt?

MERCUTIO
Ay, ay, a scratch, a scratch; marry, 'tis enough. Where is my page? Go, villain, fetch a surgeon. *Exit Page*

ROMEO
Courage, man; the hurt cannot be much.

MERCUTIO
No, 'tis not so deep as a well, nor so wide as a church-door; but 'tis enough,'twill serve: ask for me to-morrow, and you shall find me a grave man. I am peppered, I warrant, for this world. A plague o' both your houses! 'Zounds, a dog, a rat, a mouse, a cat, to scratch a man to death! a braggart, a rogue, a villain, that fights by the book of arithmetic! Why the devil came you between us? I was hurt under your arm.

ROMEO
I thought all for the best.

MERCUTIO
Help me into some house, Benvolio, Or I shall faint. A plague o' both your houses!
They have made worms' meat of me: I have it, And soundly too: your houses!

Exeunt MERCUTIO and BENVOLIO

ROMEO
This gentleman, the prince's near ally, My very friend, hath got his mortal hurt In my behalf; my reputation stain'd With Tybalt's slander,—Tybalt, that an hour Hath been my kinsman! O sweet Juliet, Thy beauty hath made me effeminate And in my temper soften'd valour's steel!

Re-enter BENVOLIO

BENVOLIO
O Romeo, Romeo, brave Mercutio's dead! That gallant spirit hath aspired the clouds, Which too untimely here did scorn the earth.

ROMEO
This day's black fate on more days doth depend; This but begins the woe, others must end.

BENVOLIO
Here comes the furious Tybalt back again.

ROMEO
Alive, in triumph! and Mercutio slain! Away to heaven, respective lenity, And fire-eyed fury be my conduct now!

Re-enter TYBALT

Now, Tybalt, take the villain back again, That late thou gavest me; for Mercutio's soul Is but a little way above our heads, Staying for thine to keep him company: Either thou, or I, or both, must go with him.

TYBALT
Thou, wretched boy, that didst consort him here,
Shalt with him hence.

ROMEO
This shall determine that.

They fight; TYBALT falls

BENVOLIO
Romeo, away, be gone! The citizens are up, and Tybalt slain. Stand not amazed: the prince will doom thee death, If thou art taken: hence, be gone, away!

ROMEO
O, I am fortune's fool!

BENVOLIO
Why dost thou stay?

Exit ROMEO

[1] Vincentio Saviolo. *His Practice.* p 7.
[2] For a full study of the duel see Baldick, Billacois, and Kiernan in the bibliography.
[3] Vincento Saviolo. *His Practice in Two Books.* First Book. First Part.
[4] An edict passed in Lyons in 501 established judicial combats a regular form of trial, equivalent with trial by ordeal. See R. Coltman Clephan, *The Medieval Tournament*, (Methuen & Co, Ltd., 1919. Reprinted by Dover, 1995) p. 146
[5] Witchcraft was sometimes used, both for protection and to cause injury or harm to one's opponent.
[6] Law exempted some people. For example, in England, exemptions existed for the citizens of London, who were excused by their charter, the clergy, and the blind. See *Origines Juridiciales*, p. 79
[7] Women could challenge, and be challenged, to judicial combat. While there is no evidence of noblewomen using anything other than a champion in such claims, common women did take part in judicial combats. For an iconographic depiction of such a combat see Hans Talhoffer's 1467 *Fechtbüch*, reprinted in Mark Rector, *Medieval Combat*, pp. 242-250.
[8] British Musuem, Sloane Ms. 1710, f. 162.
[9] See, for example, the account of a judicial combat fought by a Burgundian tailor in Clepham, p. 163, or that fought in the reign of Edward III in Vulson de la Columbiere, *Theatre des Honuer,* p. 459
[10] See Mark Rector, *Medieval Combat.*
[11] See Clephan, p. 147
[12] Sir John Froissart, Chronicles of England, France, Spain (London, 1849) vol. ii, chap 46.
[13] Such as the *Theatre of Honour and Knighthood,* (Paris, 1616).
[14] V.G. Kiernan, *The Duel in European History.* p 37. Robert Baldick also notes the Jarnac – Chastaigneraye duel as the last duel of chivalry. See Baldick, *The Duel.* p 29.
[15] Francois Billacois, Chapter 5.
[16] Ibid. See also Baldick, p. 29 and Alfred Hutton, *The Sword and the Centuries.* pp. 73 - 74
[17] Francois Billacois, Chapter 8.
[18] As reminiscent of the famous fencing match at the end of Shakespeare's *Hamlet*, Act 5, Scene 2
[19] Baldick, pp. 50 - 51
[20] See Hutton, pp. 133 – 134
[21] Hutton, p. 135
[22] Livarot's adversary had apparently neglected to bring a second, to his undoing. As he made to leave, he was stabbed in the back and killed by Livarot's groom. Hutton, p. 138
[23] Baldick. pp 51-52.
[24] Andrea Alcino, born in 1492, a lawyer whose works found readers all over Europe, was one of the first to compile a regular code to define the circumstances in which a gentleman ought to feel a duel encumbent on him. Girocamo Muzio's treatise *Il Duello*, published at Venice in 1550, became the best-known of all. Like all synthetic ideas produced by complex social situations, Honor as presented by such theorists had multiple starting points.
[25] See for example Giovanni da Legnano, *Tracatus de bello, de represaliis et de duello,* edited by Thomas Erskine Holland, Buffalo, 1995
[26] While this helps detail the response to the rapidly escalating popularity of dueling, this sort of threat was hardly a new practice. In the 12th and 13th centuries the Church had attempted to forbid tournaments in the same fashion, with similar ineffectiveness. See Richard Barber and Juliet Barker, *Tournaments.* pp. 140 - 42
[27] Robert Baldick, *The Duel.* p 52.
[28] Filipo Vadi, *De Arte Gladiatoria Dimicandi* (1482), Cap. 3.
[29] Translation by the author of part of Chapter 213 of Achille Marozzo's *Arte dell'Armi.*
[30] Vincentio Saviolo, His Practice, Book II, p. 79
[31] Frederick R. Bryson. *The Sixteenth Century Italian Duel.* p 87.
[32] George Silver. "Paradoxes of Defense". 1599. London.
[33] While the term today may conjure images of the Roman gladius, the term *short sword* in Elizabethan English means the simple, single-handed "arming" sword. This distinguished it from the *long*, or *bastard* sword. Silver's short sword has a blade of some 34 – 36" of length, and a basket hilt.
[34] Billacois, p. 32.
[35] For examples, see *Romeo and Juliet,* which hints at the changing martial culture in England, by putting rapiers in the hands of Romeo and Tybalt, while the traditional sword and buckler has been relegated to the Capulet and Montague serving men. Likewise, Mercutio's taunt that Tybalt is "the very butcher of a silk button seems to refer back to Saviolo's boast that he could teach a man to hit any button on a man's doublet. For a full list of Shakespeare's plays see http://the-tech.mit.edu/Shakespeare/works.html
[36] Francois Billacois. *The Duel.* pp 33-40.
[37] Billacois, *The Duel.* p. 38.
[38] Ibid. p. 42.
[39] Ibid.
[40] Francois Billacois. *The Duel.* pp 46-47.
[41] Vincentio Saviolo. *His Practice.* Book I p 7.
[42] Achille Marozzo, *Arte dell'Armi*, Chapter 1. Author's translation.
[43] Ibid. Chapter 6. Author's translation.

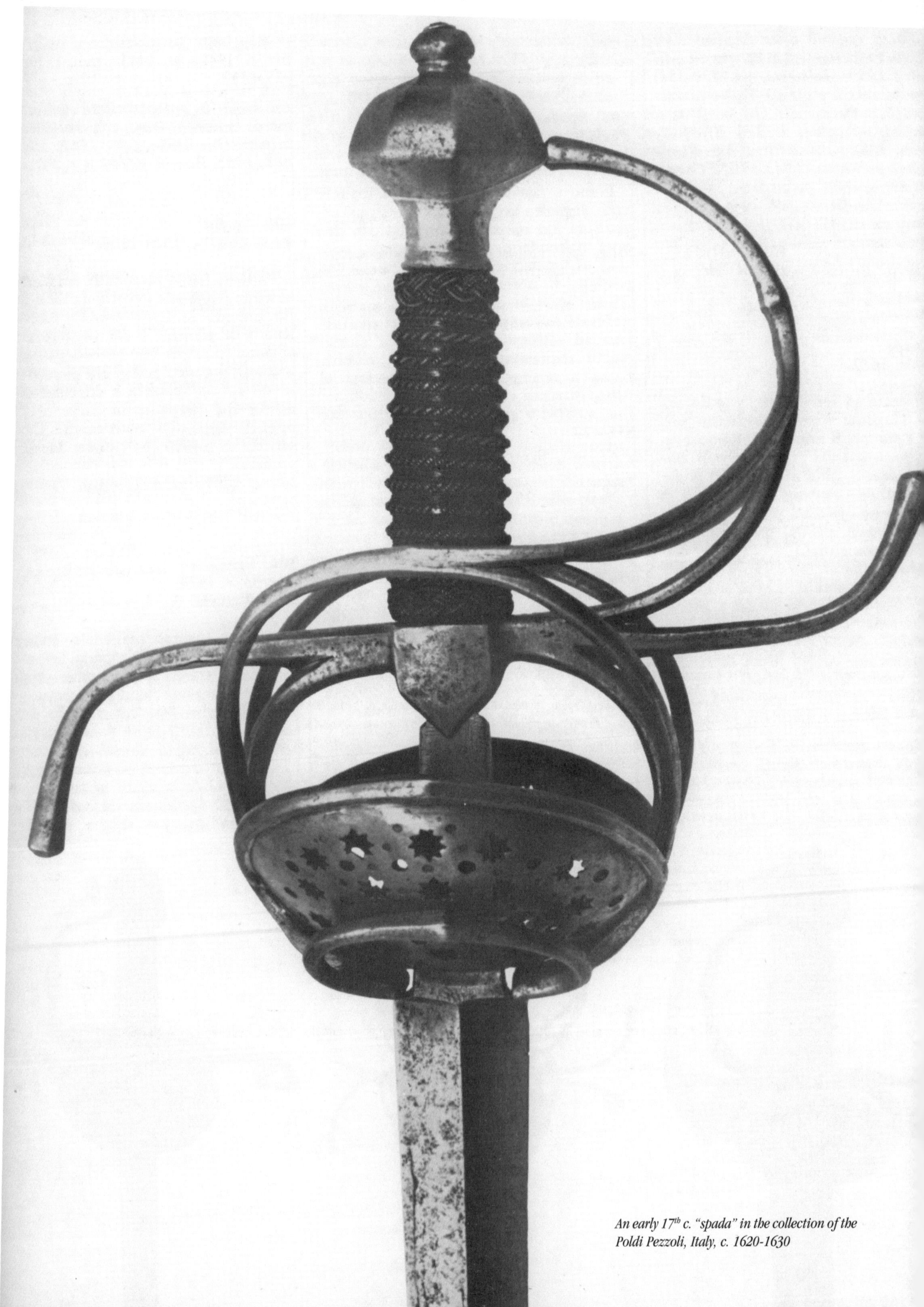

An early 17th c. "spada" in the collection of the Poldi Pezzoli, Italy, c. 1620-1630

The Ring of Steel
A look at the Rapier

"Of all the weapons devised by Man in the long lapse of the centuries, the sword is the only one which combines effectiveness in defence with force in attack, and since its Bronze Age beginnings has gathered round itself a potent mystique which sets it above any other man-made object."[1]

-Ewart Oakeshott

The question of "what is a rapier" constantly arises when studying 16th and early 17th century civilian combat. Defining the rapier is not as easy as it sounds, even for expert armourers and sword-collectors. Indeed the term *rapier* was not used in Italy, the weapon's supposed birthplace. To the average reasonably well-read modern swordsman or collector of arms and armour, a "rapier" would be a swept-hilted, long and narrow sword intended primarily—though not exclusively—for thrusting and dating from the late 16th or 17th century.

In reality what we think of as a "rapier" would have been known to an Italian fencing master simply as a "spada," (Italian for "sword") that bore characteristics of style according to both fashion and function. But the long, swept-hilt thrusting sword we think of as a rapier developed from a long line of progressively more specialized thrusting swords that began perhaps in the 14th century. Surprisingly, however, this line of development existed in parallel with and coexisted with less specialized, shorter swords that emphasized the cut, the sort of "short" sword advocated by George Silver.[2]

Another problem is that the development of such "swept" hilts were sometimes fitted to relatively shorter, broad blades and the hilts of long, thrusting weapons might have looked more at home on a longsword or shorter arming sword. To make matters even *more* complex, broken or newly fashioned blades or hilts might be interchanged by successive owners several times over the "sword's" working lifetime. And finally, the demand for historical weaponry throughout the ages has fed a rich market for forgeries and questionable restorations that are sometimes very difficult to identify. And so, when we speak of the rapier's development throughout this chapter, we will be discussing the development of the hilt, and, to a lesser degree, characteristics of various blades that might be fitted to these hilts. Unfortunately, although there are two excellent works on the development of the hilt—A.V.B. Norman's *The Rapier and Smallsword, 1460-1820* and Eric Valentine's 1968 pamphlet, *Rapiers*—there is to date no equivalent scholarly work tracing the development of blades, so our work here will be simply to catalog the various shapes and characteristics without attempting to develop the much-needed timeline for their historical development.

Defining the Rapier: Military & Civilian Context

We know that the term "rapier" might not have been used by the swordmasters themselves, but Claude Blair has suggested that the term may have been of Spanish origin, relating to a civilian sword, *espada ropera* (literally "robe-sword"). The renowned Mr. Blair presents the term from a 1468 inventory, "Otra en los bienes muebles que tenia el duque don Alvaro de Zúñiga" and in another inventory from 1503.[3] Mr. Norman makes his case in *Rapiers and Small Swords* that the sword may have been more commonly worn with civilian dress on the Iberian peninsula than elsewhere, based of necessity (owing to the lack of precisely dateable surviving specimens) upon iconographic representations,[4] though they are common enough in English, Italian and French examples.[5]

Without question, as plate defenses came into use and military deployment during the 14th century, the shape of the sword became correspondingly more pointed, probably so that the point could be used against the few remaining gaps present for reasons of mobility and visibility at the joints and face. There are, for example, many examples of these swords catalogued by Ewart Oakeshott in his landmark study, *Records of the Medieval Sword,*[6] and we will see several of these as we attempt to follow the development of the civilian sword through to the "rapier" favored by the Italian masters. As thrusting weapons became more specialized, the "estoc" or "tuck"—both intended almost exclusively for thrusting—came into brief fashion, though they do not appear to have dominated the battlefields of Europe during the centuries when plate predominated.[7]

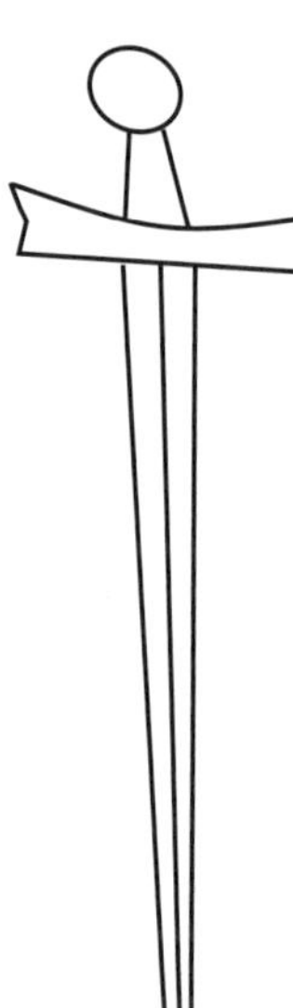

But alongside the development of the military sword, with its circular development cycle based on a constant iteration of new defenses and new weapons designed to exploit weaknesses in those defenses, civilian weaponry faced no such defensive equipment to overcome. Indeed, the earliest known fencing treatise—the afore-mentioned Royal Armouries. MS. I.33, shows unarmoured combatants in guards or positions emphasizing the point with swords tapering to an acute point (see illus. left). This German manuscript is usually dated to sometime c. 1300, clearly illustrating some kind of civilian fencing tradition emphasizing the point as early as the dawn of the 14th century.

Civilians, as we have seen in the first chapter, did require a defensive weapon for use in the street, on the road or, as the 16th century progressed, in an increasing possibility for an encounter in a duel. And the sword, more than any other weapon, proved a powerful weapon for both attack and defense, clearly the "queen of civilian combat" until the refinement in the reliability of firearms was achieved during the 19th century.

While civilian swords faced no defensive technology in the form of armour (other than wool or possibly leather doublets, or the occasional brigandine, all best defeated by a thrust), civilian technology was based on a growing corpus of technique by the masters discussed in Chapter One and presented in more detail in the chapter that follows. New defensive techniques and responses to what was being taught in the popular civilian fencing schools of the 16th and 17th centuries created their own kind of arms race based on technique, range and speed. Indeed, as the thrust developed, guards with the sword began to drift forward, probably to reduce the time needed to reach the target. Concurrently, the length of blades increased also, probably also to reduce the time needed to reach the target with a thrust—and the thrusting attack was generally believed to be faster to the cut.[8]

And so, as Mr. Blair and Mr. Norman have shown, the term "rapier" came to be known as a civilian sword,[9] one that brought about new tactics and new techniques for its employment, but one that also came about as a result of these same trends. Added to these developments were the exigencies of fashion; for the style of hilt and blade were due perhaps as much to what other prestigious and renowned swordsmen were wearing as to the new combat realities they were required to meet. As the 17th century came to a close, so too did the heyday of the rapier. It was replaced by the shorter and much more nimble *smallsword*, itself a response to changing fashions and techniques. We will of necessity restrict our survey to "pre" smallsword rapiers, leaving the survey of the much more internationalized smallsword for

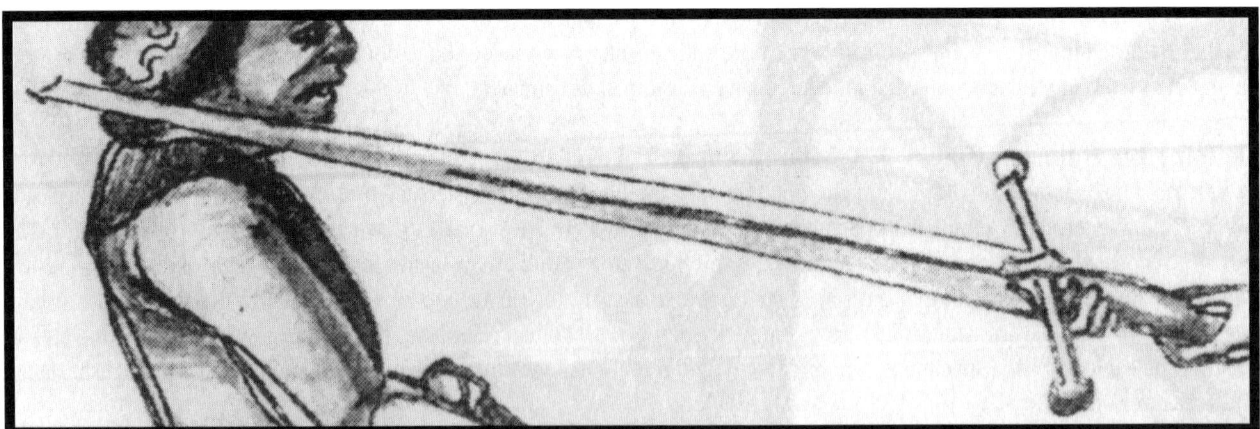

A longsword from Talhoffer's 1467 fechtbuch, showing the classic cruciform sword as taught by medieval swordsmen.

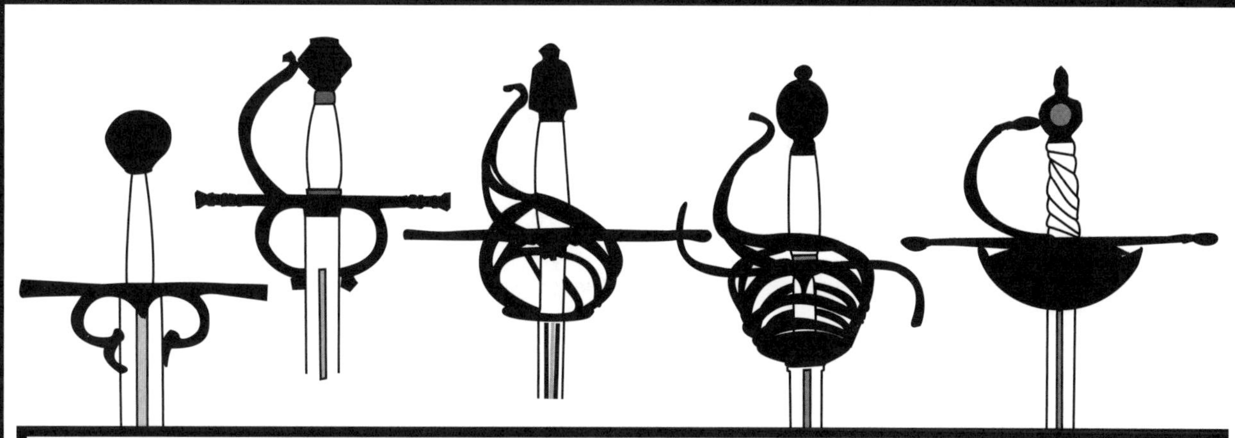

Rapier hilt examples from the 15th - 17th centuries. It is important to note that although there appears to be a "development" from the cross hilt, through the swept hilt to the "cup" hilt, to make such a conclusion would be wrong. Cross-hilted weapons persisted well into the 17th century while various forms of "swept" hilt existed side by side for nearly one hundred and fifty years. Fine hilts from older weapons would also have been fitted to new blades, and fine blades rehilted with newer hilt designs. Paintings and other forms of art that can be solidly dated that happen to have rapier hilts incorporated are the only solid sources for the purposes of dating a particular hilt. Similarly, blades did grow narrower, especially for civilian swords, but the broader cut & thrust or spada da lato *coexisted throughout the period.*

other authors specializing in this fascinating era. Our tour of representative swords and hilts that led to the development of the civilian sword—the rapier—will traverse the Middle Ages and take us into the Renaissance with some of the many forms of the sword popular in Italy, France, England and Spain.

Illustration of a classical medieval cross-hilted sword hilt from the 14th century, this one a fine reproduction from Del Tin Armi Antiche, Italy.

The Medieval Sword (Spada, Espee, Schwert, Espada)

To the untrained eye the sword has changed little since its Bronze Age appearance. At base the sword is a lever-arm that extends the combatant's ability to channel the force of a body-powered strike and deliver a cutting or crushing blow along the edge. Or, if tactically convenient, the point could extend the attack further from the combatant and strike sooner into an unprotected joint or simply into a beckoning target of flesh.

Medieval swords retained these qualities throughout the whole period of their use, and while there were interesting developments in the physical shape of the blade, their balance and techniques of employment, such developments are beyond the scope of this book. The generalized form of medieval swords is important, however, to understanding that the rapier did not spring wholecloth from the air, or to a newly evolved form of fighting. Thrusting swords were known to the Romans and to all subsequent European swordsmen, but some antecedents to the relatively radical developments of the 16th century do underline the importance of an iterative development process lasting not decades, but centuries.

Without question Ewart Oakeshott has won for himself preeminence as the world's authority on medieval swords. His typology of swords, developed in several works but culminating with the already cited *Records of the Medieval Sword*, provides a solid classification scheme for swords from the fall of Rome until the late 15th century. The citations and typologies referred to below apply to his classification.[10]

Medieval swords all follow the "cruciform" (cross-shaped) pattern, the various configurations of hilt ranging from straight across to gracefully (or more urgently) curving towards the blade, an effect that yields less interference with the wrist than does the classic cross-hilted arming or longsword.

For our purposes, it is necessarily only to look at certain developments in the cruciform hilt that presage the development of the quarter to full swept or cupped-hilted and more familiar rapier of the period.

Blades

While we will focus in this section on the development of specialized blades for thrusting, the classic "balanced" sword intended both for cutting (or smashing) and for thrusting remained popular throughout the period—and indeed up into the 19th century. Recall George Silver's admonition against the increasingly specialized weapons articulated as late as 1599.[11]

There are clear examples, however, of major trends in the design of the blade towards a strong emphasis on thrusting. Oakeshott presents many examples of these blades, and we can follow his typology through the development of these swords which do seem to be featured on military effigies and portrayals from the early 14th century (when armour of plate first became a significant presence upon the battlefield).

OAKESHOTT TYPE XIV: The blades on type XIV swords tapered strongly to a "sometimes very acute"[12] point. The grips are characteristically short, and the blade is often fullered for the first half. They are longer than the Type XII swords they are frequently found illustrated alongside from the 12th – 15th centuries, and they would seem to be better at thrusting than their Type XII counterparts. The hilts are uniformly cruciform or elegantly arched downwards, with no enhancements present. There are few examples of these swords surviving that can be positively identified, though they seem to have been a very popular military arming sword of a "classic" shape for the duration of the 14th and into the 15th centuries.

OAKESHOTT TYPE XV: Mr. Oakeshott heavily emphasizes the parallel development of this category of sword-blade with the development of plate armour; one can see in an instant that the more acutely tapered blade emphasizes the point; but such swords could also have been used effectively for civilian defense and it is tempting to classify the Royal Armouries MS. I.33 swords into this category. Interestingly, many of the fifteen swords he categorizes that fall into this group feature crosses that turn downward—even if very slightly—at the ends. Perhaps this is a modification brought about also by the increased use of the point? Note that the pommels are usually still of the rondel variety, though a few (such as XV.13)[13] presages the pommel types common during the whole of the 16th and 17th centuries. The single-handed variety of these swords can be found from the early 14th century through the 15th, but similar shapes can be found on *espee bastarda* throughout the 16th, 17th and even into the 19th century. They are similar to other, swords, namely the type XVII swords, all hand-and-a-half swords that bear strongly tapering blades and an interesting variety of pommel shapes that presage development during the 16th century. Similarly, the type XVIII swords—single-handed *spada*—are also strongly tapered, but have a startling variety of hilts that run the gambit from the famous German "branch" swords to the "fishtail" pommels to the more conservative disk-shaped pommel.[14]

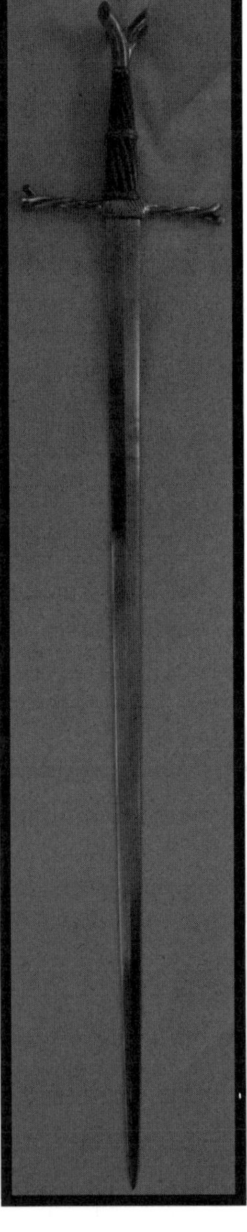

A type XV sword by Arms & Armor of Minneapolis, MN. Note the sword's relatively narrow profile emphasizing the point. While a sword like this would have been useless for smashing against armour of plate, its point could effectively exploit gaps in the articulation.

Hilts

While no linear progression of hilt designs—even for strictly medieval swords—has been done or may even be possible, given how conservative designs persisted for a very long time alongside multiple newer ones, the following drawings should serve to summarize the design of various hilts from the mid-14th century to innovations present all the way up to 1600.

Ewart Oakeshott's typology for medieval swords relates primarily to blades, while most rapier classification attempts refer to hilts. Sadly, there is no blade schema for the rapier, but we will cite Vesey Norman's hilt typology extensively in the discussion that follows.

OAKESHOTT TYPE XIX: Although the blades on these swords—all originating from the Hall of Victories arsenal at Alexandria—are uninteresting for our present purposes, two of them demonstrate extremely interesting developments in the hilt that eventually build upon the more intensive hiltwork of the following century.

Royal Armouries A.5738, with a 32" blade, an Oakeshott type G cross-hilt, but with an interesting single enarme that coils up and is intended for the swordsman's index finger (classifying it as a Norman Type 4),[15] defending it against damage in the bind or parry with the forte. Such single enarmes are not common, but they do seem to have come into use fairly early: Norman gives the first example as dating from 1340-50 in the "Master of the Codex of Saint George,"[16] though as both Norman and Oakeshott point out, the blades normally affixed to hilts of this type were generally employed for cutting or hewing, not for thrusting. They persist as late as 1500.

The next type XIX sword also posseses an Oakeshott Type G hilt, but this one has two finger openings, which Norman classifies as a Type 15.[17] Dating from the third quarter or later of the 15th century, it offers a second ring, the purpose of which remains unclear. Like the example above, it was fitted to a sword not particularly specialized for thrusting.

Shown here from Norman's typology of rapiers and taken from a turn of the 16th-century painting by Marco Marziale, the addition of the knuckle bow-while perhaps rare, was an important step in the development of the full "swept" hilt commonly associated today with the term "rapier."

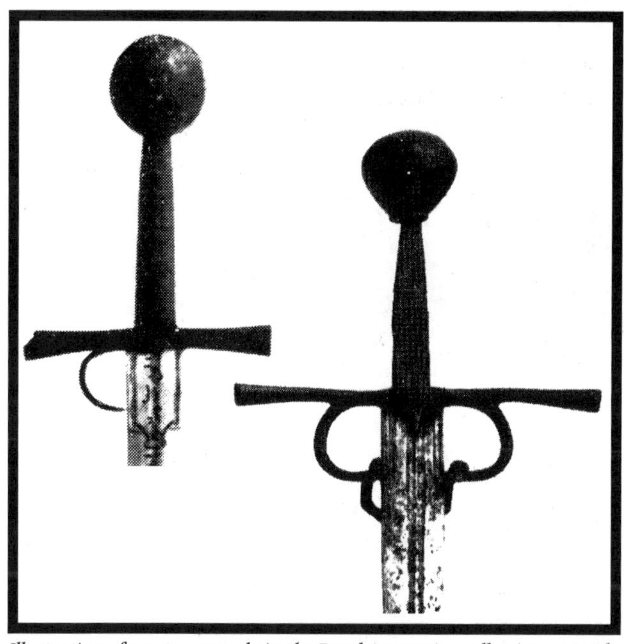

Illustrations from two swords in the Royal Armouries collection at Leeds; RA A.8 (top) and RA A.5738/1. The early finger-rings evolved first during the 14th century, but were later extended into elaborate defenses for the hand though simple examples such as these persisted as late as 1500.

Type 8: Although none of this form survives, Norman cites two sources for what is obviously a transitional development in the addition of a knuckle-bow to the Oakeshott Type XIX ring-guarded hilt. This example, known only from an obscure painting by Marco Marziale (1463-1507), is complimented by another two which were found in the 1544 Iventario Iluminado of the Spanish Real Armeria.

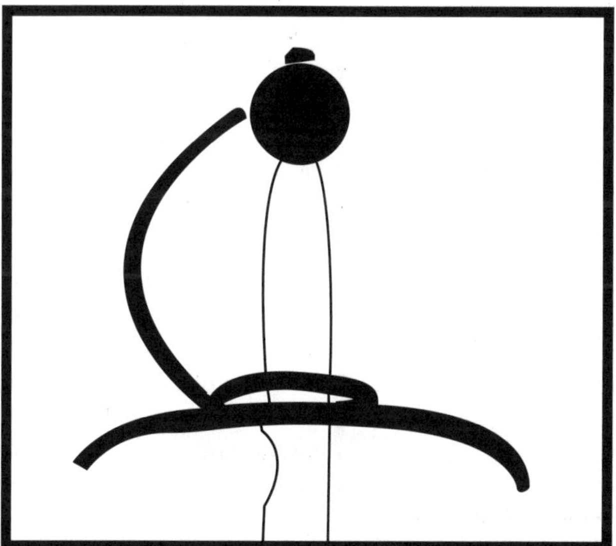

An illustration of the Norman Type 14 sword, which can be found in many museums. This example, taken from the Crucifixion by Ulrich Apt and dated to 1517, shows the knuckle-bow and thumb-ring together on a single example, and this style is far more common than the Type 8.

Similar defenses are more commonly seen in the Norman Type 13 and 14 classifications, where the addition of a knuckle-bow is well-documented in paintings from 1515 or so.[18] It should be noted that all three of these swords feature relatively wide blades well-qualifying them for both cut and thrust use, rather than for simply thrusting alone. The Wallace Collection sword A528 is similar but has a more thrusting-oriented blade, underlining the idea that developments in the blade and hilt did not necessarily run together, but probably varied wildly by region and personal taste.

Estoc, Germany, c. 1500-1525. Steel, wood and leather, L. 156.6 cm. © The Cleveland Museum of Art, 2002. Gift of Mr. And Mrs. John Severance, 1916.686

Swords with similary arranged combinations of the knuckle-bow, enarmes and thumb-rings persisted alongside the development of the civilian rapier right down to 1700.

The Tuck (estoc)

> "*Howbeit I have seene some both men at arms, and dimilaunces vse tocks very coueniently worne after the Hongarian Turkie manner under their thighs; which Tocks are long narrow stiffe swords onlie for the thrust.*"[19]

A great deal of ink has been spilled by writers attempting to trace the development of the sword from the long, narrow and exclusively thrusting "tuck" or "estoc." Mr. Norman brings out much evidence to dispel this idea, citing military manuscripts, proclamations and fighting treatises to make the point that the rapier and estoc were not only quite distinct, but that the square-bladed estoc was a military weapon of utility, whereas the rapier was an exclusively civilian weapon.

Tucks or estocs, when they are referred to or even more rarely seen in a collection, feature a shape very similar to the military longsword, saving that the blade is exceptionally narrow, as with the example shown left. A very similar weapon exists in the Wallace Collection, A504.

How the estoc was used, beyond that it was for thrusting, remains a mystery as their use is not documented in any fighting treatises. Indeed, early fighting masters up through Marozzo emphasize the edge rather than the point.

The Sidesword (*Spada da Lato*)

As we will see in Chapter Four, Achille Marozzo and the masters previous to him advocated a sword that was used equally for cutting and thrusting--hence the moniker popular in recent years "cut and thrust" sword--though it should be emphasized that this term is now falling out of favor.

To the Italian writers and, presumably, to the fencing masters themselves and to their clients, the "sidesword" was simply a "spada," sometimes referred to with more precison, the "spada da lato."

The sidesword is longer than the Type XV swords that it appears to have descended from and are perhaps just a bit heavier. Remember that the spada da lato evolved alongside the rapier for two centuries, the raging almost religious debate amongst swordmasters as to which was better wonderfully immortalized in the play, "Worke for Cutlers," of 1615 (see page 30) for an excerpt from this poignant articulation of the argument.

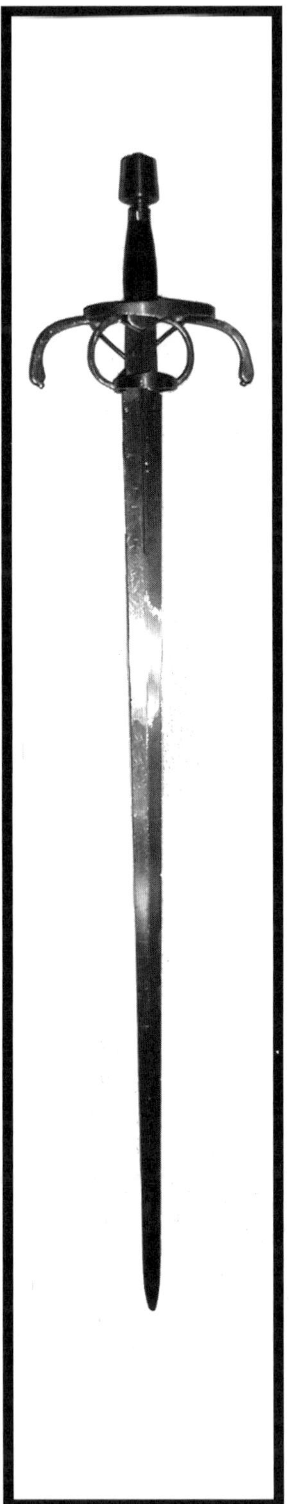

An example of a sidesword by Darkwood Armoury.

Modern arms & armor experts continue this debate today; there is no agreement on the terminology employed nor is there agreement upon whether a particular specimen might be a civilian *spada da lato* or a military cross-hilted sword. For our purposes, suffice to say that the *spada da lato* appears from illustrations in Marozzo and other masters of the period to a range of 32 to 36 inches with a cross hilt that sometimes sported rings and early swept defenses for the hand. Eventually these defenses became complete, as with the Scottish Claymore. The weight on a typical example might range, based on similar swords surviving in modern collections, between 2.2 and 3.0 lbs..

The Rapier

We do not know what the "robe sword" referred to in the Spanish accounts might have been, nor can we survey in a work as brief as this all of the various forms that this weapon might have taken from the late 15th through the 17th centuries, even if a classification scheme for both hilt and blade existed--which they don't. Rather, I would point the interested reader at Norman's landmark work, and present below various aspects of the weapons we think of as "rapiers."

For the purposes of collectors, and for this book, a "rapier" is a relatively thin-bladed, light weapon the use of which emphasizes but does not exclusively rely on the point, and featuring some adornments to the hilt designed to protect the unarmoured hand.

Rapier Blades

The rapier was most decidedly not a fencing foil; nor was it much like an epee. Rapier blades were reinforced and should be regarded as potent both in the cut and thrust. In general, blades run from 3/4" to 1 1/4" in width, and seem to have ranged from 3/32" to 1/4" thickness, usually with a "distal" taper (this means that they are thinner near the point, as well as narrower). Rapier blades are generally longer than one might expect, ranging in length from 40" all the way to nearly 60".

Blades were reinforced in a variety of ways, including through the use of the central ridge common to Type XV swords; through the use of one or more fullers, or in more sophisticated forgings with an exterior rib extending at least partway down the forte of the blade.

Rapier Hilts

From the 15th century onwards, the addition of swept bars, rings, enarmes, and sometimes cups were developed in a dizzying world of defenses for the hand and index finger. Since the civilian's hand--unlike the knight or the military officers'--would not normally have been defended by a gauntlet, protecting the hand was likely a major design concern, as evidenced by the plethora of defenses attempted.

In general, as time went on more and more sweeping bars were added, though the form of this increasing defense varied wildly not only by nationality and time, but also by personal style.

What follows is a survey of high-grade modern reproductions designed to give the reader an idea for some of the weapons loosely classified as "rapiers" and that are appropriate for the techniques shown in the rest of the book. The list is by no means exhaustive, nor is it necessarily representative of what most historical fencers are using--this is the creme of the crop; something to shoot for, high-grade equipment that will help the fencer not by looking better, but with a better-performing tool.

Modern Reproductions

Although a skilled swordsman can make use of even the poorest quality blade, learning the sword is a sufficiently difficult path that does not need to be complicated by blades that are of poor quality, or worse, that are inaccurate in terms of weight and performance.

Rapier reproductions available to the modern historical fencer vary wildly in terms of quality of the composite steels (indeed, some are barely more than iron!), proper flex in the blade, an edge and point appropriate for reconstruction and competition, the all-important point of balance and the overall feel of the weapon--not to mention their historical accuracy.

In years past, in a tradition that grew from the 19th century reconstructionists, fencers interested in historical swordplay have usually employed the blades of epees or foils and hilted them with Renaissance "ish" hiltwork. Such weapons, while sometimes beautiful for their attention to craftsmanship and passion, suffer as there is insufficient weight in the blade to effectively use many of the historical techniques. This, in turn, has had a negative effect on the reconstruction attempts that have often been attempted both by reenactment groups and by part-time historical fencers.

When shopping for a tool appropriate to the daunting yet wonderful task of studying the Italian rapier, here are a few things to keep in mind:

Safety
The quality of the steel in the blade must be of paramount importance, for it is not difficult for a blade that is either over-soft or over-brittle to break or bend sufficiently to cause a catastrophic failure that could end someone's life. You should secure a blade from a vendor that has a strong reputation in the Historical Fencing community (see the Appendix C for some providers), and one that has seen a good deal of testing in the hands of fencers you either know in person or by reputation.

Historical Accuracy
As mentioned above, it is impossible to learn the Italian rapier with something that has qualities different from the originals. Use the guideline examples included herein and look for specifics on the historical model a blade you are considering is modeled upon, taking note of such details as historical versus reproduction weight, blade shape, and if you can manage it, distribution of the weight and balance point. A more historically accurate weapon will serve you much better than will a dim impression of one.

Weight
For women and fencers of lesser strength, a blade on the light side of the historical spectrum will serve better than will a heavy one--there is no need to complicate things further by fighting the weapon as well as yourself and your opponent. Before buying, try out various rapiers from other students of a similar stature to yourself, and get the opinion of your fencing instructor.

Balance
Now, as in history, the proper balance point for a rapier was and is a matter of debate. In reality, the proper balance is one that allows you to wield the weapon effectively and to employ the broadest spectrum of historical technique.

Cost
Today, rapier reproductions range in price from $200 to $800 USD and up, depending upon the quality and manufacturing techniques employed, as well as the material. Anything much below $200 is probably junk, while anything over $800 will likely take too long to get and be so nice that you won't want to nick it while learning. Plan to spend somewhere around $350-$600 and you're talking a really nice piece of equipment that will last many years.

Availability of Replacement Parts
Sometimes, vendors will use blades ground in mass such that a damaged blade can be replaced. This is a great potential money-saver if you manage to break the blade--which is possible. Again, ensure that the blade used is well-respected in the community and well-tested.

Individual Flair
One of the really pleasant things about Renaissance weaponry is that almost every one is different, and this allows for a great deal of personal expression when choosing a weapon's design. Pick something that is "you" and that reflects the period of fencing or historical reenactment that interests you, then learn enough to bring honor to the blade and to yourself.

Avoid "Innovations"
Do not look for modern "innovations" to improve your winning statistics--such as the pistol-grip--these "improvements" to the weapon serve as dangerous crutches. If you were really in a fight and had learned to rely on a pistol-grip, but had left your trusty pistol-gripped rapier at home, whatever would you do? Stick to the historical basics--they are already optimized for the style.

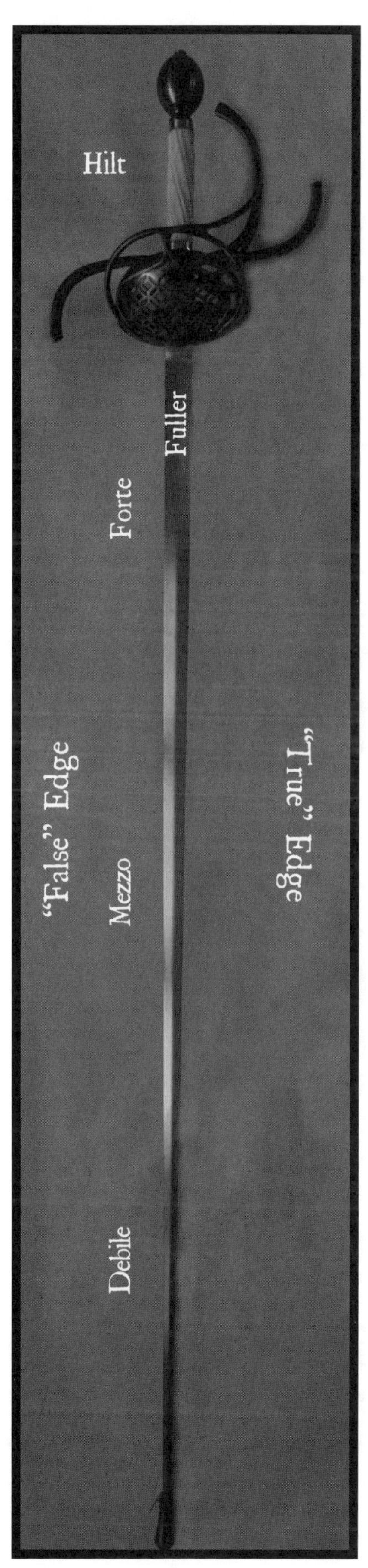

Parts of the Rapier

Hilt: The whole of the *grip*, *quillion,* and *pommel*; everything that does not fit into the sheath. The *cross*, *pommel*, *handle*, *enarmes*, *rings*, *diagonal swept bars*, and the *Turk's Heads* are all part of the hilt. From the fencer's point of view, the hilt mostly functions for defensive purposes and to keep the weapon balanced, but the pommel, knuckle-bow and cross may all be used to strike as well.

Tang: The portion of the hilt under the grip, quillion and pommel, a critical region to the blade's overall strength.

Fuller: Some rapiers had shallow grooves--fullers--forged into them, not as a "blood channel" as one sometimes hears, but rather to lighten the blade without significant loss of strength. Some rapiers even featured piercings in the fuller, lightening the blade still more. Still others were engraved or even stamped with various mottos.

Maker's Mark: Some blades featured a mark of manufacture, usually found on the ricasso, but sometimes found under the hilt on the tang.

Forte: The first quarter or so of the blade, also known in English as the "strong." This is the he most usual place for a parry to be made.

Mezzo: The "middle" of the blade.

Debile / Foible: The "weak" of the blade, where it is most easily controlled if crossing with an opponent's *mezzo* or *forte*.

False Edge: The "back" of the blade, aligned with the fencer's wrist.

True Edge: The "front" edge of the blade, aligned with the fencer's knucklers.

Point or Tip: The sharpened end of the rapier designed to enter the opponent and cause him great discomfort.

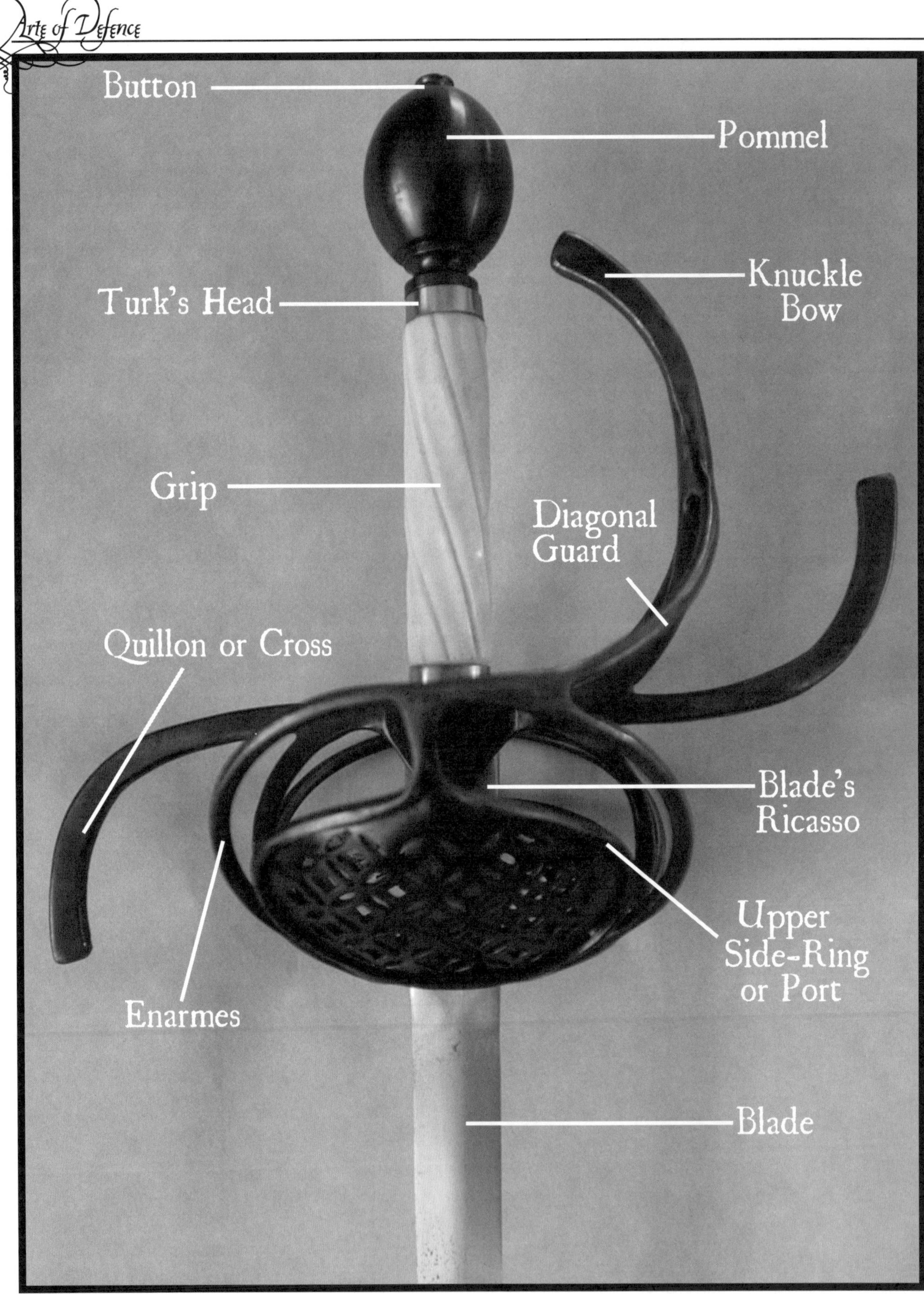

Hilt of an Italian style rapier by Darkwood Armoury made for Brian Price.

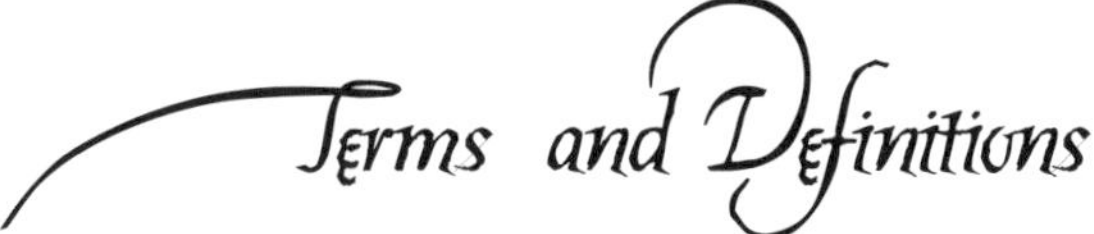

Terms and Definitions

Blade: The blade is used for offense and defense. It has a point and two edges. The blade is divided into three major sections: the *forte* (strong part of the blade near the hilt), the *mezzo* (middle part of the blade) and the *debile* (weak part of the blade near the point). The part of the sword blade that is used to attach the grip and guard is the tang. The tang is the section that goes through the grip and should be of sufficient strength to not break during fencing. The *forte* is the strongest part of the blade closest to, and forward of, the guard. This portion of the blade is used for parrying. The *debile/foible* or weak part of the blade is closest to the point and is used for cuts and the point for thrusts. The blade has two edges. The true edge (right/forward) is aligned with the knuckle bow and forward quillon; your knuckles are on the true edge side. The false edge (rear) is aligned towards your wrist when you grip the weapon. The length of the blade will depend on the height of the fencer. With the point of the sword on the ground the quillons should come to the belly button on the fencer.[19]

Button: The portion of the tang that is piened (riveted) over to secure the whole blade together. On some weapons this is actually a nut, while on many reproductions this is a cosmetic "bump" added instead to the pommel.

Diagonal Guard: The "swept" bars that defend the back of the metacarpal and lower portion of the fingers; the sweeps can create a very beautiful and flowing enhancement to both defense and appearance.

Cross: Another word for *quillons.*

Enarmes: The ring defenses that are situated in line with the blade; evolved from the first finger-rings found in the 14th century.

Grip: The grip is the portion of the weapon that you hold on to. On modern replicas the grip should be made out of a good hardwood, bone or metal that is resistant to cracking.

Pommel: The counterweight to the blade; the weight of the pommel is a critical factor in making the blade balance effectively.

Ports Are another word for *siderings.*

Ricasso The first portion of the blade that is generally unground and rectangular, where the index finger and thumb grasp the blade.

Siderings These are the "rings" of the "ring-hilted" rapier. As many as twelve or fifteen are found on some later examples, while the siderings were a part of the very earliest innovation to a *quillion* or *cross*.

Quillons Also known as the cross; the quillons are used in defense.

Worke for Cutlers:
A Merry Dialgoue betweene Sword, Rapier & Dagger, A.D. 1615[20]

Rapier. S'foot thou shalt know that Rapier dares enter: nay Backe-Sword.

Enter Dagger, he holds Rapier's hands behind him.

Rapier. Whose this behind me?

Dagger. Tis *Dagger*, Sir; what will you never leave your quarreling?

Rapier. Well, *Sword*, *Dagger* hath defended you a good many times; but that is no matter, another time shall serve: shall I get you out *Sword alone,* that I may have you *Single-sword.*

Sword. Yes, if youle be single *Rapier* too.

Dagger. Nay, *Sword,* put the *Case of Rapiers* aside, that there were two of them, I hope you were able to buckle with them.

Sword. I'll tell you what, if I goe into the field with him, hans *Sword* up if I do not cut *Rapier's* poyntes, and lash him when I have done: nay, you shall finde *Sword* mettle to go the very back; 's foot, my teeth be an edge at him.

Dagger. If you offer but to thrust against him, *Rapier,* I'll strike you downe.

Sword. Hang him, I defie him base Spaniard.

Rapier. Defie me? Sirrah, *Sword, Rapier* spits i' thy face: dar'st meet me i' the fields, currently Capon?

Sword. Capon?

Rapier. I Capon, so I say sir.

Dagger. Why any man may see that thou art well caru'd *Sword*; and yet mee thinks that *Rapier* should not speak of that, for its an hundred to one if he be not gilt too.

Sword. Well, *Rapier*, if thou goest into the fields with me, I'le make a Capon of you before I have done with you, you shall nere come home uncut I'll warrant you.

Dagger. Nay, you shall find *Sword* a noble cutter.

Rapier. He a cutter? alas he nere went into the fields yet, but he was foundly hacked before he came out.

Sword. Nere talke you of hacking, for it's a hundred to one if you have not the Foyle-Rapier.

Rapier. 'S foot if you be so *Short-Sword*, *Rapier* nere feares you: come a long.

Dagger. Nay nere goe, for if you doe, Ile fende one after you, which shall scowre you both. The *Cutler* can doe it. I have seene him handle you both bravely.

Sword. The *Cutler*, alas wee are the best Friends hee has, and if it were not up for us, the *Cutler* might soon shut up his shoppe.

Dagger. Alas *Sword*, you need not talke of his shutting up of Shoppe, and if it had not beene for him, you had broken by this time. *Sword*, nay, nere talk: For you know hee can holde your nose to the Grind-stone, when he list.

And as for you, *Rapier*, you knowe hee brought you up first, and if you had stayed with him still, it might have been better for you.

Rapier. better for mee? Alas hee knewe not how to use mee.

Dagger. Hee used you too well indeede: for when you were with him he furnished you with Siler and everything, but now you are wone out of all fashion. You are even like a Lapwing, you are no sooner Hatcht *Rapier*, but you runne abroad presently from him.

Rapier. Yet I scorne to run away from him.

Sword. But if iwere more wisdom then to stand: for the *Culter* is a man well Armed as any man I knowe, and has good skill ins weapons.

Rapier. Ha, *Sword*, is the winde in that Doore? Faith nowe I see which waye you stand bent, *Sworde*, you had rather sleepe in a whole skinne, than to goe into the fields to try yourself.

Sword, Syr, *Sword* has been proov'd before now, and yet heele proove himself againe with you, if you dare follow him.

Dagger. Doe you hear *Sworde*? If you goe, look for *Dagger* at your backs presentlie; for I am a Justice of the Peace, and I am sword to keep and defend the Peace....

Today the student of historical fencing has many options when it comes to selecting one or more rapiers for their reconstruction study and fighting pleasure.

On the following pages are a sample of works produced by two fine sources for historical rapiers in the United States.

Arms & Armor, of Minneapolis, MN. produces many stunning pieces of weaponry relating both the Rennaissance and the Middle Ages. Their work represents the best of the manufactured blades available today, pieces either drawn directly from a specific historical example or from a very well documented set of features appropriate for a given period.

Darkwood Armouries of Panama City, FL. is in many ways the main provider of weapons to the reenactor and historical fencing communities. Their work is excellent and affordable, usually a pleasant blend of stylistic elements that yield original yet recognizeable pieces.

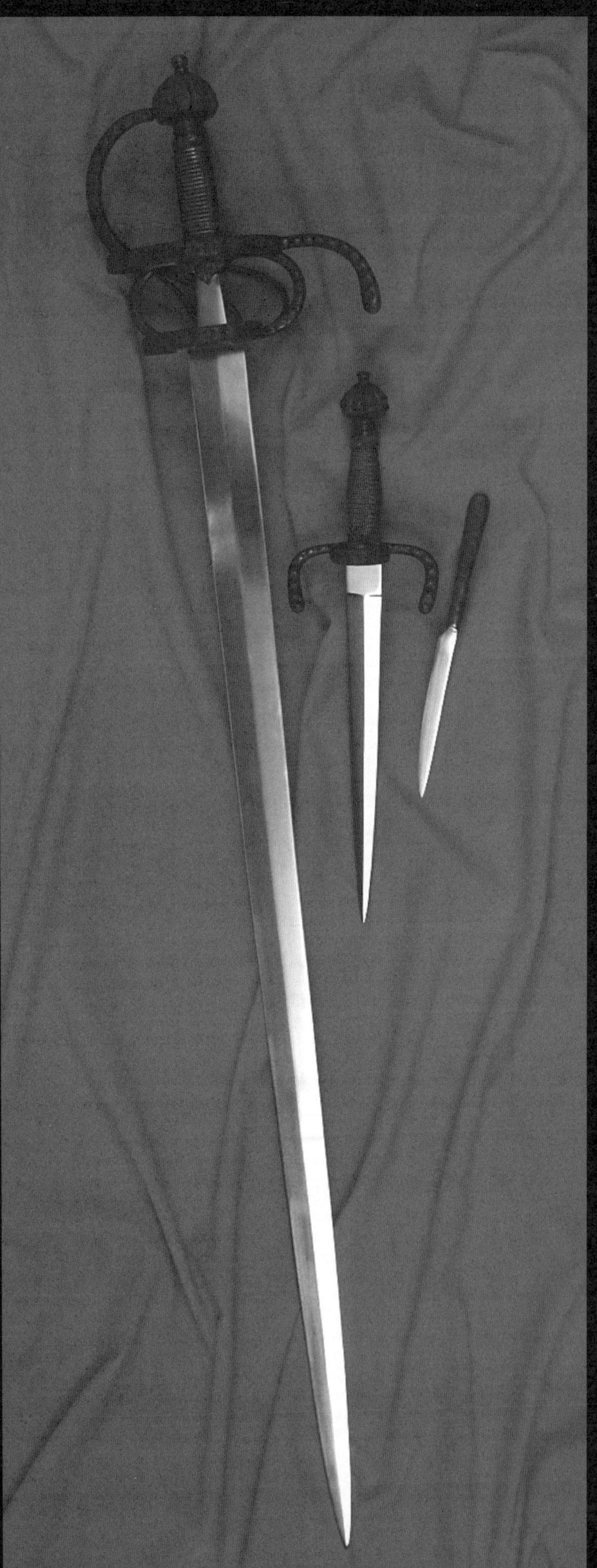

"Dresden" rapier c. 1590

Crafted by Arms & Armor

Carried as personal weapons by the body-guard of Christian I (1586-1591) Elector of Saxony. The hilt was probably constructed in Dresden. The blade has the Milan town mark on the original, but this is fairly certain to be a German forgery. The blade is wider at the hilt then most rapiers and is in fact what many people would consider a broadsword blade. These extremely heavy rapiers were often used as calvary side arms. The hilt is finished with a wavy chiseled pattern in steel. The fore ring is filled with a pierced plate. The grip is wire bound.

Original: c. 1590 Saxon (Dresden)
M. 34, Victoria & Albert Museum, London.
Blade Length: 37.375" BW: 1.75"
Overall Length: 51.5" Wt: 3: 13

Hilted by Darkwood Armory, simple swept hilt designs like this one persisted into the 17th century. Although knucklebows are believed to have been more common after 1560, though similar hilts without the knucklebow can easily be found dating to 1520.

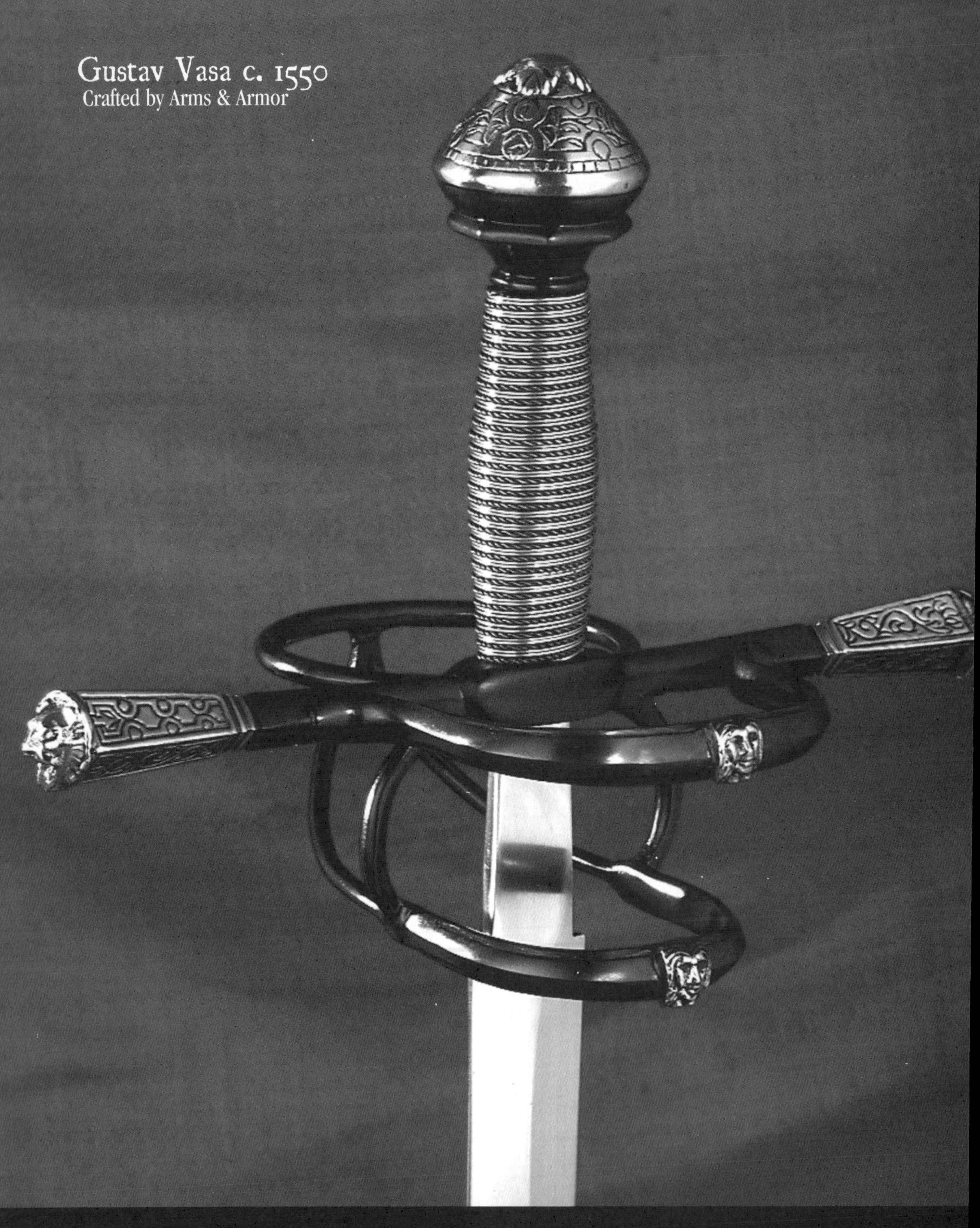

Gustav Vasa (1494-1560) was elected King of Sweden on June 6th 1523, and led the Swedish people to independence from the Danish King. This elegant replic depicts the personal weapon of King Gustav. It is an excellent example of the early style of rapier designed for the cut and thrust fencing. This steel replica i blued and accented with bright steel lion and medusa heads on the guard. This reproduction is fitted with a black and silver wire grip. Original: c. 1550@ German Hilt, Blade possibly Swedish, Royal Armory (LRK 13502), Stockholm.

"Milanese" Rapier c. 1570

Crafted by Arms & Armor

chille Marozzo and Camillo Agrippa would be quite familiar with this particularly fine sword. It is a classic style with two horizontal side rings and can be sed by either a right or left handed swordsman. Its highly distinctive hilt is blued and mounted with a wire grip crowned by turk's heads. The broad rapier lade is designed to give excellent service for both the cut & the thrust.

riginal: c.1570 Milan, Italy. Museo Poldi Pezzoli (2575)

Popular in England during the period 1580 to 1610, this form of hilt probably originated on the continent, but was introduced to England by craftsmen who immigrated in this period. Distinctive features of this type are the large globular pommel and medallions on the bars of the hilt. The pommels and guards are often covered in floral and figural details in silver over a russet or blackened finish. Arms & Armor has produced this rapier with vines, sunbursts and faces in burnished steel over a blued background. It is fitted with an authentic twisted wire wrapped grip using fine blackened and steel wire. The single bar inner guard has a graceful sweep to the guard and a loop at the front. This rapier is based on an original German rapier (A597) from the turn of the 17th century now in the Wallace Collection, London.

Cup-hilt rapier c. 1650
Crafted by Darkwood Armory
A fine example of what kinds of hilts can be fitted to the commercial "rebated" rapier blades such as those manufactured by Del Tin Armi Antiche.
Cup-hilt rapiers like this one appear to have originated in Spain during the middle of the 17th century and might have occasionally been seen borne by the Spanish in Italy.

"Writhen" rapier c. 1625

Crafted by Arms & Armor

A fine example of a relatively simple rapier of the late 16th or early 17th century. The heavily roped hilt brilliantly reflects the light and will impress friend and foe alike. This swept hilt rapier has a steel hilt and pommel with a twisted wire bound grip that is crowned with turks heads (a braided knot at top and bottom). The Italian original dates about 1625, though this style was seen as early as 1580's.

Original circa 1625, Italian.
(A602) Wallace Collection, London.
BL: 34-1/4" BW: 1" OL: 43-3/8"

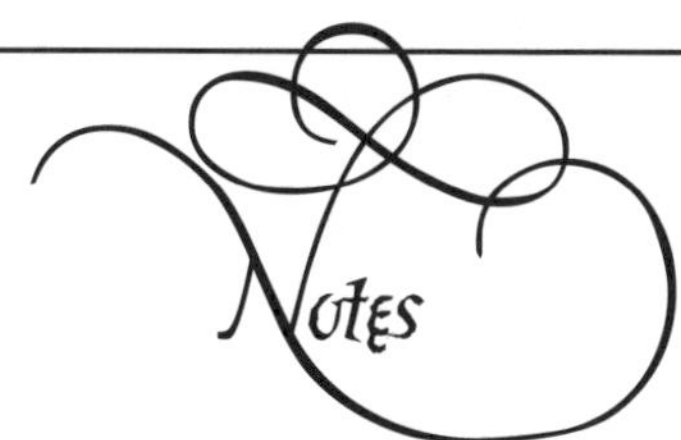

[1] Cited in Oakshott's *Records of the Medieval Sword*, Boydell Press, 1991.
[2] The use of the "short" sword, which was the direct descendant of the medieval arming sword, was detailed in George Silver's "Paradoxes of Defence" (1599) and his unpublished "Brief Instructions Upon My Paradoxes of Defence." Silver described a weapon that was broad-bladed, capable of severing limbs and with a keen point. He recommended the blade be fited with one of the new basket hilts (as opposed to a cross-hilt), but failing that a cross-hilt used with an armoured gauntlet was acceptable.
[3] Blair, Claude. *European and American Arms*, pp. 6-7, cited also in Norman, p. 20. The case is convincingly made in both presentations; the reader is strongly recommended to seek out both for a fuller treatment of the term's development.
[4] Because the weapons themselves are notoriously hard to date—few bearing anything like a date or even maker's signature—scholars of arms must rely upon iconographic sources to try to date many forms; in most cases a painting, sculpture or illuminated representation of a rapier will be sufficiently exact to instill confidence in its accuracy and the work itself may be more easily attributed to a known artist working at a given time and place.
[5] Norman, A.V.B., *The Rapier and Small Sword*, pp. 20-21.
[6] This work builds on his earlier work, *The Sword in the Age of Chivalry*.
[7] Indeed the esteemed Mr. Norman stated that he, "could find no evidence" tying the development of the Tuck or Estock together with the rapier, despite the common assertion by many students of arms and armour. See *The Rapier and Smallsword*, p. 21.
[8] See for example di Grassi, *Ragione di adropar sicuramente l'arme*. 3, 8 - 13.
[9] This case is convincing, despite popular culture references in the past two centuries depicting the rapier upon the battlefield, as in *The Three Muskateers*. See especially Mr. Blair's article and the analysis built upon it in Mr. Norman's book cited above, pp. 19-22. See also Dr. Sydney Anglo, *Martial Arts of Renaissance Europe*, p. 99, "there never was any general agreement as to what a rapier might be. It was only in England and Germany, around the middle of the decades of the 16th century, that *rapier* came to be used to denote a long sword which, though designed both for cutting and thrusting, placed emphasis on the use of the point rather than the edge: and in neither country has it been possible to establish a convincing etymology."
[10] Although he emphasizes the point that medieval swords must be taken in their holistic forms, he does classify them based on their blade-shape, and has less interest in the variations on the hilt.
[11] George Silver, *Paradoxes of Defence*, 1599.
[12] Oakeshott, *Records of the Medieval Sword, p. 115*.
[13] Presently in the Treasury of the Basilica of San Giovanni Battista, Monza.
[14] It should perhaps be mentioned, however, that the disk-shaped pommels of many modern swordsmiths are far too narrow. Most extant examples feature pommels that strongly balance the wider blades of these swords, and as such can be as much as 2" thick. See XVIII.1 as a particularly fine example, (Oakshott, p. 172).
[15] See Norman, A.V.B, op cit. p. 67-68.
[16] Now in the Metropolitan Museum of Art, MMA 61.200.1
[17] See Norman, A.V. B., op. cit. p. 78-80.
[18] See Norman, A.V. B., op. cit. p. 72-74.
[19] Federico Ghisliero recommended a rapier with a blade of "two armes length," and illustrated a sword whose sword reached from the ground to nearly the fencer's armpit. *Regole di molti cavaglireschi essercitii* (1587), p.18, 47. Ghisliero's measurements are almost identical to those of Capo Ferro (p. 7), while other masters recommended that the blade reach from the floor to the navel. (See Girard Thibault, *Academie de l'espee* p. 14 -15).
[20] *Worke for Cutlers: Or a Merry Dialogue between Sword, Rapier & Dagger*. "Acted in a shew in the famous University of Cambridge, 1615" ed. by Albert Forbes Sieveking. C. J. CLay & Sons, 1904. This is a wonderful play that underscores the tension that still persisted between the "short" sword described by George Silver and the civilian Rapier. The author of the original 1615 play is, sadly, unknown.

Spada da Lato

Achille Marozzo's *Arte dell'Armi* of 1536, 1540, 1550 and 1568 was to prove not only highly influential, but it was one of the last books to presented a system of fencing that relied as much on the edge as on the point. Marozzo's text, reminiscent of earlier fighting treatises, includes sections on the single *spada da lato* (the sidesword), sword and buckler, the longsword, and poleweapons.

Mystery of the Sidesword

The Foundations of Italian Rapier

As the rapier evolved, it continued to exist beside the earlier sidesword, a weapon that emphasized both point and edge. This chapter introduces the reader to early 16th century sidesword combat, which formed the foundation for the rapier fencing of the late 16th and early 17th centuries. During the end of the 15th century and throughout the 16th, there was a shift to a new form of purely civilian style combat. Military style combat did not disappear, but a new style of combat surrounding the duel of honor was developed. The foundations laid down by early masters such as Marozzo and Manciolino influenced later rapier combat. The concepts of time, how to attack via the cut and thrust, movement and the general terms used to describe fencing came from this period. So a study of these early masters will help in understanding late 16th and early 17th century rapier combat. As a full discussion of sidesword techniques can fill a book, this chapter will only touch upon some of the information that remained influential in rapier fencing for our period of interest.

One of the weapons used during Marozzo's time period was called the *spada da filo* in Italian ("edge sword"), and was primarily a cutting weapon.[1] Later, Camillo Agrippa called this sword the *spada da lato* or in English the "sidesword."[2] For convenience sake I will refer to this weapon as a sidesword.

In early 16th century Italy, Achille Marozzo wrote his *Opera Nova*, a fencing manual that covered a number of different types of weapons, one being the sidesword.[3] This is the earliest surviving book of its type and is the first known treatise covering civilian use of weapons. A number of editions of his book were published under two different titles, *Opera Nova*[4] and *Arte dell' Armi.*[5] The book is divided into five sections: section one and two deal with the sword (*spada sola*) alone or used in conjunction with the dagger (*pugnale*), round shield (*rotella*), square buckler (*targa*), round buckler (*brocchiero*), or cloak (*cappa*). Section three deals with the two handed sword (*spadone*). Section four is devoted to pole weapons including the pike, partisan, voulge and poleaxe. Section five covers the philosophy of fighting and the duel.[6]

Castle considers Marozzo "the greatest teacher of the old school."[7] This "old school" was founded by Master Filippo (or Lippo) di Bartolomeo Bardi (Neppo Bardi) at Bologna in 1413. Bardi was not only a fencing master, but also an astrologer and mathematician who taught at the famed University of Bologna. Bardi is said to have written a book on the relations between fencing and geometry, which has subsequently been lost. He died in 1464, and one of his best scholars was Guido Antonio di Luca, Marozzo's Master. Other students of di Luca included Manciolino, Francesco Altoni and possibly Giovanni dall'Agocchie (who later went on to write a fencing manual that is helpful in understanding Marozzo).[8]

The sidesword was a weapon used equally for both cutting and thrusting. Dr.William Gaugler describes this sword as having a short grip, a large, spherical pommel, crossbar (quillon), and a long slender blade that tapered to a point.[9] On the other hand, Arthur Wise describes the sword as heavy and ill balanced.[10] The sword was long, approximately half the height of the fencer (the quillons at the hip with the tip of the sword on the ground). The width of the blade at the ricasso was approximately three centimeters.[11] In my own studies of sideswords from the Howard de Walden Collection at Dean Castle in Scotland and the Royal Museum of Scotland in Edinburgh, I agree with Maestro Sinclair that the sidesword is a very agile weapon that is easily wielded. The sideswords that I examined weighed approximately one kilogram and had blade lengths from 86 to 96.5 centimeters.[12]

> "I wish thee to make thy scholar practice these things – the cuts and parries in the form of counter attacks – during four or five days with thee. As soon as he knows them well, I wish thee to begin and examine him in every guard, but

especially in those of Porta di ferro larga, stretta, o alta, also in Coda lunga e stretta. This thou shalt do as in a combat with sword and target or shield or buckler, or with the sword alone. Let this indicate to thee that in teaching a scholar to play with any of the above weapons, thou must make him understand all these guards, one by one, step by step, with their attacks and parries and everything pro and contra. Thou shalt see in these writings, and in the figures therein to be found – and therefore do not fail to succeed in teaching the same – that I make no difference in the guards on account of the weapons. But, in order not to cover too much space and to avoid repitition, I explain them merely in connection with the sword alone, or with the sword and buckler.[13]"

--Achille Marozzo

Marozzo instructed in technique on the primary cuts and thrusts used during the period. He also taught a number of guard positions. Manciolino describes the primary attacks as well as some secondary. The following is from his *Opera Nova* (1531):

"But first I will teach you the attacks. It is necessary that the name of the attacks are not secret. There are five principle and two that are not. The first is the *mandritto*. The second is the *roverso*. The third is the *fendente*. The fourth is the *stoccata* or *punta*. The fifth is the *falso*. Because the sword has two edges, that which looks towards the enemy is called the right (true) edge and that which remains towards you is called the false edge. If you throw a cut naturally towards your enemy that goes from the left ear to right knee or if you want, to any part of the left side, this is called the *mandritto*. But if you attack that which is counter, that is to his right side, high or low as you wish, it is said to be a *riverso*. And if you pull the sword between the middle of the two, that is to the head, it is said to be a *fendente*. But if the attack is from the ground against the face of your enemy, or if you want, to the right or the left side of your enemy, it is a *falso*. If you push a thrust at your enemy it is called a *stoccata*, with the left foot or the right, above or below the hand.

"Other than these five there are two that are not principle, because only in the play of sword and buckler are they seen. The first is called the *tramazzone*. This is made with the joint of the hand that has the sword. That is rising past your left side in the guise of a *fendente*. The other is called a *montante* because it is thrown rising in the manner of a *falso* that ends in the *guardia alta*."[14]

Marozzo described the cuts in far more detail than the thrusts. He categorized the cuts as *mandritti* and *roversi*. The *mandritti* were cuts delivered from the right and the *roversi* from the left. Both were issued with the right (also known as true) edge (*dritto filo*). Some of the cuts were delivered with the false or back edge of the blade. The cuts with the right edge were subdivided by the general angle of attack:

Tondo	A circular cut delivered horizontally
Sgualembrato	An oblique downwards cut
Fendente	A vertical downwards cut
Montante	A vertical upwards cut
Redoppio	An oblique upwards cut used to redouble an attack after a downward stroke.

As noted previously, cuts could also be delivered with the false or back edge of the blade. Marozzo called cuts with the false edge from the right *falso dritto* and from the left *falso manco*.[15] As far as attacks go, Marozzo said "And I tell you again that you must never attack without defending, nor defend without attacking, and if you do this you shall not fail."[16] The cut diagram from *Arte dell' Armi* is given from the perspective of the one issuing the cut. Other manuals that have similar cut diagrams show it from the perspective of the target.[17]

Marozzo uses three thrusts. The *punta* or thrust from the right is made with the sword at approximately shoulder height; the *stoccata* is a rising thrust from the right; and the *punta roversa* is a thrust from the left side. In my reading of Marozzo I would estimate that up to 50% of attacks are made with the thrust. However, most attacks begin with a cut, unless a feint is being made.

Although the term parry was used, it does not mean exactly what is termed a parry in modern fencing. According to Castle all attacks were to be countered with a counter-attack or a displacement of the body, or else they were to be warded with a buckler, cloak or dagger.[18] In my own reading of *Arte dell'Armi* I found that Marozzo details four different methods of defense:

1. **Static** – Marozzo in his section on the first assault of sword and small buckler shows the use of the *guardia di testa* as a static block. See chapter 10 part two of *Arte dell'Armi*.
2. **Expulsion with the false edge** –This defense is an expulsion or beating of the attacking blade to knock it out of line. Refer to Chapter 10 part five of *Arte dell'Armi*.
3. **True edge parries** –Refer to Chapter 10 part 6 of *Arte dell'Armi* for an example of the true edge parry.
4. **Stop cuts to the arm** –Refer to Chapter 15 of *Arte dell'Armi*.

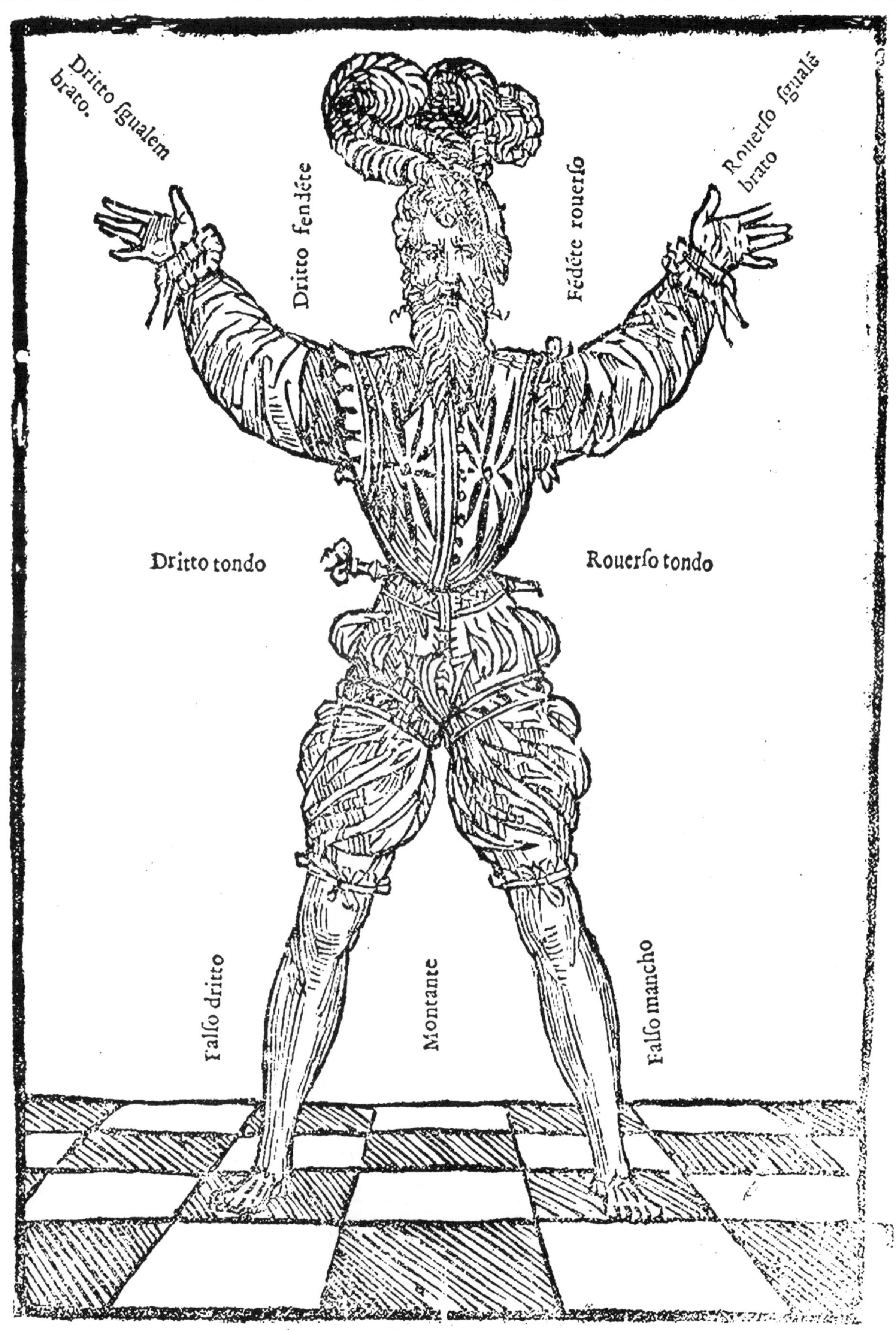

Cutting diagram from the 1536 edition of Marozzo's Arte dell'Armi, *showing the principle cuts. Note the continued emphasis on the cut rather than the thrust or* punta.

Principles of Sidesword Fencing

- Principle of the Hand and the Foot. In chapter 5 Marozzo said that the hand should go with the foot and the foot with the hand.[19] i.e. when the hand moves to attack or defend the appropriate foot will also move.
- Learn swordplay first and then add wrestling. Chapter 8.
- To know how to fence is good, but knowing how to fence *and* to teach makes one a double master. Chapter 8.
- If you are the active *agente* (the one initiating the attack), always start in the *guardia alta*. Chapter 10.
- Attack where the foot points. Chapter 10 part 6.
- Feint with *tramazzoni* (cutting attacks issued from the wrist with a circular cut) and thrusts. Chapter 15.
- When fighting with sword and dagger take up a guard with the left foot forward and open your combat with cuts to the hand. Always try and be the active *agente* when using sword and dagger. Chapter 37.

Marozzo's work is quite extensive. A comprehensive discussion of Marozzo's sidesword is the subject of a future work but I include it here for the sake of completeness and so that the student of the rapier might know something of what went before.

Guardia di Becca Cesa from Marozzo's 1568 edition. Note both the strong cutting orientation and the nature of the spada da lato itself; clearly oriented at cutting over thrusting.

Marozzo's guard positions are more invitations or positions to launch an attack from than true parries. The only exception may be the *guardia di testa*, used as in number one above.

Foot movement was used to maintain a proper fighting distance from an opponent. A number of specific steps were noted and others can be inferred from Marozzo's text. Footwork was generally natural and circular, involving steps off-line at both 45 and 90-degree angles.

Marozzo showed fifteen guards through illustrations and text. These guards were described with the single sword or with the sword and buckler. Fanciful names like *porta di ferro* (iron door) were given to the guards. Marozzo's manual uses the guard names to indicate starting and final positions. Sidesword combat should flow smoothly with the combatants moving from guard to guard, blades engaged at times and moving with absence of blade at others. The different guards must be learned and internalized so that they are used subconsciously to close lines and to provide invitations.

For modern swordplay I have distilled a number of principles from *Arte dell'Armi* that may be used for sidesword combat (chapter references are from *Arte dell'Armi*):

Marozzo's Guardia Porto di Ferro Stretta

Marozzo's Guardia di Faccia

Marozzo's Guardia di Testi

Marozzo's Guardia Alta

The title page to Camillo Agrippa's important treatise.

THE END OF SIDESWORD AND THE MOVE TO RAPIER

During the mid to late 1500's there was a shift in sword technique from cut-oriented combat to more focus on the thrust. This trend is most pronounced in the works of Camillo Agrippa and Giacomo di Grassi. However even Giovani dall'Agocchie who taught a system very similar to Marozzo indicated that the thrust was superior to the cut. On page 9 of his *Opera Necessaria* (published in 1572), he classifies the thrusts as:

> "Coming to the thrusts, that which is made with the hand high is the *imbroccata* and with the hand low is the *stoccata*. When it comes from the left side it is called the *punta roversa.*"[20]

In regards to cuts and thrusts he had this to say on page 14:

> "The one and the other are good. However, the attacks of the thrust are best. Because the thrust is of less time, is closer to the enemy and is more deadly."[21]

Dall'Agocchie was also a proponent of the use of the single sword. He indicated that it was preferred over other weapons.[22]

Camillo Agrippa published his book *Trattato di Scienza d'Arme* in 1553 and although the sword he used was a *spada da lato*, his theories set the stage for later, thrust-oriented rapier combat. According to Jacopo Gelli, Agrippa was not a master but a brilliant amateur.[23] Agrippa was a well known mathematician and architect, penning numerous books including his work on fencing. His *Trattato di trasportare la guglia in su la Piazza di S. Pietro,* published in 1584 is famous in architectural circles. His use of geometric diagramming, illustrations showing movement of the body, and the detailed descriptions of the movements in the text show a more scientific approach, in keeping with his profession as an architect, than prior writers.

> "The fundamental error of fencing in the 1500's had been, and was, the multiplicity of the guards...."[24]
>
> -Jacopo Gelli, 1906

Agrippa's contribution to fencing of the era was to simplify the many guards of Marozzo[25] and others of Marozzo's time period down to four fundamental guards that would be used by a number of later masters such as Fabris and Alfieri.

Agrippa's Guards

Agrippa started a shift to a more scientific approach to fencing and simplified the number of guards down to four. He also was instrumental in setting the stage for a move from cut-oriented swordplay to a more thrust-oriented style.

"Not being a teacher, he was not shackled by any conventionalities, and, accordingly, his book is original, and much in advance of the popular notions of his days. As an engineer he studied the link movements performed by the various parts of the human anatomy in the actions of the various parts of the human anatomy in the actions of thrusting and cutting, and his mathematical mind reveled in geometrical figures and optical diagrams devised for their explanation. No doubt his "philosophical dialogue" on that subject is very tedious, but "theory" led him to the useful practical result of discarding, on most occasions, the cut in favor of the thrust."[26]

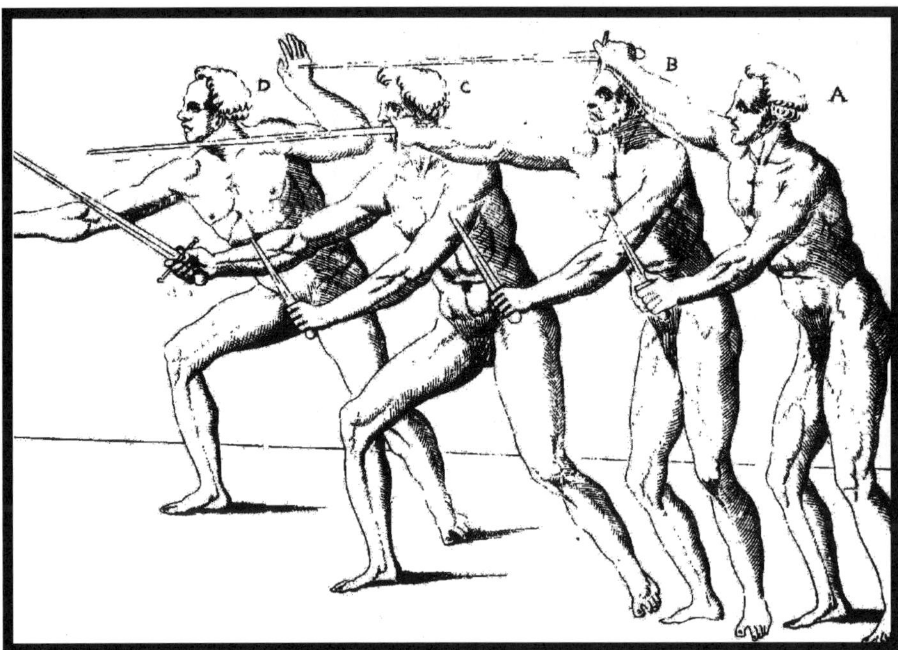

Agrippa's Four Guards shown in a single plate, not only a significant simplification of Marozzo's twenty guards, but also an increasing emphasis on the point, rather than the edge.

Agrippa's first guard came from the First position (*prima guardia*) that could be taken upon drawing the sword from the scabbard. The hand is high, above the head with the palm facing the right and the point directed at the opponent. "the prima guardia has to be the one that the fencer takes naturally, drawing the sword from the scabbard...[27] This guard is used to threaten an opponent.

Agrippa's second guard (*seconda guardia*) is made by lowering the hand and turning the palm down slightly. This guard is less tiring than the guard of first.

The third guard (*terza guardia*) is made by dropping the hand and raising the point. The palm of the hand is turned to the left. The feet are farther apart in this guard than in the prior two. In my opinion this guard is the most relaxed and least fatiguing of Agrippa's guards.

The fourth guard (*quarta guardia*) is made by turning the hand with the palm slightly up and moving the hilt across the body to guard the left side.

The Fight of Agrippa

Engagement of the blade was an integral part of Agrippa's fight.[28] Engagements in first and third were used and as the combatants circled each other, they looked for openings where a thrust could be made. Castle indicates that thrusts were delivered "by fully extending the arm, bringing the right shoulder forward, so as to be better covered, and slipping the left foot back.[29]" The face was also turned back and away when making the attack.

As with prior instructors and masters of fencing of the time, Agrippa taught that attacks were made on the pass. While, Gelli feels that the greatness of Agrippa's approach is much exaggerated,[30] I feel that Agrippa presented a basis in the science of fencing that later masters could build upon. This foundation is the basis of all Italian rapier play for the late 16th and early 17th centuries. We now turn to the study of a practical approach to a generalized system of Italian rapier fencing in the manner of this era.

[1] Achille Marozzo. *Arte dell'Armi.*

[2] Camillo Agrippa. *Trattata di Scienzia di Armes.* p 7.

[3] In chapter 31, Marozzo also refers to the arming sword or *spada di arme* in Italian. This was one of the military weapons of the time. He specifically mentions the arming sword in his Third Assault of sword and small buckler.

[4] Published in 1536, 1540, 1550, and 1568.

[5] Published in 1568, 1615, and 1892.

[6] Earlier manuscripts have been located from Italy as well as other countries that cover both swordplay and combat with other weapons. The earliest of the Italian texts is *Flos Duellatorum* by Fiore di Liberi (1409). This manual covers unarmed, dagger, arming sword, longsword and armored combat. Fiore himself claims to have read many fencing treatises, but none of these XIVth century treatises has yet come to light. The *Arte Dimicandi Gladiatoria* of Filipo Vadi (c.1482), the *Collecteana* of Pietro Monte (1509), and the *Opera Nova* of Manciolino (1531) are all multi-weapon systems that predate Marozzo.

[7] Egerton Castle. *Schools and Masters of Fence from the Middle Ages to the 18th Century.* (London, 1892) P. 48

[8] Francesco Novati. *Flos Duellatorum in armis, equester, pedester;* p. 108

[9] William Gaugler. *History of Fencing.* P. 2

[10] Arthur Wise. *History and Art of Personal Combat.* P. 36

[11] Personal communications with Maestro Andrea Lupo-Sinclair during 2001.

[12] I viewed the swords with Master Paul Macdonald of Edinburgh Scotland in June, 2001. As a representative sample here are the measurements of a sword from the Howard de Walden Collection: early 16th C. sidesword - overall length 40 1/8 inches with a blade length of 33 ½ inches. The ricasso is 1 inch wide and the shoulder of the sword is 1 3/8 inches. The balance point is 3 ½ inches from the cross.

[13] Egerton Castle. *Schools and Masters of Fence from the Middle Ages to the 18th Century.* (London, 1892). P. 52. Achille Marozzo. *Arte dell' Armi.* Cap 137.

[14] Antonio Manciolino. *Opera Nova.* p. 10.

[15] Egerton Castle. *Schools and Masters of Fence from the Middle Ages to the 18th Century.* (London, 1892). p. 49

[16] Achille Marozzo. *Arte dell' Armi.* Cap 2. "Et anchora te dico, che tu non gli dia mai ferire senza il suo parato, et cosi parato senza il suo ferire, et se cosi farai non portrai fallire."

[17] For example Salvator Fabris. *Sienz e Practica d'Arme*, (Copenhagen, 1606). p. 30.

[18] Egerton Castle. *Schools and Masters of Fence from the Middle Ages to the 18th Century.* (London, 1892) p.50

[19] Original Italian from Arte dell'armi Capitula 5: "...et insegnarli d'accompagnare la mano con il piede, et il piede con la mano, ..."

[20] Translation by the author.

[21] Translation by the author.

[22] Giovanni Dall'Agocchie. *Opera Necessaria.* 1572. p. 13.

[23] Jacopo Gelli. *L'Arte Dell'Armi in Italia.* 1906. p. 86.

[24] Gelli. p. 88. Translation by author. Original Italian reads: "La errore fondamentale della scherma del Cinquecento era stato, ed era, la molteplicita delle guardie,..."

[25] Gelli notes on p. 88 of his book that Marozzo had some 24 different guard positions.

[26] Egerton Castle. *Schools and Masters of Fence...* London. 1892. p. 60.

[27] Jacopo Gelli. *L'Arte Dell'Armi in Italia.* 1906. p. Translation by author. Original reads: *la prima guardia abbia da essere quella che lo schermitore prende naturalmente, appena tratta la spada dal fodero...*"

[28] Per Maestro Andrea Lupo-Sinclair, from personal conversation and from a class on Agrippa/Sidesword at the Lansing Swordsmanship Symposium, July 2001.

[29] Egerton Castle. *Schools and Masters of Fence..."* London. p. 66.

[30] Jacopo Gelli. *L'Arte Dell'Armi in Italia.* 1906. p. 86. "La Opera dell' Agrippa ebbe, fino dal suo apparire, il favore dei piu; ed anche dai critici moderni di oltra Alpe dell' arte delle armi il merito del libro fu esaltato sino all' esagerazione."

"In Truth this science of arms is merely the science of deceiving your adversary with subtlety."
--Salvatore Fabris, 1606

"Fencing is the Art of Defending oneself with the sword." --Ridolfo Capo Ferro, 1610

When fencing with a partner, you must wear correct protective gear. If you are not familiar with groups such as the *Association of Historical Fencing*, the *Tattershall School of Defense*, or the *Society for Creative Anachronism* (SCA), you should try to find a chapter of one of these organizations in your area. The AHF, TSD or SCA guidelines for protective gear will be adequate for all rapier play (see the section on armoring). These are only three examples of organizations devoted to the study of historical fencing; there are numerous others.

Or simply put, without correct protective gear you should not take part in rapier combat and practice.

Proper clothing, footwear and protective gear is important in that it both connects the fencer with the long history of the art and yields similar movements. One does not, for example, move the same in a 16th century doublet as they do in a fencing school t-shirt. Nor can one lunge effectively in tennis shoes. Similarly, there is no replacement for a rapier of quality, for an epee is not a rapier, and while a perfectly valid modern weapon, it handles nothing like the historical rapier and should thus not be substituted for it. Acquire a quality weapon and take good care of it!

When studying historical fencing, you must transcend physical movement and learn to make the sword an extension of your own body. Additionally, many of the early masters incorporated philosophy along with the technical aspects of swordplay. The philosophy of fence, especially of the period covered by this book (late 16th to early 17th centuries), included the concepts of honor and how the swordsman thought about not only taking part in the duel, but when the duel was justified at all.

Each teacher of fencing codified his or her own system, but based on the common underlying principles of the Italian school, and often with a common teaching style. Following in this tradition, this book presents a set of guidelines and techniques that you may use when fighting in a Renaissance style with the rapier. This system is my own, based upon the philosophies and techniques that I have learned through my study of primary sources. After you have gotten a general feel for the Italian style of rapier (the style given in this book), I would suggest that you make an advanced study of one of the historical masters.

You must not only master the use of the single rapier to be proficient at rapier fencing, but also the rapier and dagger, rapier and cloak, rapier and buckler and case of rapiers. However, prior to taking a weapon in hand the stance and footwork must be learned. Without a proper guard (stance or *ward*) and footwork the fencer is at the mercy of a more experienced opponent. Therefore, the first step in studying the Arte of Defence is to learn how to take the rapier into the hand, and move with it.

NOTE: The examples, illustrations and descriptions given in this manual are all referenced for a right-handed fencer unless otherwise noted. Please reverse all instructions if you are left-handed. Also, I have chosen to include a female fencer in the photographic reconstructions of these texts. As the modern practice of rapier fencing is open to and popular with both genders, the decision was made to dress the woman *as* a woman, rather than disguising her as a man. While this is an anachronistic conceit, I believe it better maintains the tone of the photography than dressing her in modern attire.

Stance and Foot Movement

"You cannot lose if you are not hit, and you will not be hit if you are not there."

--William Wilson's First Axiom of Fencing

Movement is critically important in rapier combat. Until the sword was used as much for defense as for offense, one basic defensive technique was to dodge an opponent's attack (historically called *voiding*).

Guard and footwork are paramount in learning the Art of Defence. Both arise from having a strong stance.

The stance is your base and all movement originates from it. To make your stance, face your opponent with your right foot forward, the toe of said foot pointing at your adversary. The left foot should fall behind about a shoulder's width with the toes pointing out perpendicular to the front foot (the rear foot may be turned up to 45 degrees towards the front). The knees should be slightly bent with the knees generally over the insteps of the feet and the body held upright. Depending upon which guard/ward you will use, the right arm will be in a slightly different position, as will the body. Your off-hand (left hand) is held loosely in front of your chest with the edge of the hand (fingers together) facing your opponent. Do not position your hand out too far from the body or it may be injured. The right arm is held loosely in front of the body and dipping towards the ground with the palm to the left, the hand approximately at the level of the hip. This is the basic stance.

Your head and upper body should remain upright except in very specific circumstances. The arms and body should also be kept as loose as possible to facilitate smooth movement. Masters from the time period taught to hold the body many different ways. For example Salvator Fabris had his students lean in various directions based upon what they were doing.

> "When you understand how to control the figure and stand without strain, to stand low is more useful. But if you cannot do this it is better to stand upright, for if you are in a strained posture you cannot be quick to move. Whereas a body bent at a suitable angle and well balanced on the feet is much securer being less exposed, and can be defended with little movement of the weapons. The forces are more united, and this union generates vivacity and swiftness of movement in one who is well used to this position. To take up this position in the required manner needs practice and entails fatigue. But afterwards it will be found more quickly and easily; you will be readier and safer in every case, will defend yourself without getting into disorder, hit more swiftly and reach further."[22]

Stances in the guard Quarte compared in Salvatore Fabris (left) and Ridolfo Capo Ferro. Note how Salvatore advocates a leaning position, while Capo Ferro seems to prefer a more upright stance. For beginners, I generally recommend a position more like Capo Ferro's.

Ridolfo Capo Ferro also advocated leaning a little.

> "In remaining on guard and searching for measure, the body should be stooped and leaning to the rear as if at an angle that is made with the right thigh....And with the left thigh to be made with an obtuse angle such that the left shoulder is in line with the left foot and the right separated by half a pace."[3]

In Capo Ferro's illustrations of the guards--see pages 66-69--he shows the guard of Third made in this fashion with the body leaning back a little. In other guards such as Fourth or First he shows the body leaning forward a little. Fabris' guards and body positioning are similar.

I advocate keeping the body upright for the beginning fencer to aid in balance. With an upright stance you can center your weight which will make your movement easier as a beginner. Shifting weight is an advanced technique that you will study at a later point in your study of historical fencing .

Once you have practiced the basic stance, the next step is to master movement. I advise begining your footwork practice without a sword in hand at least the for first few weeks of your instruction. This will allow you to concentrate on your footwork and gain a firm foundation in movement before having to worry about what you are doing with the weapon in your hand. Once you are comfortable with the basic steps, then you should move to doing the same with a weapon in hand. Movement is your foundation and without a good foundation you will not be able to fence effectively.

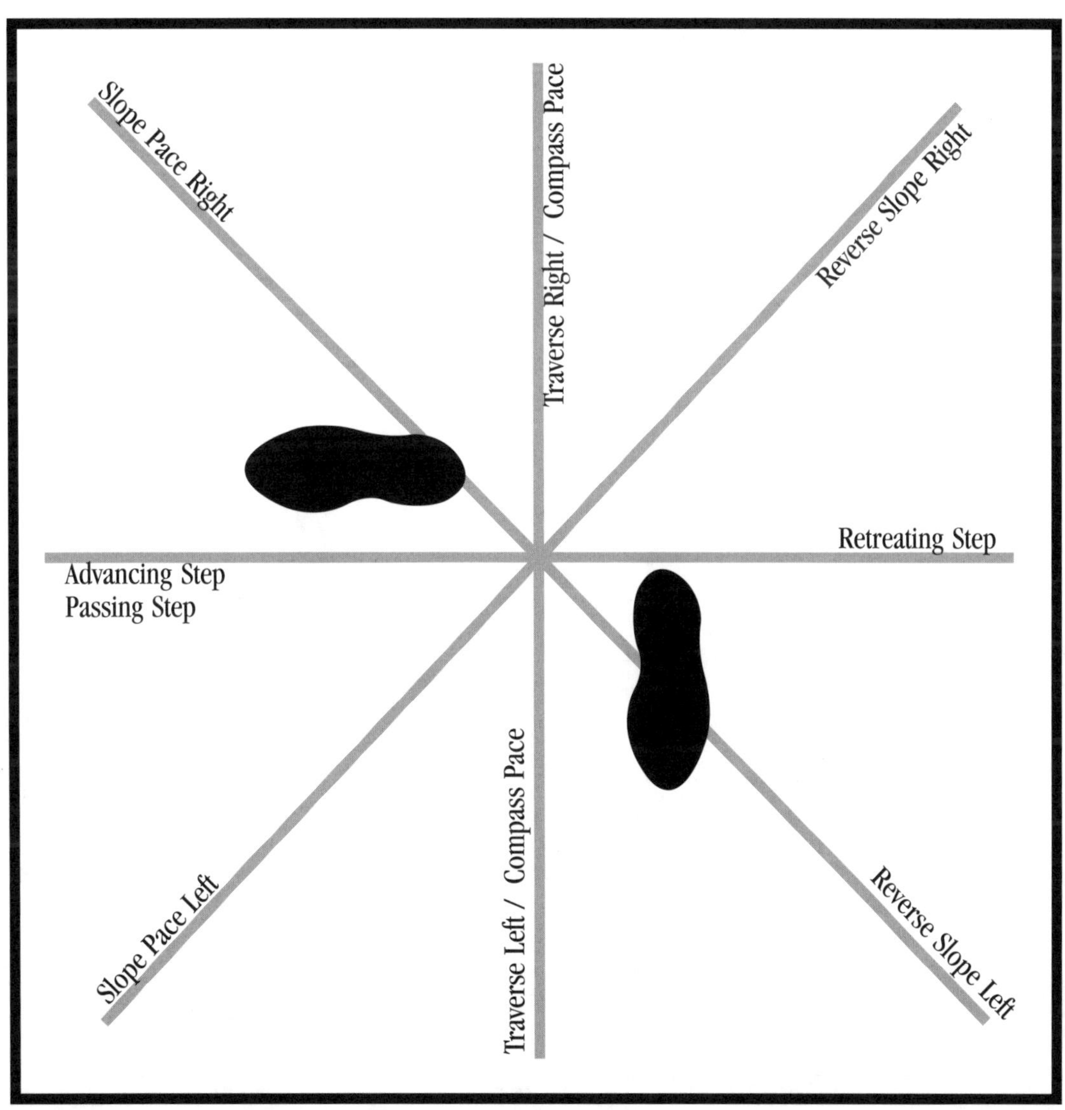

The basic stance and simple step directions in Italian rapier. While modern sport fencing emphasizes advancing, retreating and passing steps, the rapier requires a great deal of "off-line" movement, a characteristic common to medieval swordsmanship as well.

The historic manuals cover a number of different methods for taking and losing ground. In general these may be broken down into three distinct movements: advance, retreat and the pass.

The Advance

You will advance by moving the leading foot forward and following it with the rear foot. This type of fencing step was advocated by Capo Ferro:

> "in movement the left foot always accompanies the right and step in a straight line, one foot chasing the other, the forward then the rear."[4]

Only move your rear foot the distance that your leading foot went forward. Do not bring your rear foot right up against the heel of the leading foot. Also, be careful not to take too big of a step. In so doing you may be caught off-guard by a sudden attack from your adversary and you will not be able to retreat in time. I would suggest beginners keep their weight centered between the legs. Do not lean forward or back. Historical masters advocated placing more weight on the forward or rear leg. For example Saviolo taught:

> ". . . he shall cause him to stand upon his ward; as the teacher shall deliver the rapier into his hand and shall cause him to stand with his right foot formost, with his knee somewhat bowing: but that his body rest more upon his left legge, not steadfast and firm, as some stand, which seem to be nailed to the place, but with a readinesse and nimbleness; as though he were to perform some feate of activity."[5]

Di Grassi[6] also taught to place more weight on the left (rear) leg. I advocate centering the weight between the legs for beginners as it facilitates easier movement with either foot for the various foot movements. While I do not have definitive proof that this was advocated in period, I have found that it is a useful technique for a beginning fencer to use when fencing in a generic Italian style with the rapier.

The Retreat

To retreat, step back with the trailing foot and follow it with the forward foot. Be careful to only move the forward foot back the distance that the trailing foot moved as with the advance. When moving the trailing foot do not drag the foot or step too high; barely skim the ground. Precipitate moving the front foot with a raising of the toes. All movement is from the heel of the foot. Do not fight from the balls of the feet for it will drastically alter your balance. Your center of gravity should be between your legs. Do not lean forward or backward in your stance until you are comfortable with the standard movement.

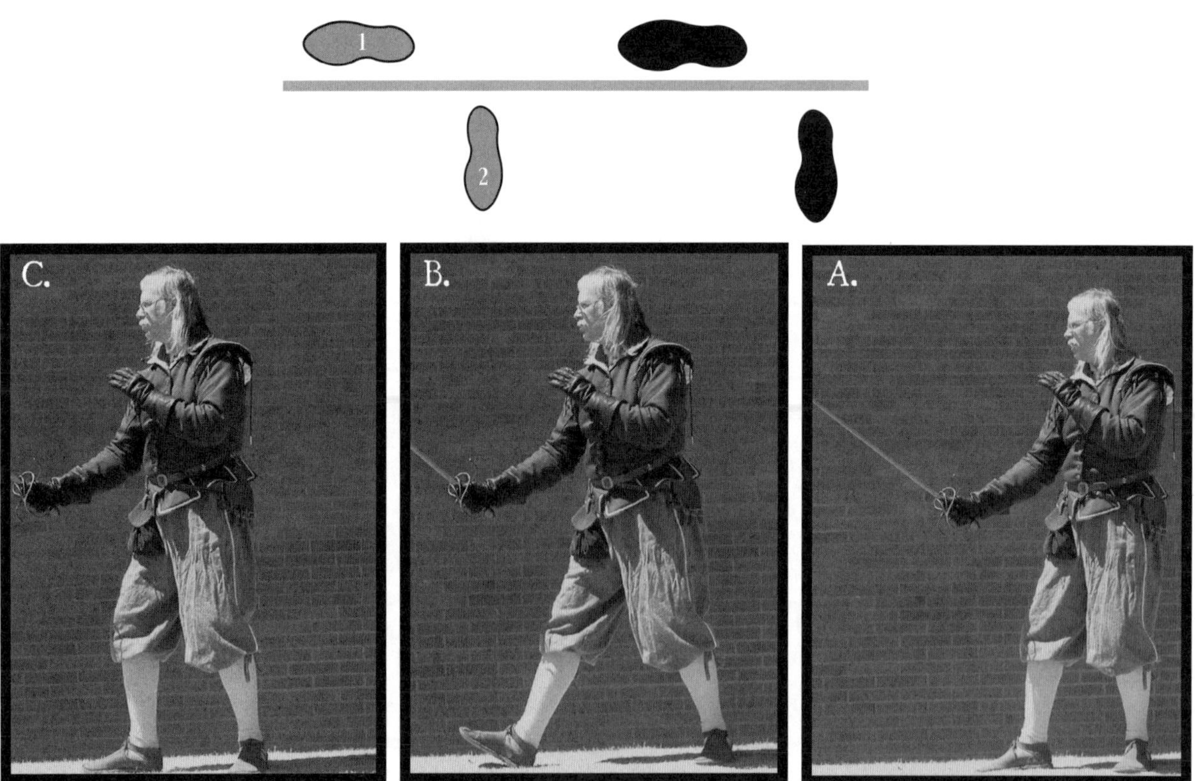

Bill Wilson excecutes a simple advance. Starting in the 3rd ward, the front foot is moved forward, followed by the back foot. To execute a retreating step, simply move the back foot first, then follow with the leading one.

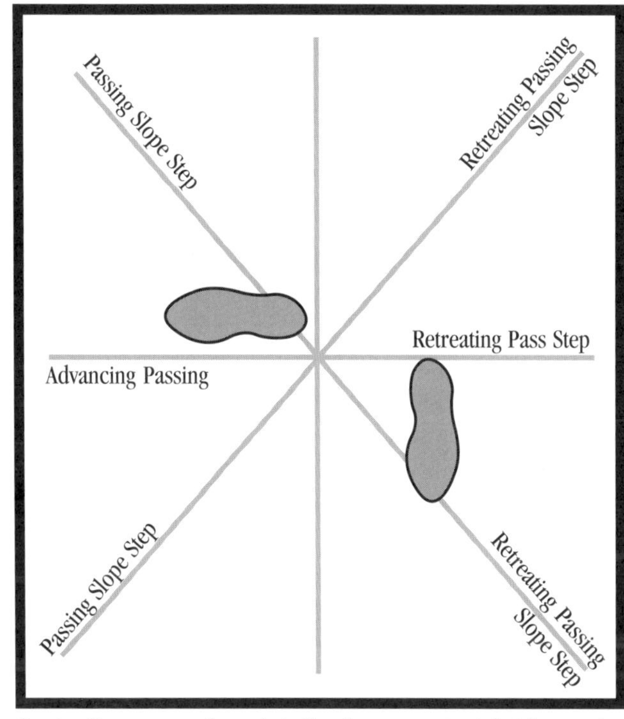

Passing Steps are usually made in the advance or retreat, but they can less commonly be used to move rapidly in a sloping direction, either forwards or backwards. Depending upon the movement of the left foot when it is brought forward it can be placed with the toes pointing forward or up to 90 degrees to the left, as shown above.

The Pass

The pass or passing step is used to cover ground quickly. When executing a forward passing step move the rear foot ahead of the forward foot. Immediately follow by moving the forward foot to the front again. In a retreat the forward foot is moved behind the rear foot and the trailing foot is immediately moved back into its normal position. This type of movement in a retreat may also be used to displace your body out of the way of a cut or thrust from your opponent (by voiding or dodging the blade). With passing steps your footwork should feel natural, like walking, only more balanced.

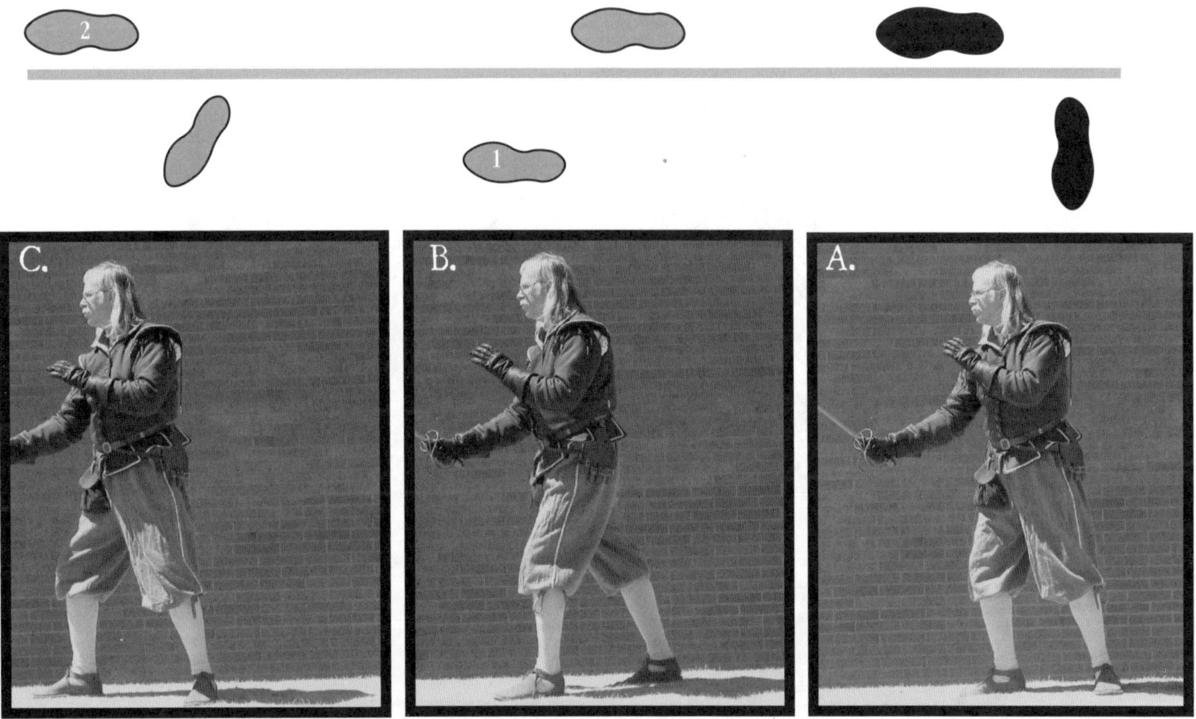

Wanting to cover ground quickly (A), William now executes a passing step in the advance, bringing the back foot across the front foot (B), then resetting the front foot to its normal "en guard" position (C).

The Half Pace

di Grassi taught a type of step called the *half pace*. To do this step one foot is moved such that it does not pass the other foot. For example, if I make a half pace with the rear foot, I would bring the foot forward up to, but not past, the lead foot.

> "Now the middle of these back and fore paces, I will term the half pace: and that is, when the hindfoot being brought near the forefoot, does even there rest: or when from thence the same foot goes forwards. And likewise when the forefoot is gathered into the hindfoot, and there does rest, and then retires itself from hence backwards. These half paces are much used, both straight and crooked, forwards and backwards, straight and crooked."[7]

This step is useful in both offense and defense. For defense it may be used to move the forward leg back out of the way of a cut. This keeps the body in the same relative position so that you may reach your opponent with a counter-attack as their blade passes by where your forward leg used to be. In offense it may be used to bring the rear leg forward so that you may take a long forward step with the leading foot to make an attack (i.e. the lunge). This allows you to close distance with your opponent quickly.

You must also keep from bouncing, hopping, or dipping when you move. Any odd quirks that you develop can, and most assuredly will, alert your opponent to your actions. Di Grassi was explicit on this subject:

> "And above all, not to skip or leap, but keep one foot always firm and steadfast: and when he would move it, to do it upon some great occasion, considering the foot ought chiefly to agree in motion with the hand, which hand, ought not in any case whatsoever happen to vary from his purpose, either in striking or defending."[8]

Once you have learned the simple advance and retreat and have studied passing steps you will move on to other movements.

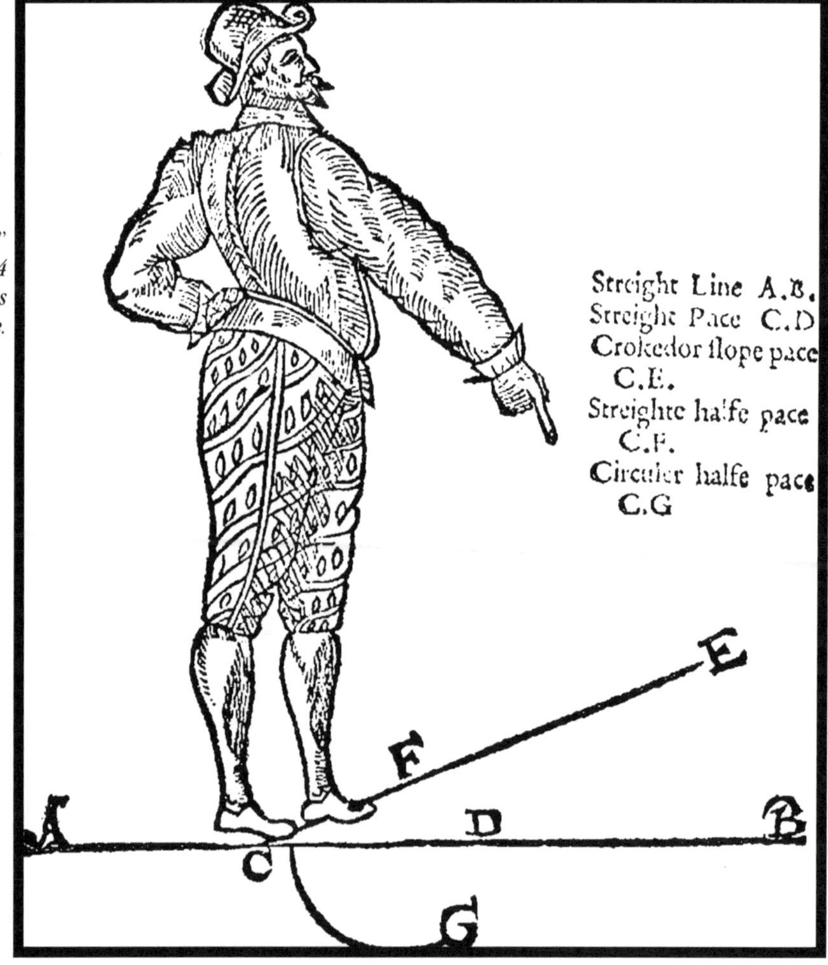

di Grassi's "Of Paces" *diagram from the 1594 English edition of his fencing treatise.*

Drills

Move back and forth with the advance, retreat, pass and half-pace. With a partner you must learn how to keep your distance. The distance is how far away from your opponent you will stand. Pick the distance that you want to maintain and then as your partner moves use your footwork to maintain that distance.[9] This is not a dance where they take one step and then you do. If you are shorter than your partner you may need to take two steps to their one, etc. Work on this as often as possible so that keeping the same distance from your partner becomes second nature.

Practice

Even after you feel comfortable with your movement keep practicing! Working on your footwork with and without a partner will increase your ability to move smoothly. As a partner you may also help point out deficiencies in a new fencer's footwork. In particular you should look for:

! Taking too large of a step
! Bobbing or dipping of the upper body
! The arms waving about while stepping
! Turning in of the front toe

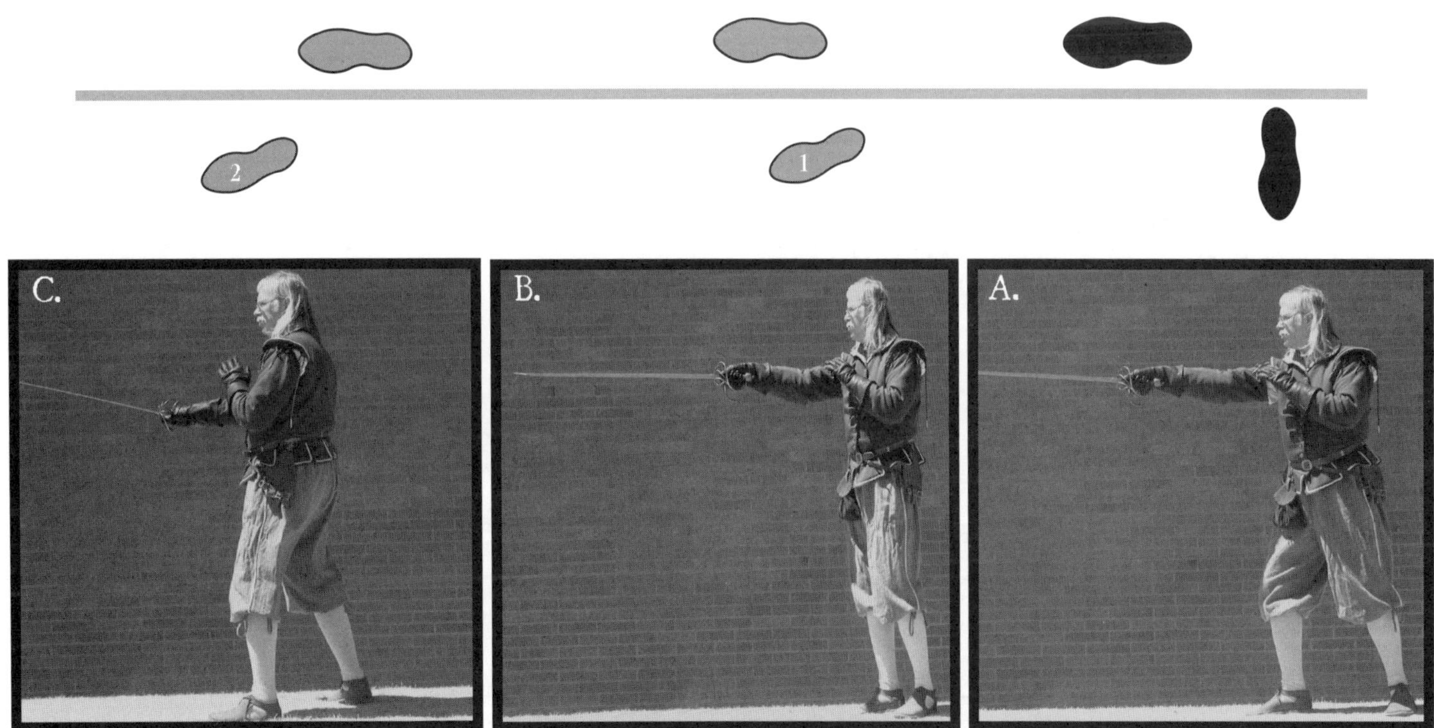

William begins in a high 3rd ward (A). A half-pace is made to gain distance (B)...followed by a passing step in a traverse to the left with a turn of the hand into 2nd ward (C).

Sloped Paces

A sloped or crooked pace is a step that is made off the straight line, that is, an angular step. In the Renaissance, the slope was used to gain an advantage via angle of attack. Stepping on a forward angle to the right or left would take your body away from the incoming attack while bringing your own weapon into a better position to counterattack.

In an orderly retreat you may also use a slope pace to the right or to the left to maximize the potential for you to hit as well as to minimize the possibility of being hit yourself.

> "It is to be knowen that the feete move either streightly, either circulerly: If streitly, then either forwardes or backwards: but when the move directly forwards, the frame either a halfe or a whol pace. By whole pace is understood, when the foot is carried from behind forwards, kepinge stedfast the forefoot. And this pace is sometimes made streight, sometimes crooked. By streight is meant when it is done in the streit line, but this doth seldome happen. By croked or slope pace is understood, when the hinderfoot is brought also forewards, but yet a thwarte or crossing: and as it groweth forwardes, it carieth the bodie with it, out of the straightline, where the blowe is given."[10]

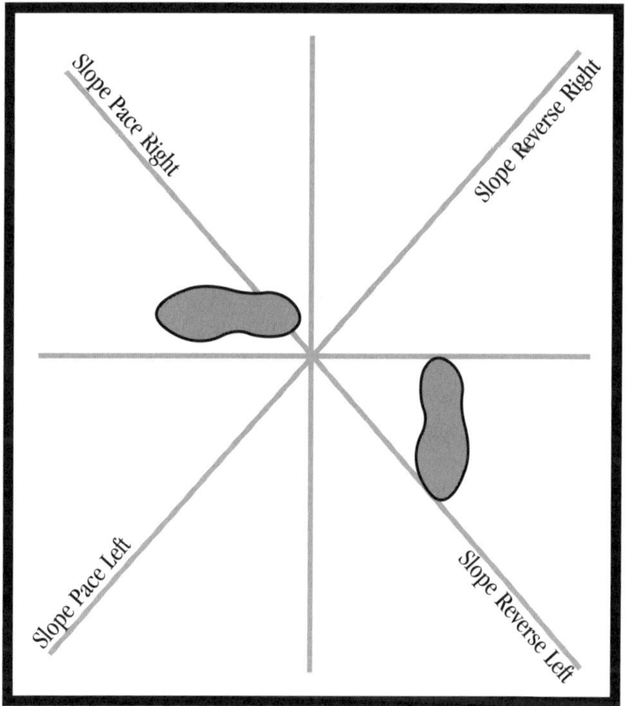

Slope paces are very effective--and very fast--at moving the body or the blade offline; they are a core step in the mechanics of Italian rapier and should be practiced extensively.

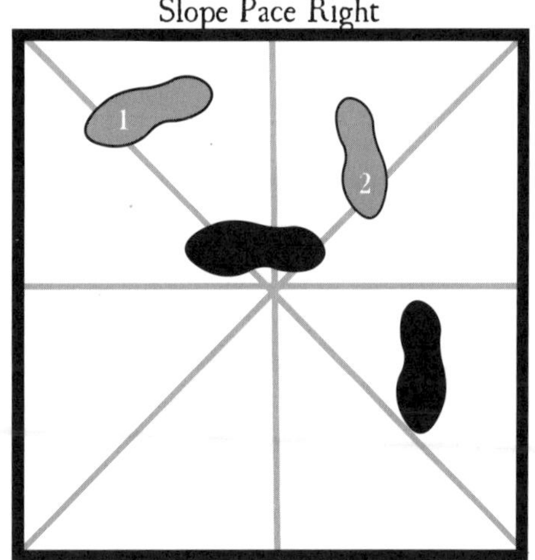

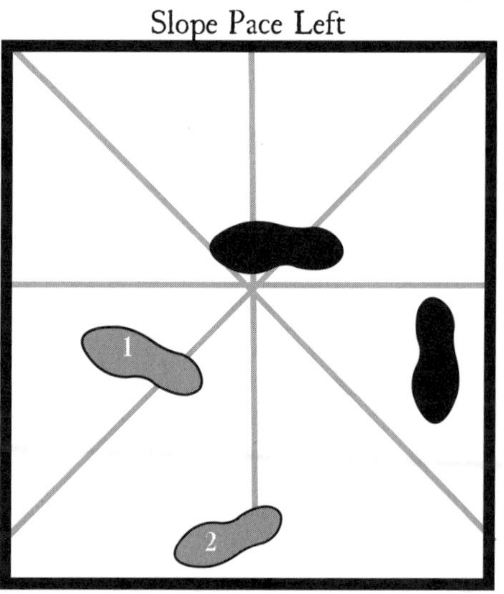

Note that as the sloping step is made either to the left or to the right that the orientation of the body changes with respect to the target. Not only does this have the effect of moving the body out of line for the opponent's attack, but it also changes the distance to the target. Like all aspects of footwork, one of the main objectives for footwork is to control the distance to the opponent, ever-critical with the very small movements necessary to score a thrust or a cut. The examples as shown above portray only the sloping movement done with an advancing-type step forwards; sloping steps may also be combined with passing steps to gain distance faster, or to retreat.

Traverses

Hutton described the traverse as a step to the side where you shift your feet sideways. To traverse to the left, the left foot moves first and vice versa. Traverses were heavily used by di Grassi and Saviolo. Saviolo advocated the side-step "circle-wise" to be used almost exclusively:

> "V. At the selfesame time the scholler must remove with the like measure or counter-time with his right foot a little aside, and let the left foote follow the right, turning a little his bodye on the right side, thrusting with the point of his rapier at the belly of his teacher, turning redily his hand that the fingers be inward toward the body, and the joint of the wrist be outward. In this sorte the saide scholler shall learne to strike and not be stricken, as I alwaies advise the noble men and gentlemen with whome I have to deale, that if they cannot hit or hurt their enemy, that they learn to defend themselves that they be not hurt. Then to make the scholler more ready, the teacher shall cause his scholler firste to part, wherefore he shall remove with his right foot on the right side a little in circle wise as the maister did before to the scholler."[11]

Traversing Pace Right

Traversing Pace Left

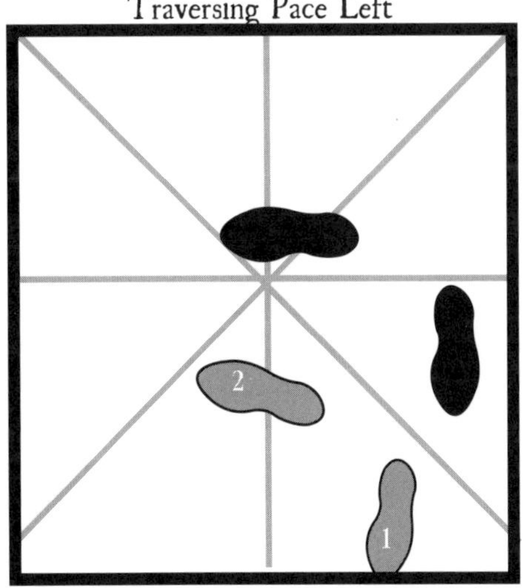

Di Grassi called this movement a *compass*:

> "Circuler paces, are no otherwise used than halfe paces, and they are made thus: When one hath framed his pace, he must fetch a copaise with his hinder foote or fore foote, on the right or lefte side: so that circuler paces are made either when the hinder-foot standing fast behinde, doth afterwards move it selfe on the lefte or right side, or when the fore-foote being setled before doth move likewise on the right or left side: with all these sort of paces a man may move everie waie both forwardes and backewardes."[12]

Circular movement used in conjunction with slope paces will give you better angles of attack on your opponent. For example if your opponent attacks with a forward step on the straight line and you step at an angle to the right, letting your opponent's point pass by you to where you used to be, you will be closer to your opponent on their inside line.

As you move you must vary your pace (take different sized steps) so as to throw off your opponent's distance. When an opening then presents itself you attack.

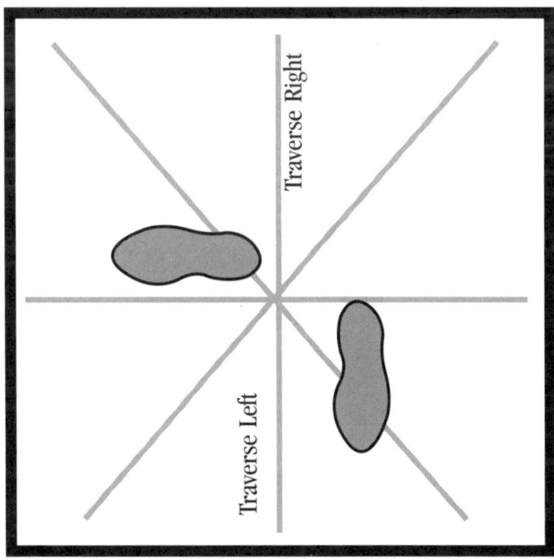

Traversing steps--called "compass steps" by di Grassi and strongly advocated by Master Saviolo; when connected together, they have the effect of moving the combatants in a circle.

Note that traversing or compass steps to the right begin with the right foot--as in the illustration above-left--while those to the left begin with the left foot and are followed with the right.

It is frequently the case during a good bout that one fencer will take a traversing step and will be immediately answered by his opponent; if he takes one to the right, for example, his opponent counters with one to the left. In this way the two circle in a subtle challenge of movement before the swords cross.

The Importance of Basic Footwork

As mentioned before, both distance and time in rapier combat are controlled by the positions of the feet; hence, solid footwork is more than just fundamental to fencing with the rapier--it is impossible to fence well without it.

Each instructor will devise many drills to continually build and enhance the student's footwork, no matter that the students are beginners, intermediates or advanced in their skills. Drills can and should always be emphasized in practice to steadily refine the fencer's movements over the course of years.

The drills given below are just a few of those that could be devised for basic footwork; you should set aside a portion of each practice to work on footwork, and the payoff will be great when you find yourself able to execute very subtle movements under the stress of the engagement without conscious thought.

Footwork Drill #1
Simple Advances & Retreats

Assuming their guard, students attempt to maintain distance while responding to advances and retreats by their opponent. Each student directs the action for a while, then the roles are changed and the other initiates the action. There is no victor; both students should strive for elegant movement with small motions and great efficiency.

Footwork Drill #2
Slope & Traversing Step

The master puts the student in the basic stance. The master then attacks along the straight line at the student's belly. The student steps to the right and forward with the right foot followed by the left, letting the point pass by his body.

The advanced footwork drills may be done without a sword in hand, then repeated once the guards are understood with sword in hand.

Footwork Drill #3
Traversing Step Counters

Master and student both face one another in their chosen guard. Each takes turns making traversing steps to both sides and the other counters with the appropriate steps. Movements should be smooth and elegant, not jerky and awkward. Eventually, there will be very little if any delay apparent and the two should appear to move as one.

Notice how, when the counter is not made, the angle of attack will change and opportunities arise.

Footwork Drill #4
Distance & Stepping

As with the traversing step drill the master will take a passing step and the student will maintain distance. The master should alternate between normal advances and retreats and the passing steps so that the student may practice maintaining distance.

All footwork in fencing with the rapier should be made with elegance, yet surety. Steps are not clunky, but should be smooth and as efficient as possible.

It is easy, with sloppy footwork, to place one's self in danger by moving inadvertantly into range or to move inadvertantly out of your own striking range. Similarly, inefficient movements cause deficits in time that can be very costly; under the stress of an engagement, every *fraction* of a second counts--not just the seconds themselves.

An Advanced Foot Movement: The *Incartata* or *Volte*

The *incartata*, or *volte*, is a defensive move that will be employed in a *stesso tempo* (single time, to be discussed later) defense where the body is moved out of the line of attack while at the same time thrusting in quarta with opposition against the incoming attack.

> "To Voltere is, when thine adversary doth thrust at thee, and thou first parering his thrust, doest just upon the approaching of his thrust turn thy body round about towards thy left side out upon thy right leg, so that thy back cometh towards thine adversary, and thy left leg between thy right, and thine adversary's right leg, and thrusteth him with a Quarta at his right breast: But this is a trick altogether full of danger, unless it be used to avoid the Passade withal."[13]

In this movement your back actually faces your opponent. This move takes a lot of agility but can be used effectively against an aggressive opponent who launches strong thrusts.

Fabris taught this technique but did not call it an *incartata*. He simply described the movement. In the section where he describes the variations of the guard in Quarta he said:

> "This is another extension in Quarta, made with a turn of the left foot. It may be used in the time when your adversary tries to hit on the inside in Terza or Seconda, or to pass below."[14]

One page 70 of *Gran Simalucro* Capo Ferro describes this move, which is shown in plate 19.

> "Figure D being on guard to the outside and disengaging to give a thrust to the face of C, C attacks in quarta with an avoidance of the body passing the left leg crossing behind the right as may be seen in the figure."

Drill For the *Volte*

The master brings the student on guard in the basic stance. The master thrusts at the student's left breast, who turns the body counterclockwise, taking the left foot behind and to the right of the right foot, letting the point of the master's sword pass by the body.

Stepping the *Volte*

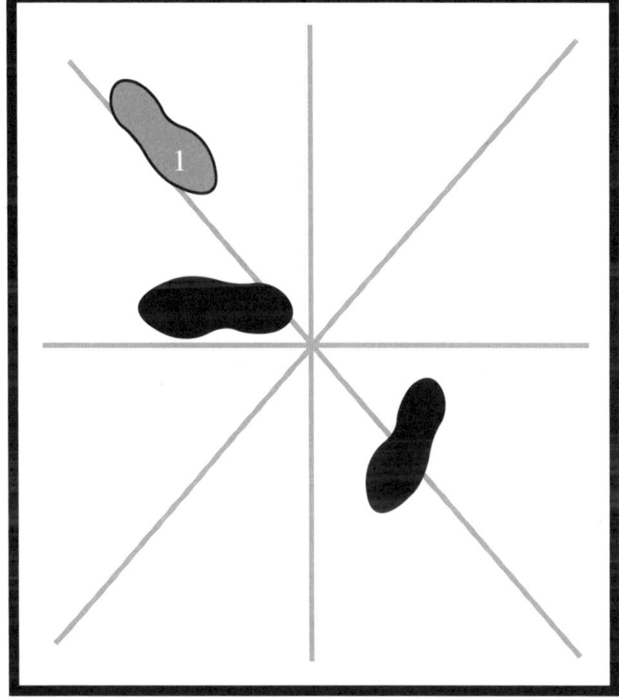

The Volte *or* Incartata *is a very sexy and effective motion that is used to move your body out of line of an incoming attack while simultaneously gining an angular advantage.*

Ridolfo Capo Ferro illustrates the incartata.

The Guards

A good guard is the second pillar of rapier fencing. Having gained some expertise in movement, you will next learn how to hold the sword. Your stance and how you hold your sword (the orientation of your weapon) is your guard. It is used to guard part of your body. The term *ward* was also used in England and means the same thing as guard.

> "Wards in weapons are such sites, positions or placings which withstand the enemies blows, and are as a shield or safeguard against them."[15] --Giacomo di Grassi, 1594.

Grip

Before any ward can be taken, we must look briefly at how to hold the sword. Grip the sword by taking the rapier loosely in hand and by placing the index finger over the forward quillon and wrapping the remaining fingers and thumb around the grip. It it important not to "choke" the sword with too firm a grip--this is a waste of energy and also reduces your ability to "float" the point --but it is equally important not to hold too loose a grip lest the weapon be easily twisted from your hand. The grip should be natural, but firm.

The rapier should be gripped with a natural, firm yet relaxed hand; one that is sufficiently nimble to maneuver the point with precision, yet one that maintains control of the blade under the press of the encounter.

The sword will be held in various positions based upon the wards that you will employ. I suggest that as a beginner you practice all of the wards but start with mastering the Third Ward, as I find it the most natural, least fatiguing and most defensive guard. With this are positions of the hand that will normally relate to the guards. The figure to the right shows the four standard hand positions. First – the palm is to the right, Second – the palm is down, Third – the palm is to the left, and Fourth – the palm is up. These hand positions will be used later in the text to help clarify hand positioning during specific techniques.

> "The four guards arise from the four faces of the hand and the sword, that is to say the two edges and the two surfaces; and these produce four different positions."[16]

I will use Fabris'[17] descriptions of the wards, with information from other historical masters used to help illustrate similarities or differences in style.

The description of each primary guard will start with a quote from Fabris.[18] The four primary guards were first taught by Agrippa and were used in one form or another by various succeeding historical masters. Each of the masters taught variations of these wards with different stances, left or right leg leads, etc. I will present what I consider a good starting point for a beginning fencer. As you study the historical masters you may adopt some of their alternate techniques in your own study of rapier combat.

"*Guardia* are called a sure posture with the hilt of the sword which when placed above the shoulder forms *Prima* and when lowered equal with the shoulder it makes *Seconda*, and when it is lowered outside the knee to the right side it forms *Terza*, and *Quarta* is made when the hilt is inside the body. And these four guards are called *principle*."[19]

Gary holds the hand in the First *or* Prime *position.*

Seconda *or* Second *position.*

Terza *or* Third *position.*

Quarta *or* Fourth *position.*

First Ward, *Prima*

Cappo Ferro's Guard in Prima.

Prima (First, high ward)[20]

"Prima is that position which the hand takes in drawing the sword from the scabbard, when the point is turned towards the adversary – all guards especially with the sword alone must be formed with the point so directed."[21]

The high ward is an offensive ward. The ward is made by holding the arm straight out from the body with the palm of the hand to the right. The true edge of the sword will be up. The hand should be positioned above the level of the head and the point towards the opponent. Allow the point to drop slightly below the hand. There is a tendency to fatigue the hand and arm with this ward. Di Grassi advocates holding the hand behind the head, while Agrippa and Fabris show the hand forward of the head. With the hand in front of the head and the point threatening the opponent you are placing yourself in a more aggressive stance. This guard is also good against cuts to the head and shoulders. I suggest using this guard while approaching your opponent.

Guard of *Prima*

Rhys and William take the First Ward, also known as First Position or the guard of Prima. Note how the feet are relatively close together, the body upright and the sword hand above the shoulder. Also note that the point is forward and would be trained at the opponent's face or chest.

Second Ward, *Seconda*

Seconda (Second)

"When the hand is turned slightly upward we have seconda,"[22]

Cappo Ferro's Guard in Seconda

Seconda is similar to *Prima*, except the hand is lowered to shoulder level with the palm of the hand towards the ground. The true edge of the sword will be to the right. This ward is also very aggressive, since you are threatening your opponent with the point as in the *Prima* ward. As your arm starts to fatigue a little from the *Prima* ward you should rotate your hand and lower it into *Seconda*. This ward may also be used when approaching your opponent.

Guard of *Seconda*

Rhys and William now take the Second Ward, also known as Second Position or the guard of Seconda. Note how the feet are a bit further apart and the hand is turned so that the palm is down with the hand at shoulder level.

Third Ward, *Terza*

Cappo Ferro's Guard in Terza

Terza (Third, low ward)

"... and terza when the hand is in the natural position and is neither up nor down."[23]

The low ward is made by keeping the sword hand low and in front of the knee and by holding the weapon with the point towards your adversary and with the blade either parallel to the ground or the point held above parallel, pointing at the adversary's right shoulder. The palm of the hand is towards the left and the true edge towards the ground. Some descriptions of the low ward (Lovino[24] & a variation of *Terza* by Fabris) show the point dipping towards the ground. I suggest you use this guard position when you take your stance and prepare to fence.

Guard of *Terza*

Rhys and William take the Third Ward, also known as Third Position or the guard of Terza. Note how the sword hand is now lowered and is in a natural position with the palm towards the left. The fencers' feet are spaced approximately a shoulder width apart and his left hand is held in a defensive position.

Fourth Ward, *Quarta*

Quarta (Fourth, inside ward)
"When the inside of the hand is turned upwards we have quarta."[25]

Cappo Ferro's Guard in Quarta.

The stance is made by holding the sword on your left side with your sword arm slightly crossing your body. The point of the sword is angled up towards your opponent's right shoulder. Your hand should be in the Fourth position (palm up). This ward is best used when engaging an opponent's sword on the inside and against adversaries who prefer cutting attacks to your left side. This guard position is more defensive in nature, although you may use it to engage the inside of your opponent's blade and set up for attacks that employ opposition to the enemy's blade.

Guard of *Quarta*

The fencers take the Fourth Ward, also known as Fourth Position or the guard of Quarta. Note how they have now turned their palms up and have shifted the sword towards the left side of their bodies. Foot positioning is similar to Terza or the Third Guard.

Prima

Seconda

Terza

Quarta

Which foot forward?

All of these wards may also be made with the left foot forward. This left foot forward stance is best used with daggers, bucklers or cloaks in the off-hand. Putting the left foot forward when only employing a single rapier brings your body closer to your opponent's blade, thus placing yourself in jeopardy of being injured. It also takes your blade further back away from your opponent. One move that can be used from this position with some chance of success is the pass followed by a slight lunge.

You should practice your foot movement enough so that you do not need to think about what your feet are doing while you are moving. Once you have integrated stance, footwork and guards, you are ready to go on to more advanced topics.

As a final note to this section, St. Didier,[26] a French master of note, said:

> "None of the demonstrators, when they define the said guards start at the high. As for me, I start at the low, in view that all things start at the foundation: as for example, learned men will not start to teach the sciences at complex things, nor masons when they go to start to build buildings, do not start at the tiles, but at the foundation. And thus I start at the low, which is the foundation which one must guard well."[27]

A Drill for Practicing Footwork

These footwork drills may be done alone or with a partner.

Go on guard in the Third ward.
Advance with a normal step. Retreat.
Advance with a passing step. Retreat
Traverse to the left.
Traverse to the right.
Circle to the left (pivoting on front foot).
Circle to the right.
Go on guard in the First ward.
Advance with a normal step. Retreat.
Advance with a passing step. Retreat
Traverse to the left.
Traverse to the right.
Circle to the left (pivoting on front foot).
Circle to the right.
Go on guard in the Second ward.
Advance with a normal step. Retreat.
Advance with a passing step. Retreat
Traverse to the left.
Traverse to the right.
Circle to the left (pivoting on front foot).
Circle to the right.
Go on guard in the Fourth ward.
Advance with a normal step. Retreat.
Advance with a passing step. Retreat
Traverse to the left.
Traverse to the right.
Circle to the left (pivoting on front foot).
Circle to the right.

Defense

You should always fence as if your life depended on it. In this way you will avoid foolhardy actions and you will improve your chances of defeating your adversary. I feel it is important to have an understanding of defense before discussing offensive actions. You should read this section first and then the chapter on attacking with the single rapier. You should then re-read this section before practicing the offensive and defensive technique.

Targets

The body (target) is divided into four areas delineated by inside, outside, high and low. The outside is to the right of your weapon hand for a right-handed fencer; Inside is on the left. High is above the bottom of your sternum and low is below.

Specific targets may be the head, upper body, stomach, arms, lower body and legs. The placement of the blade will guard these primary areas. No matter how you parry (defend), it is of utmost importance for you to keep the point of your weapon trained at your opponent as much as possible. The further you move your point the slower your riposte or counter attack. Using the strong portion of your blade (i.e. the *forte*) will help with this. Parrying with the weak portion of your blade (the *debile*) will take your point offline and does not offer the mechanical strength to effectively parry.

> "The forte is for parrying and the debile for wounding."[28]

Single vs. Double Time Defense

The historical fencing masters taught concepts of time on to how to counter the attacks your adversary uses. The Italians called these *stesso tempo* (single time) defense and *dui tempi* (two time) defense.

The debate in the 16th century was which of the two were better. *stesso tempo* is a parry and riposte[29] executed simultaneously in one action by forcing the attacking blade out of line with the defender's counterattack. *Dui tempi* is a parry and riposte in two consecutive actions. In the end, it was decided that *stesso tempo* was generally preferred.[30]

> "It has been our experience that most of those who observe this rule of '*dui tempi*', if they can engage the adversary's sword, generally beat it in order then to proceed with the stroke. This would be successful but for the danger of being deceived."[31]
>
> --Salvatore Fabris

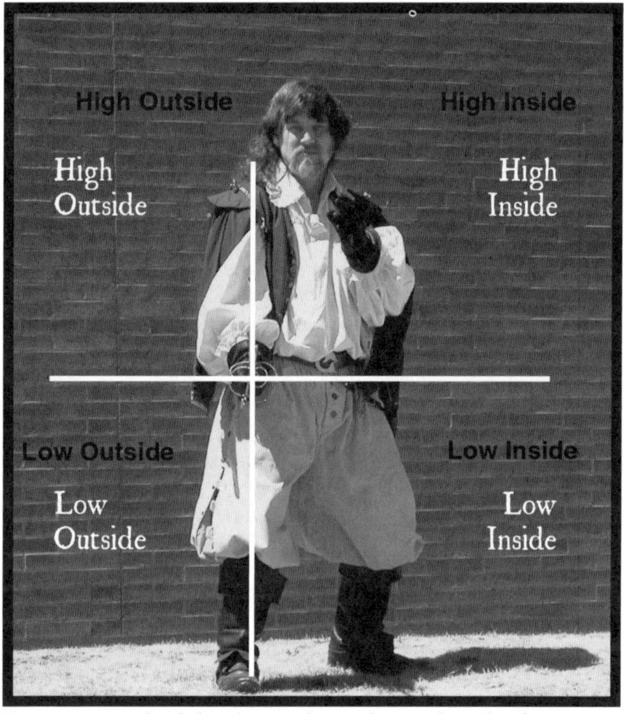

Target zones as divided at the sword; outside is to the right of your weapon while inside is to the left.

Employ both *stesso tempo* and *dui tempi* maneuvers for different circumstances. Learning what circumstances to use each under takes experience. Each should be practiced and used in your repertoire of skills.

When defending you may use opposition from your rapier, your empty off-hand, your dagger, buckler or cloak, or you may use voids (dodging). For cuts you will use the forte (part closest to the guard) of your rapier blade or body voiding. Fabris particularly advocated the void:

> "From this you may deduce the principle that, when possible, it is always better to let cuts pass without parrying them, so that you may not be put into subjection and the danger of being deceived while parrying."[32]

Sword Parries

No matter what, if you must parry an incoming attack with your sword you should use the *forte*, as it is the strongest part of the blade. Di Grassi divided the blade into four parts:

> "I have said elsewhere, that the sword in striking frames either a Circle, either a part of a Circle, of which the hand is

the center. And it is manifest that a wheel, which moves circularly, is more forcible and swift in the circumference than towards the Center. The which wheel each sword resembles in striking. Whereupon it seems convenient, that I divide the sword into four equal parts of the which that which is most nearest the hand, as most nigh to the cause, I will call the first part the next, I will term the second, then the third, and so the fourth which fourth part contains the point of the sword. of which four parts, the third and fourth are to be used to strike withal. For seeing they are nearest to the circumference, they are most swift. And the fourth part (I mean not the tip of the point, but four fingers more within it) is the swiftest and strongest of all the rest for besides that it is in the circumference, which causes it to be most swift, it has also four fingers of counterpiece thereby making the motion more forcible. The other two parts, to wit, the first and second are to be used to warde withal, because in striking they draw little compass, and therefore carry with them small force And for that their place is near the hand, they are for this cause strong to resist any violence."[33]

Giacomo di Grassi's division of the sword into four parts.

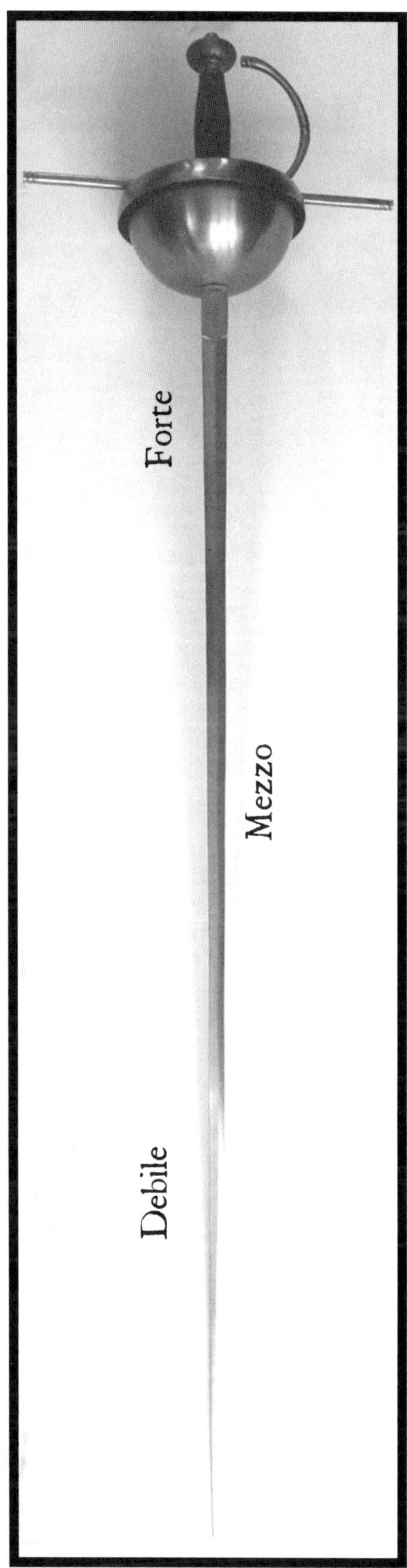

Divisions of the blade on a modern rapier in the Spanish style by cutler Dennis Graves. The forte *is always stronger than the* debile, *a concept well articulated in the literature of Masters both medieval and Renaissance.*

William (right), having "gained the sword" from Richard prepares to attack in single time from wide measure. "Gain the sword" means that he has made contact and has the blade under control; in this case using the mezzo *of his blade against Richard's* debile *or* foible.

William completes his lunge with a turn of the hand to Fourth to make sure that he is not subject to a counter-thrust during the attack.

Gary (right) makes a parry in Second forcing Richard's sword point high and to the right.

While many masters relied on the left hand to parry attacks, Fabris taught that the sword should be used for defense, as the left- hand may be deceived. I suggest first learning to defend with the sword and then later adding hand parries and parrying weapons, such as the dagger.

Two basic parries may be performed with the sword: the parry in second and the parry in Fourth. The parry in Second should be used for attacks coming to your outside line and the parry in Fourth to attacks coming to the inside line. For example if you are in the Third ward and your opponent attacks you on the outside of your sword to thrust you in the right shoulder, you will turn your hand to Second and you will use just enough pressure to his blade to force his point out past your body. The same holds true if your opponent attacks you in your inside line to the chest or belly. You will turn your hand to Fourth and exert just enough pressure on your opponent's blade to force the point past you on the inside. Parries in First may also be used if your head is attacked. Parrying in first will take the point up and above your head.

When you parry it is imperative that you not throw your own point to the side during the parry, but keep your point trained at your opponent. The further your point moves from your opponent the slower your riposte or counter- attack. See di Grassi's first rule in the section on the Single Rapier, below.

Gary makes another parry in Fourth taking Richard's sword point out of line to the left.

Richard (left) shows an incorrect parry. He has lowered his hand and is bending his body forward--two common mistakes made by both novice and even some intermediate fencers.

Hand Parries

The simplest parries are performed against thrusts to the inside (left side of body for right-handers). If the thrust comes in towards your face or extreme upper body, you will use you off-hand to push the blade out and away to the left. If the thrust comes in below your off-hand you will sweep the incoming blade down and out to the left. Never sweep the blade across your body. There is a chance that you will be struck in the process. Even if a fencer was not wearing gauntlets, it was considered prudent to take a slight hurt to the hand rather than suffer a grievous injury.

> "L. But I praye you tell me, is it not better to breake with the Sworde, then with the hand? for (me thinketh) it should be dangerous for hurting the hand.
>
> "V. I will tell you, this weapon must bee used with a glove, and if a man should be without a glove, it were better to hazard a little hurt of the hand, thereby to become maister of his enemies Swoorde, than to breake with the swoord, and so give his enemy the advantage of him."[34]
>
> --Vincento Saviolo

Drill

Both the student and the master come on guard in Second. The master will thrust at the student's left breast (*imbroccata*) and the student will parry the thrust with their hand to their left side.

The student comes on guard in First and the master in Second. The master rotates their hand to Third and thrusts to the student's belly (*stoccata*). The student uses their left hand to parry the thrust out to the left.

During your parries you will typically want to move to one side or the other, or even to give ground, to safely remove your adversary's threat.

Rhys executes a parry wih the hand, moving his opponent's cut offline while executing a counterthrust of his own.

Gary (right) and Richard both start in Second with wide measure.

Richard thrusts in Second while Gary parries with the left hand and counter-thrusts. Ricahrd also parries with the left hand.

Gary recovers in Second while Richard recovers in First.

Richard moves his left hand to Third and thrusts at Gerry's belly. Gary parries the thrust with the left hand and begins a counter.

Finally, Gary thrusts between Richard's left hand and his face to finish the fight with the thrust to the face.

"Do not automatically riposte after you parry. Only riposte (or counter-attack when using stesso tempo defense) when you think you have a good chance of hitting your opponent and not being hit yourself!"

--William Wilson's Second Axiom of Good Fencing

Although cuts were delivered from all angles I would suggest that you concentrate first on those delivered to the head, neck, flank (right side) and chest. Flank, chest and neck cuts are parried in a similar fashion. No matter which type of cut you are parrying you should always place the knuckle-bow in the direction that the cut is coming from. This assures that you use the true edge of the sword blade to make the parry. Never parry with the flats of the blade. The hand wrist and arm are naturally built in such a way that the hand when pushed from different angles has varying mechanical strength. Do this: hold your hand in front as if you are going to shake hands with someone. Have a person press on the back of the hand and see how it feels. Next have a person press up against the bottom of the hand. I find when I do this that I have much more strength with the edge of my hand over the back. Di Grassi was also very specific in this regard:

> "So that he which is in the lowe warde may very easily withstand the downright blow, and the reverse by giving a thrust, for that he shall hit him first, And if he would onely oppose his sworde, and not strike also therewithall, he must encounter the enimies sword with the edge of his owne, and turning the same edge fetch a reverse, striking at the face of the enimie."[35]

> "Because both the down-right blowe, and the reverse are verie easily defended in this warde, I will not stand to speake of any other then of the thrust, restraining my selfe thereunto. The which thrust, if at the first it be not withstoode, may prove verie mortall & deadly. Therefore, when this thrust is given within, it must be beaten inwardes with the edge of the Rapier, requiring the turne of the hand also inwards, and the compasse of the hinder foote, so farre towards the right side, as the hande goeth towardes the right side."[36]

To parry a cut to the head bring your rapier up over your head and hold it with the knuckle-bow held up and slightly forward (hand in the first position). The blade of your rapier should be parallel to the ground with the point aimed generally at your opponent. Do not lock your arm out. Hold it with the elbow slightly bent and the blade about six inches above and just forward of your head. If you took a full cut on a locked/straight arm you could end up with a broken wrist. The bent arm acts like the spring shocks on a carriage.

Salvatore Fabris illustrates a hand-parry in his plate 42 of the 1624 edition.

To parry a cut to your flank (right side) you will move your hand out to the right of the body and a little more forward than a normal low ward (hand in Second position). You should raise your point, aiming at your opponent's head. Catch the cut in the forte of your blade as close to your guard (hilt) as possible. To parry a chest cut you will bring your hand across your body, catching the opponent's blade in your forte (hand in Fourth position).

Drills for parrying a cut to the head

The student comes on guard in the Third ward. The master makes a downwards-arcing cut to the student's head. The student brings their hand up into the First position above the head and stops the cut with the *forte* of the sword.

The student comes on guard again in the Third ward. The master makes an angular downward attack (*roverso sgualimbrato*) to the student's right shoulder. The student will move into the Second guard stopping the cut on the *forte* and hilt of their sword.

Again with the student in Third, the master makes an angular downwards (*mandritto sguamlimbrato*) or horizontal (*mandritto tondo*) cut to the student's chest. The student moves into the Fourth guard stopping the blow on the *forte* and hilt of their sword.

A. Gary (right) comes en guard in Third and Richard assumes his guard with sword held high. B. Richard now cuts at Gary's head; in response Gary raises his sword hand to First while keeping the point in-line with his opponent. C. Having maintained the line, Gary simply finishes the thrust to Richard's chest.

Gary (right) parries a downward cut to the head in First.

He now parries a cut to the cheek in Second.

Finally he cuts a parry to the cheek in high Fourth.

Voiding

Another tactic that may be employed in your defense is called voiding. This is where you dodge your opponent's blade as they attack. You may use steps to the side to dodge thrusts or cuts. A fast retreat may also be employed. Practice dodging the blade and use this tactic to your advantage. When performed properly your opponent will not be in a position to strike you while you may be in reach of them. More on voiding is in a later section.

No matter what, your rapier is your deterrent. Always "hide" your body behind your weapon and keep your point towards your opponent as best as you are able.

Capo Ferro shows the advantages of a voiding defense in plate 17. Note that the voiding movement is very small, not large and exagerrated.

Salvatore Fabris also shows a void, a strike in Fourth while turning the body.

Preparing for Combat

Preparing the Mind

Being fully proficient in rapier is not simply a matter of learning mechanics. A certain mindset must be attained and philosophy learned to become fully proficient with the rapier. It is my opinion that two of the most important principles are timing and distance. I will discuss these later.

Rapier may be fought at a certain metaphysical level where certain actions taken by the body are automatic based on the threats that are given. Footwork and defense should be automatic. Your timing should not be cogitated over; you should know subconsciously when you may most easily offend or be offended by your opponent. This is not instinctive. It is a trained response, so regimented practice and drills are critical.

Distance

Distance is a crucial element that goes hand in hand with timing. If your distance is too great to be able to offend your opponent in a timely manner then you are too far away from your opponent. If your distance is too close, your opponent may more easily offend you. In the Italian tradition there are two distances that you may find yourself in. In Italian these were called *misura larga* and *misura stretta* or wide distance and narrow distance. Capo Ferro described these measures (distances) in Chapter Three of his book. He indicated that the measure takes a certain distance[37] and that the measure is a "just distance" when it is possible to wound your opponent with the point of the sword with simply an extension of the arm.[38] This is *misura stretta,* or narrow distance.[39] Of *misura larga,* or wide distance, he said that it is when with an increase of the right foot (i.e. a lunge) it is possible to wound the adversary.[40]

Your normal measure (distance) from your opponent should be *misura larga*, wide distance.

The Misura Larga, *or wide distance, at which most rapier combats begin. At this range much of the stepping and counter-stepping is done and, with the right kind of advance in the right time, the opponent can still be reached.*

The Misura stretta, *or close distance. Richard (right) can make a thrusting attack with a simple extension of the arm or by bending the body slightly forward.*

Timing

Timing is also very important. If you see an opening but your timing is off in pressing the attack, you are at risk of being injured yourself. The same is true in defense. You must defend in a timely manner to be able to save yourself from harm's way. Learning time takes years and definitely requires consistent and rigorous practice. The following quote from William Gaugler in talking about Capo Ferro helps illustrate the concept of time:

> "And in Chapter Five he tells us that the word "time" (*tempo*) in fencing signifies diverse things, but primarily, it means a correct choice of time to realize one's aim."[42]

He goes on to give this example from Capo Ferro:

> "...the first tempo is...when I find myself at tight or wide distance, I am able to wound the adversary with a single movement of the sword; similarly, one knows that wounding in two tempi requires at least two movements of the sword; half tempo is when at wide distance I wound the adversary in the forearm... counter tempo is when in the same tempo that the adversary wishes to wound me I counter in a briefer *tempo...*"[43]

Fabris also talked on time and counter-time. Of time he said:

> "Tempo demands that the motion (movement) of the adversary is in distance because those (motions) that are far away (out of distance) can not be called anything other than movements or a change of perspective. Tempo in this art only signifies the occasion to wound or to take advantage over the adversary and for no other reason is this given the name of tempo."[44]

Basically what this says is that if you are within distance you may time an attack on your opponent to wound them in one movement or tempo. The timing of your attack may be on one of his movements to catch him in mid-movement, making it harder for him to defend. This movement may be attempting to take or bind your blade, to move around you, etc.. If you are out of distance, then a movement that would take one tempo when in distance will take more than one tempo, as you must first move into distance taking at least one tempo, followed by the time of the attack. This is why Fabris states that tempo signifies the occasion to wound or take advantage over the adversary. In very simple terms, counter-time is when you hit your opponent with a counter attack during the time that they attack you, while at the same time covering the line that they attack you in so that you are not hit in the meantime.

Learning timing takes years of practice, so you will need to work on your timing *every* time you fence.

What to watch?

As you fence with your opponent or partner, you must consider what to watch. Fabris was quite explicit in this regard. "One must always have the eye on the sword hand."[45] All attacks will issue from the sword hand. So, you must watch it. However, you must also be aware of the body positioning of your opponent as well as what type of footwork they are using. With a simple extension of the hand can they hit you? Will it take a step with the extension? You must be cognizant of the whole person while paying special attention to the sword hand.

Attacks with the Single Rapier

"Learn the Single Rapier First: for it is the basis of all rapier combat."
--William Wilson's Third Axion of Good Fencing

The single rapier is the basis for all rapier combat. Fabris, and other historical masters, indicated that learning the single sword first was important . The single sword is the foundation; learning it before adding in other defensive and offensive weapons will greatly increase your skill in the long run. Capo Ferro stated that the single sword is the queen of all weapons and is the foundation upon which all other play at arms is based.[46]

Simple attacks comprised of the thrust, cuts, and attacks with opposition, should be studied first. These attacks may be aimed at the head, torso, arms or legs. Avoid attacks to the legs as they may put you at greater risk than attacks to the other targets. If a thrust is aimed at the legs simple geometry shows that the fencer that is thrusting at the leg of their opponent may be counter-thrust in the chest before the thrust to the leg will land. Think of this as a triangle where the targeted knee that is one point, and the body and arm of the target makes a right angle. The incoming sword and arm of the attacker forms the hypotenuse of the triangle, which is the longest line.

I recommend the following five cardinal rules, as presented by Giacomo di Grassi :[47]

"First, that the right or straight line is of all other the shortest: wherefore if a man would strike in the shortest line, it is requisite that he strike in the straight line.

"Secondly, he that is nearest, hitteth soonest. Out of which advertisement a man may reap this profit, that seeing the enemy's sword far off, aloft and ready to strike, he may first strike the enemy, before he himself is striken.

"Thirdly, a circle that goeth compassing beareth more force in the extremety of the circumference, then in the center thereof.

"Fourthly, a man may more easily withstand a small than a great force.

"Fifthly, every motion is accomplished in time."

The "true" distance to the head is shorter than the "false" distance to the feet or leg. If an opponent attacks the lower body, the best counter is to slip the forward leg black and counter-thrust in Stesso Tempo.

Towards the end of the 16th century it was agreed that the thrust was both quicker and deadlier than the cut. Attacks in the straight line with a thrust were thus considered to be the best attacks. Also, in utilizing the thrust instead of the cut the point of the sword remained trained on the opponent; as they moved their arm back to cut it was possible to hit sooner with the thrust, as the point was both closer and in line. Cuts will cause the most damage with the part of the sword closest to the point. As the sword is swung it describes an arc and at the circumference of this arc is the most force delivered. Since it is possible to withstand a smaller force than a larger one you should move in and stop a cut before it reaches maximum velocity. Lastly, all attacks must be done in proper time.

These basic rules will help in understanding how some of the attacks were, and are, to be performed.

Simple Attacks

The nomenclature of cuts and thrusts was laid out by three 16th century authors. Antonio Manciolino and Giovanni dall'Agocchie were instrumental in defining the attacks used at the time, while many latter masters adopted Achille Marozzo's cutting diagram and nomenclature.

Dall'Agocchie also helped to define the attacks:

> "The mandritto demands this, that it commences from the right side. It is called fendente when it cleaves the head to the feet in a straight line. But the sgualembrato is so called as it passes, that is from the left shoulder to the right knee of the adversary. The tondo or traverso demands that it turn a traverse. The redoppio is that which goes rising with the true edge and ending at the point of the shoulder of the enemy. The tramazzone is that which is made with the joint of the hand in the guise of a molinello. The riversi are so called because they are opposite of the right, commencing on the left side. They are similar to the mandritti, that is they are of the same nature. But coming to the punta, that which is above the hand is called the imbroccata, and that which is below the hand is the stoccata, and that which is from the left side is the punta riversa."[49]

Plate 8 from Capo Ferro demonstrates that if one loses the measure of the attack to the leg. "A" figure that demonstrates when if one loses the measure to attack the leg. "C" having reached the sword of "D", D is able to attack in riverso, *make a* stramazzone *to the arm or a thrust to the face that is too far forward. D throws the right leg behind in the attack.*

The Thrust

The first type of attack that all scholars should learn is the thrust. The scholar should be able to thrust just hard enough so that a real rapier would enter the body up to three finger-widths in depth.

> "Without all doubt, the thrust is to be preferred before the edge-blow, as well because it striketh in less time, as also for that in the said time, it doth more hut. For which consideration, the Romanes (who were victorious in all enterprises) did accustom their soldiers of the Legions to thrust only: Alleging for their reason, that blows of the edge, though they were great, yet they are very few that are deadly, and that thrusts, though little and weak, when they enter but iij fingers into the body, are wont to kill."[50]

The advised depth of three fingers to the torso is all it takes to puncture most major organs. Bernard Knight in an article entitled *Some Medicological Aspects of Stab Wounds* indicates that with a very sharp knife, it takes as little as 1.1 pound to 6.6 pounds of pressure to pierce the skin.[51]

All attacks are a coordination of the hand and the foot. It is the extension of the arm with the point towards your opponent that threatens your target.

> "In 1606 Nicoletto Giganti, in his treatise "Scola overo teatro," explained that when executing a thrust one must extend the arm. A contemporary of Giganti, Ridolfo Capo Ferro, was in agreement. In "Gran Simulacro dell'arte e dell'uso della scherma," he wrote that to deliver a thrust, the sword arm should be extended in a straight line. Attacking with a bent arm was considered a bad practice to which Salvatore Fabris felt a need to draw particular attention. In "Scienza [sic] e practica d'arme," he cautioned that "there are some who, wishing to attack with the point, launch the arm with violence to give it greater force, [but] such a manner is not good... [for] one may be wounded in the time of this withdrawal of the arm."[52]

Mechanics of the thrust

A thrust is nothing more than preparing an attack by extending the arm and threatening a target; then using the body (or foot movement) to take the point to the target. To extend the arm, move the hand smoothly forward so that the arm is almost straight out in front of you. Do not lock the elbow so that you may more easily move the arm if necessary. The hand should be at shoulder height on the extension. Thrusts may be made with the hand in First (palm to the right), Second (palm down), Third (palm to the left), or Fourth (palm up). I suggest using either Second or Fourth as they facilitate opposition. Your extension of the arm during the thrust should not be made as a jabbing motion, but should be made as smooth as possible. At narrow measure you will hit with just the extension of the arm on the thrust. At wide measure during the extension of the arm you may lunge or use a passing step to get close enough to hit.

Richard (left) begins a thrust toward's Rhys' lower leg. Rhys slope-steps slightly right, lunging into a counter-thrust in single time.

Richard (left) attacks in Second. Rhys counterattacks in time with an off-line lunge to the right, followed by a counter-thrust in Third.

This time Richard attacks in Second. Rhys counterattacks in time with a passing slope step to the left, also closing the line with the left hand.

In the early schools movement was not linear, as it is in both classical and modern fencing. The fencer would use circular and angular movement to come closer to his opponent. Di Grassi called angular movement the *crooked pace*. Others during the late 16th century called this the *slope pace*. However, once we enter the 17th century this philosophy changed, and a more linear form of combat came into vogue.

Note that when teaching or attempting to learn the thrust, pinpoint accuracy must be developed; to do this, the fencer must have spent a large amount of time practicing thrusting at various targets, first while immobile and later accompanied with different steps and combinations of steps.

As such, one cannot over-emphasize the importance of drills to develop this accuracy. Using a wooden pole, or a target of some sort, the student should spend time each day---or at least two or more times per week--working on accuracy and smoothness of movement in the attack.

Drill for developing the Thrust

The master brings the scholar on guard in the Third ward. At the master's command the scholar extends with the hand, going into Fourth and steps towards the master, making sufficient contact with the point to cause injury in a duel. The scholar should practice hitting different areas on the torso, the head, and the arms. The student should also start in the various guard positions for this drill.

The Lunge

As combat philosophy turned from a circular to more linear footwork, the use of a technique called the lunge began to come into play. Vigianni is the Italian master first thought to have described the lunge in 1575. He called this movement the *punta sopramano*. Giganti's *stoccata lunga* and Capo Ferro's *botta lunga* further refined this technique for delivering the point to one's opponent.

> "In executing the long thrust...after one is placed on guard, one must first extend the arm, and then carry forward the body in one tempo, so that the thrust arrives, and the enemy does not perceive it...In recovering back one must first carry the head back followed by the body, and then the foot...Whoever wishes to learn this art must first know how to deliver this thrust, for knowing this it is easy to learn the rest..."[52]

Mechanics of the Lunge

"The attack is the ultimate offensive action of fencing, in the which it arrives when I am in narrow measure. I move the body, with the leg, and with the arm all in one *tempo*, thrusting forward to be able to wound my adversary. And this with a firm foot or with an increase of a step [with the forward foot]..."[53]

The lunge is made with the whole body. Capo Ferro called this *l'incredibile accrescimento della botta lunga* which means the incredible increase of the long blow [attack]. From the guard position, the arm is extended and immediately the body is propelled forward by the back leg. The rear foot should remain firm and flat on the ground and the front foot will come down on the heel and roll forward so that the front foot is also flat on the floor. The rear leg will be straight. The front knee should end up over the foot. No further than the toes as is shown in the figure of the lunge above. The body should not lean too far forward. You

The lunge in Capo Ferro:
A-left shoulder
B-knee of the left leg
C-planting the left foot
D--an ordinary step
E--planting the right foot
F--thigh and leg to the shoe
G--hand and right arm
H--increase of the right arm
I--Increase of the right knee, almost a step
J--no entry in the original text
K--increase of a step, a little more than a foot
L--increase of a left foot, with its turn
M--increase of the left knee, with a half pace

A thrusting attack...

Margo (left)--and Gary en guard in Third. Each fencer will look for an opening to make an attack on the straight line while trying to close off any attack along the same line. Opportunities might appear such as an opponenent changing his guard or lifting a foot to take a step.

Gary now performs a double disengage to try and gain an open line; Margo attacks in time during his movement. The Fencer should time his attacks so that they will land when your opponent is busy doing something else.

Another thrusting attack...

Margo starts in First with Gary in Third. Margo will wait for Gary to move his body or change his guard--then she will immediately counterattack.

Margo takes advantage, and thrusts in Second.

A thrusting attack from Fourth

Margo takes her guard in Fourth while Gary remains in Third. Since she has closed the line and also has a straight attack she engages his blade to attack.

Since Gary doesn't react quickly enough, Margo is able to slide down his blade and complete the lunge.

A thrusting attack from Second

On guard in Second, Margo waits for Gary to make even the smallest movement from his favored Third position.

Gary begins an attack by shifting his weight, but Margo attacks in time staying in Second, keeping her hand in a position of defense to deflect Gary's possible counter-thrust.

should be balanced and be able to move easily. To recover from the lunge, bend the back knee and force yourself backwards with the front foot. Push with the heel and not with the toes. The non-sword hand may either be kept in front of the body for defense or may be thrown back behind the body as advocated by Capo Ferro.

Rhys takes his guard in First and prepares to lunge by shifting his weight.

Moving his right foot forward, Rhys starts the lunge. He lowers his hand to Second for the thrust and keeps his left hand in a defensive position for as long as possible before completing the attack.

Completing the lunge, Rhys throws his left hand back and moves his right knee over the instep.

Targeting the Thrust

Thrusting attacks may be made above or below (*imbroccata* and *stoccata*) the opponent's sword arm, or from the left side (*punta riversa*). Attacks to your opponent should be made so that it is harder for them to counter-attack[54] in time to wound you or perform a double-hit. When you attack your foot should hit the ground as your point contacts the target. You will always cover distance by making a series of simple advances or passing steps.

"Never open with a cut!"

--William Wilson's Axiom on Cutting

Cuts

After the scholar has gained a mastery of the thrust the next step is to study the cut or blow. Di Grassi taught three types of cuts: cuts from the shoulder, the elbow and the wrist. In practice the first two cuts must be practiced carefully to avoid excessive blows to your opponent/partner. When performing cuts I would suggest that you use primarily wrist cuts. Although the wrist cut does not deliver as much force it is faster, allowing you to keep your hilt in front of you helping to guard you from counter-attacks.

Although Di Grassi taught that the thrust was superior to the cut, he did teach how to effectively use the cut. His philosophy on the cut or edge-blow is best summarized in his own words:

> "I have said elsewhere, that the sword striking frameth either a circle, either a part of a circle, on which the hand is the center. And it manifest itself that a wheel, which moveth circularly, is more forcible and swift in the circumference then towards the center: The which wheel each sword resembleth in striking."[55]

The cut performed with only the wrist was called a *stramazzone* in Italian. The Italians perfected the *stramazzone* and examples of special rapiers crafted with flared tips may be found in European collections. I was able to handle such a one at the Royal Armouries in Leeds, England. The balance on the weapon seemed to lend itself to cutting. Although I have not read any scholarly reasons for such flaring, my opinion is that it is for augmentation of the damage done by the *stramazzone*. Normal cuts are performed so that the "point of percussion" of the sword (the sweet spot) strikes the intended target and the force of the blow is substantial because of the swing of the cut. The point of percussion is a spot a number of inches back from the point that will deliver the most impact with least vibration to the hand on contact.[56]

You must also assure that your opponent's blade is immobilized or not in a position to hit you during a cut or you will most assuredly be struck at the same time. Di Grassi taught that as part of the cut the sword should be made to slide after impact to increase the damage of the cut:

> "And if one would in delivering of a great edge-blow, use small motion and spend little time he ought as soon as he hath stroken, to draw or slide his sword, thereby causing it to cut: for otherwise an edge-blow is to no purpose, although it be very forcibly delivered, especially when it lighteth on any soft or limber thing: but being drawn, it doth every way cut greatly."[57]
>
> --Giacomo di Grassi

Using Cuts

Although cuts should be part of your repertoire, you must be very careful when employing them in an assault. Cuts should not be used as the opening attack in an attack sequence. Your first attack should be a thrust.

Cuts may be used as the second or subsequent attack in a sequence or they may be used as an attack following a parry when your point has drifted away from target during the parry. The thing to remember is to only use the cut when it will be faster than a thrust.

> "He who wishes to make a cut with safety, must wait a fitting opportunity, since he cannot make the strike in a moment, and the time might have passed before the sword arrived."[58]

Cuts may also be used as the final attack after making a feint with a thrust (see section on using feints). Although the mechanics of the cut are relatively basic, mastering when to use them is advanced. It takes impeccable timing to use a cut effectively and not be hit yourself in the meantime. This may take years of practice to perfect.

> "You can make a feint in order to put the adversary in subjection, and whilst he is parrying the cut, thrust at him, or make a feint of a thrust and cut."[59]

As with the thrust, cuts should be practiced exhaustively to develop precision. They should next be married to combinations of cuts, thrusts and footwork to form useful "phrases" of attacks strung together. As with everything else, this must be done keeping in mind the need for defense; no combination of attacks will be effective if you're already sporting three feet of steel from your chest.

Margo and Richard come on guard. Margo in Third, Richard in Second.

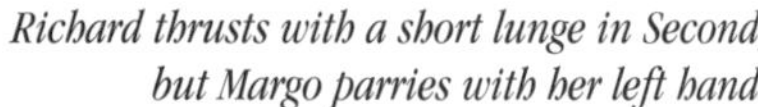

Richard thrusts with a short lunge in Second, but Margo parries with her left hand.

Maintaining pressure against Richard's sword with her left hand, she cuts to his cheek.

A drill to develop the cut

The master will bring the scholar on guard in Second on the inside. The master will then thrust at the scholar who will then parry the thrust with the off-hand and will cut the master on the face, sword arm or chest/stomach using a *stramazzone*.

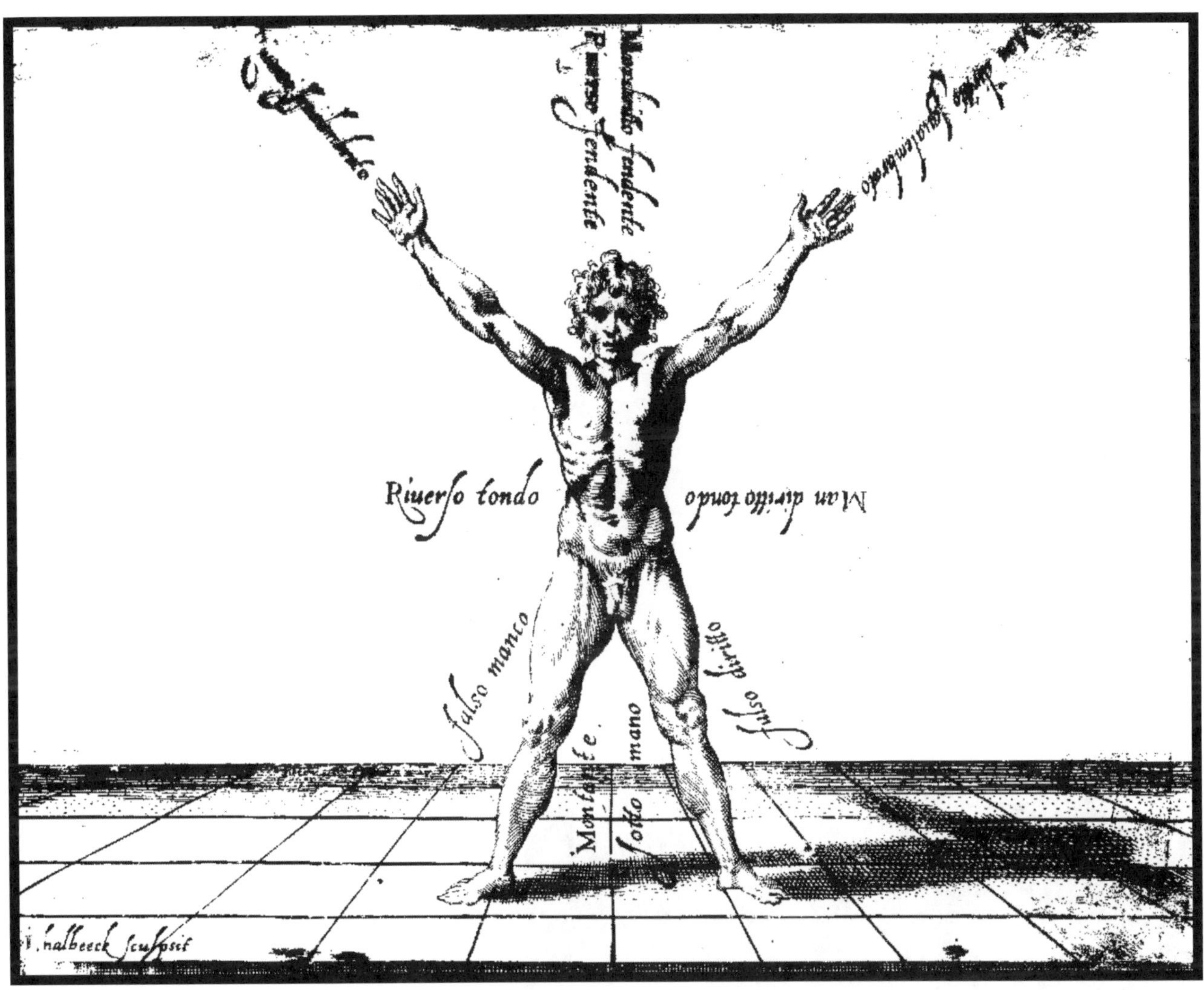

Cutting diagram from Salvatore Fabris

Drill for the develpment of the use of the Cut

Both master and student begin in Third. The student extends the arm and pulls the point back slightly. The student immediately makes a small circle with the point from left to right and cuts the master's left cheek (*mandritto sgualimbruto*).

Rhys (right) starts in the Second ward, while William begins in the Third.

Keeping the guard in its original position, Rhys makes a counter clockwise circle with his point while rolling his palm up.

Rhys lunges and cuts to William's left cheek while keeping the line between his opponent's point and his chest closed. Note that Rhys' knee is not over the instep on the lunge, a very common error for both beginning and intermediate fencers alike. The knee should **always** *be over the instep of the forward foot.*

Another drill for the develpment of the use of the cut

Both the master and the student begin in Third. The student extends the arm and pulls the point of the sword back slightly. The student immediately makes a small circle with the point from right to left, and cuts the master's right cheek. The studunt should lunge forward with the left foot during the attack.

Richard takes his guard in Third while Margo assumes Second. As before, Margo will wait until Richard moves to attack, counterattacking with a cut.

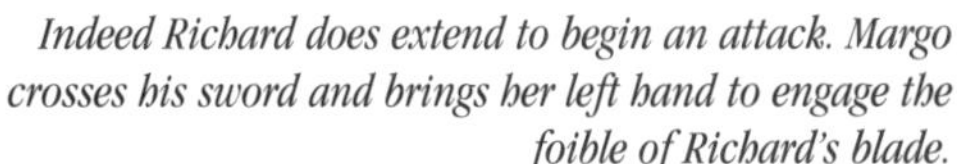

Indeed Richard does extend to begin an attack. Margo crosses his sword and brings her left hand to engage the foible of Richard's blade.

Maintaining pressure against the sword Margo cuts to Richard's right cheek. In order to make the fastest possible time, the cut is made only with the elbow and wrist.

Attacks with Opposition

This type of attack covers a wide range of attacks that involve putting pressure on your opponent's blade with your own as you make an attack while moving along his blade. In historical fencing this type of attack was typically performed as a counter-attack with pressure to the blade. Proper execution of this attack requires impeccable timing and blade control. The purpose of this attack is to carry the opponent's point away from your body and to control his/her blade in such a manner that they cannot hit you while you thrust them. Fabris called this type of attack "running along the blade."[58] In the figures below, the combatant on the left begins in Third as does the combatant on the right. The combatant on the left then engages his opponent's blade on the outside and slides down the blade, moving his own hand into First position. He thus brings his opponent's point above his head and his own point into the opponent's chest.[59]

Drill to develop attacks in opposition

The master brings the scholar on guard in Third on the inside. The master thrusts at the scholar's chest. The scholar turns their hand to Fourth and while putting pressure on the blade takes the master's point out and to the left as they thrust to the master's face or chest.

Both students stand on guard in Third, but Rhys (left) will gain Margo's sword by closing his line in Fourth.

Having gained the line, Rhys engages Margo's sword and lunges. For this action to work the fencer must use good timing, only engaging (making contact with) the opponent's blade at the last moment, and then maintain control through to the attack's finish.

Another drill to develop attacks in opposition

The master and the student come on guard in Third. The master raises his hand to Second and attacks with an *imbroccata*. The student turns their body and counterattacks in Fourth using opposition to the blade.

Both Richard (left) and William take their guard in Third; William waiting for Richard to make a straight-line attack.

As Richard makes his thrust in Second, William makes an incartata (a turn of the body) and brings his to Fourth. It is crttically important to get the hand to this position because it closes the opponent's line of attack.

Richard's attack brings his body's close to William's point. On a deep lunge the fencer initiating the attack could impale themselves on the defender's sword.

Since he does not oblige completely by impaling himself, William moves his foot closer and thrusts home. By maintaining contact with the blade, Richard's blade stays off-line, avoiding the double-strike.

Sword Engagement

An English sword and rapier manual in the Italian style, *Pallas Armata* (1639) called opposition to the blade *stringering*. Stringering was to put pressure on your opponent's blade with your own. Depending on the master, engagement was done at the weak or middle part of the blade. This may be used in preparation for a bind or to evoke a response so that you may execute a *cavatione*. Quoting from Pallas Armata:

> "Stringering is the touching of thine adversary's point with thy point, which thou art to do upon any occasion, that thou mayst secure thyself on either side from a thrust, which commonly is termed binding."[61]

Capo Ferro also defined engagement of the blade. On page 38 in the chapter *Dello Stringer Della Spada* (Of the engagement of the sword) he says:

> "The sword is engaged on coming into measure, or to uncover the adversary on the outside, inside, high or low, but always in a straight line while the adversary is set or moving. The turn is mostly done in two times (*dui tempi*), first you acquire the *debole* of the sword with a *palmo* of the *debole* of your sword. In the second time (tempo) you acquire the beginning of the forte of the adversaries sword, such that he disengages, you counter disengage, or not, I advise that you face in a straight line, and that the forte always follows the *debole* together with the movement of the leg."[62]

Stringering may be used to both harass your adversary and to keep track of the location of his sword. If he disengages to attack, you can feel the movement of the sword. Remember that when using this technique, that it is important to use very little pressure against your adversary's blade.

Another technique was called *trovare di spada*. The A.F. Johnson translation of Fabris' calls this "engagement of the sword." However, the Italian term used is *trovare*, which means "to find" and does not imply engaging or touching the blade. Fabris devoted the whole of chapter nine of his book to this subject. In this he states on page 17:

> "To find the sword is to gain advantage over it;"[63]

Fabris' method for finding the sword to gain an advantage requires that you come close to your adversary's sword but do not actually touch it. However, he does state that you should have a little more of your sword overlapping your adversary's (in the weak part of the sword blade, i.e. *debile*). This slight amount will give you an advantage.

> "It often happens that the adversary, finding his sword is not molested is not aware that you have already gained the advantage, whereas if you touch his sword he more easily realizes the fact, and can disengage or retreat or change his guard, in order to free himself, so that you lose the first advantage. Moreover if you touch his sword, you impede and disconcert yourself, so that if a time comes to hit, you cannot take it because of the resistance of your adversary's sword."[64]

This plate from Cappo Ferro, entitled Modo di Guardagnarla la spada di dentro in linea reta I transate as "the manner of gaining the sword on the inside of the straight line." This chapter deals with stringering the sword and thus gaining an advantage by controlling it.

The *Cavatione* (disengage)

The disengagement is used to out-maneuver your opponent by removing your blade from your opponent's blade after they have engaged (placed pressure on your blade with their own) yours or to gain an advantage by moving into a different line. The disengagement is made by taking the point of your weapon in a semicircular motion around your opponent's guard.

Drill for the *Cavatione*

The master comes on guard in the Fourth ward with the point aimed higher than usual and engages the scholar's blade on the inside. The scholar is in Third. The master puts too much pressure on the blade and the scholar disengages under the master's blade. Moving the sword hand to Second, the scholar then thrusts to the chest.

William (left) takes his guard in Third while Gary assumes Fourth, just touching William's sword with his own. But Gary starts to apply just a bit too much pressure...

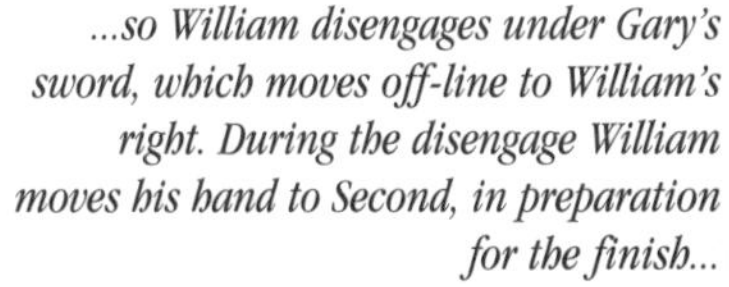

...so William disengages under Gary's sword, which moves off-line to William's right. During the disengage William moves his hand to Second, in preparation for the finish...

...so William steps boldly forward with the left foot and finishes with a thrust, still in Second.

This technique was also used to counter attacks made with opposition. In *Pallas Armata*[65] this was called the *cavare* and was used to foil binds, etc:

> "To Cavere, is to turn thy point under thine adversary's Rapier on the other side, when thou art bound, or he doth thrust at thee."

In Chapter Six of *Pallas Armata* the author went on to say:

> "Cavere took its beginning from a Cock fight; for Camillo Agrippa, a reverend Master of defense at Rome fifty years ago (who was the inventor of the Dagger) seeing two Cocks combat together, and observing, how when one of the Cocks leaped up to strike the other with his claw, the other seeing him come leaping at him went quite under him on the other side, conceived that he might make use of this in his Art, and coming home made trial of it, and found it a very useful and remarkable observation.
>
> "Cavereing is therefore only to be made use of, when thine adversary doth thrust at thee over the Secunde or weakest part of thy Rapier, because thou canst not parere his thrust, thy point being unable to resist."

Fabris devoted a whole chapter to the disengage. According to Fabris there are four types of disengage: disengagement (*cavatione*), counter disengagement, double disengagement, and the half disengage. The following is a brief description of each:

Disengagement (*cavatione*)
Changing from one line to another as your opponent tries to engage your sword or beat it.

Counter Disengagement (*contracavatione*)
As your opponent disengages from your sword you follow his disengagement to engage in the original line.

Double Disengagement (*ricavatione*)
You disengage and your opponent counter disengages. You disengage again to gain the advantage.

Half Disengagement (*meggia cavatione*)
You start to disengage and do not complete it, leaving the sword below your adversary's sword.

Many of the principles covered in single rapier may be applied when using the rapier with other weapons or parrying devices. Practice all of the moves detailed in this section and then experiment to see which attacks will or will not work for you.

Further drill for the *Cavere*

The master and the student both start in Third on the outside. The student disengages under the master's sword and moves their hand to Fourth and engages the blade. This is the simple disengage.

Both the master and student start in Third on the outside. The master disengages to the inside of the student's sword. At the same the student disengages to bring the weapons back to the same position as at first. This is the counter disengage.

Again, both the master and the student start in Third on the outside. The student disengages to take the inside line. The master counter disengages to regain control. The student will immediately disengage again to take the inside line. This is the double disengagement.

The master begins in Fourth and the student starts in Third on the outside. The master engages the student's sword by touching it, puttung a little pressure on the student's blade. The student makes a half disengagement by bringing the point of their sword in a quarter circle below the master's sword.

The Beat

The beat is a technique used to quickly take your opponent's blade out of line. This type of a preparation takes three forms, the last two related to counter-pressure. One thing that you will need to be careful of is not telegraphing your beats. Do not start your beat with a back swing of the blade or else your opponent may be able to time an attack during your preparation. To execute the beat correctly, strike your opponent's sword between the point and the middle of the blade with your blade somewhere between the midpoint and guard. This will assure that you are able to temporarily bring their point out of line. The beat prepares for either a thrust or a cut. When you beat to the inside of your opponent's blade you should turn your hand to Fourth during the beat and immediately thrust to the right side of your opponent. If your point travels too far to your left during the beat it will be quicker to give a reverse cut than a thrust. To use a beat in preparation for a cut I would suggest that you beat the outside of your opponent's blade while stepping forward with the left foot and give a mandritta (a cut from the right side) to the face of your opponent.

You may also beat your opponent's blade aside with your unarmed hand, dagger or buckler. A cloak may also be used in the same fashion. Again, your timing must be right to accomplish this.

First Drill for the Beat

The master will bring the scholar on guard, both in the Third ward on the inside. The scholar will turn their hand to Fourth and beat the inside of the master's blade taking the master's point out of line and will execute a thrust to the inside of the master's arm.

Rhys (left) and Gary take their guards in Third on the outside. Rhys makes sure that he is not touching Gary's blade in order to deny Gary information on exactly when and were Rhys will be moving.

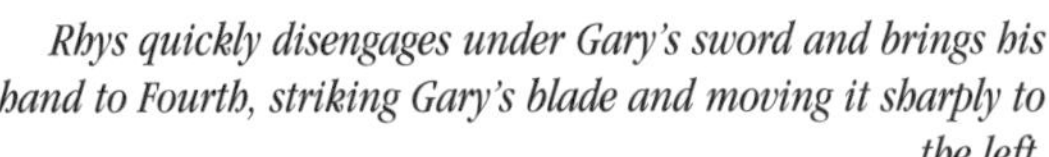

Rhys quickly disengages under Gary's sword and brings his hand to Fourth, striking Gary's blade and moving it sharply to the left.

To complete the attack, Rhys lunges while keeping his hand in Fourth to ensure that his inside line remains closed. This is very important, or a double-hit can occur.

Drill

The master comes on guard in Fourth and the student in Second. The student disengages and beats the master's blade towards the right (on the outside). As the beat is moving the master's point away the student steps forward with the left foot and cuts with a *mandritta* to the master's face. After the impact of the cut the student must assure that their guard and sword blade stay between their own body and the master's sword.

Gary (right) takes his guard in high Fourth while Margo takes Second. She will be to the inside of his sword--but if timed incorrectly, the attack will surely fail.

She first disengages under Gary's sword and beats his blade to her right in order to open a line for a cut. It is important in this maneuver for the fencer to keep their arm extended and to use only the wrist for the cut.

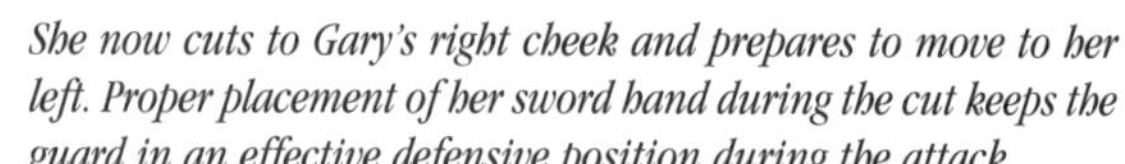

She now cuts to Gary's right cheek and prepares to move to her left. Proper placement of her sword hand during the cut keeps the guard in an effective defensive position during the attack.

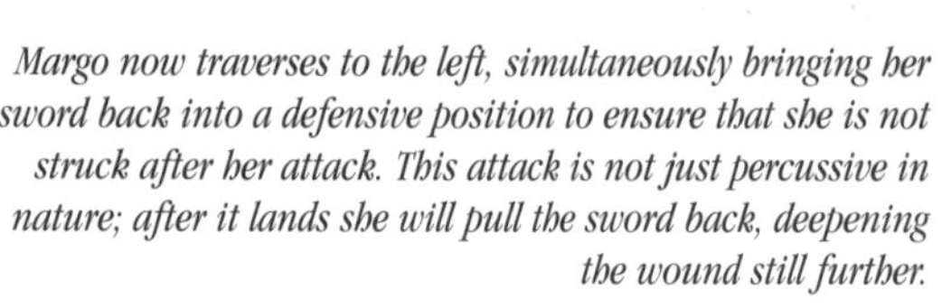

Margo now traverses to the left, simultaneously bringing her sword back into a defensive position to ensure that she is not struck after her attack. This attack is not just percussive in nature; after it lands she will pull the sword back, deepening the wound still further.

No doubt at some point you will face a left-handed fencer, or may be one yourself. The lessons in how to fence a left-hander also teach a left-hander how to fence against a right-hander. As early as Marozzo's *Arte dell'Armi* the topic of a right-handed fencer assaulting with a left-handed fencer was a topic of study. The following are the first two chapters from *Arte dell'Armi* (Capitula 147) that relates to this:

> "I want you to know that when you go to fight with one who is left handed. For your advantage you will be patiente . . ."

What Marozzo is saying here is that if you are right handed and fencing a left handed fencer you should be on guard and let them attack first. He continues in Capitula 148:

> "But know that if you want to be agente against a left hander you will step in finding him with your right leg forward (the one that goes with the sword). It should be a little towards his right and in this step you will give a thrust in falso to his face above his sword. He seeing this will in fear thrust outside towards your right side and in this you will make a mandritto to his right leg together with a roverso sgualembrato, throwing behind to its place your right leg. In this manner you will return to the guard as at first. Still to said left hander you will throw out a ponta to his face between his sword and brochiero towards his left side stepping in such time with the right foot forward. But know for his fear of the thrust he will uncover his right side and you will then give a mandritto fendente to his head ending in a porta di ferro alta. But if he responds to this with an attack to your right you will strike his attack to your outside and slice his face. Here there is a need to move your left leg forward a little in a traverse and you will make a half turn of the sword hand and you will return to the coda longa e alta as at first."

In this chapter Marozzo describes what to do in the event that you want to attack first. The first action is to draw your opponent out by thrusting at his face. In this he may counterthrust and during his action turn your thrust into a cut, stepping back for safety. In the second sequence you will also thrust at his face between his sword and buckler. If he moves his buckler to close the line he will uncover his right side a little, allowing you to make a cut to his head. Instead of just trying to cover, if your opponent counterattacks, you will beat his blade to your outside and then slice his face while stepping forward with the left foot in a traverse.

My survey of the Renaissance fencing books has revealed little else on fighting a left-handed fencer prior to the 17th century. Both Joseph Swetnam's *School of the Noble and Worthy Science of* Defence, and in the *Pallas Armata* provide sections on fighting a left-handed fencer (from chapter one):

> "Containeth the use of the four general guards against the left-handed.
>
> "The right-handed man doth thrust the left-handed man with the Prime only at the outside of his Rapier over his left arm.
>
> "The Secunde is used by the right-handed against the left-handed without, over his left arm in a long thrust, and in a Passade and in a Passade under his left arm; and is likewise used within, in a long thrust, and in a Passade.
>
> "The Tertz is only thrusted at the left-handed, at the outside of his Rapier, over his left arm.
>
> "The Quarte is thrusted at the left-handed man without, over his left arm, likewise within in a long thrust and in a Volte, and then it may be called a reverse, as having changed her property and nature."

All of the attacks made against a left-handed fencer should go over the left arm. Going over the arm, especially with a small step off to your right will help protect you from a counterthrust by your opponent. He continues in chapter two:

> "The use of the four guards against the left-handed man is particularized, how thou art to thrust with the Prime or Secunde at the outside over his left arm.
>
> "If thine adversary be open within stringere him at the inside of his Rapier, as soon as he caveres towards his right side under thy Rapier, for to thrust at thee within with a Secunde, then just at coming of his blow thrust with a Tertz, or a Quarte at the outside of his Rapier, over his left arm; if he then pareretb thy thrust with a Quarte towards his left side, then turn thy Tertz or Quarte into a Secunde or Prime, and thrust him without over his left arm at his left breast."

If you can take the inside line against the left handed fencer he will more than likely work to retake the inside line. If he does this and thrusts in Second you should counterthrust over his arm, either in Third or Fourth, while keeping opposition to his blade. If he happens to turn his hand to Fourth, you outside you should turn your hand to either Second or First to thrust him over his arm. I suggest that in doing either of these actions that you step off the line to your right to gain the advantage of angle.

> "How to passere a left-handed man with a Secunde, at the outside of his Rapier under his left arm
>
> "If thy left-handed adversary be open within, then stringere him at the inside of his Rapier, as soon as he will thrust at thee within with a Secunde, then at the approaching of his thrust make at him at the outside of his Rapier over his left arm, with a Tertz or Quarte, if he then will put by thy thrust upwards with a Secunde, then let the point of thy Rapier sink down into a Secunde under his left arm and pass behind him."

In this engagement you will again try to take the inside line. If he happens to gain the inside and thrust in Second, turn your hand to Third or Fourth and counterthrust over his sword arm. If he parries you up, turn your hand to Second and let you point circle down below his arm to thrust him below his arm.

> "How thou art to use the Secunde within at a left-handed adversary.
>
> "Stringere thine adversary at the outside of his Rapier, when he cavereth towards his right side under thy Rapier, and will thrust thee without over thy right arm, then thrust just at the coming of his thrust with a Secunde at the inside of his Rapier close to the Secunde or weakest part of his weapon, between his left arm and left breast."

In this sequence you are taking mechanical advantage over your opponent's weapon by engaging in the area of the foible as you counterthrust.

> "How the Tertz or Quarte is to be used without, over the left-handed man's arm.
>
> "Stringere thine adversary within, as soon as he doth thrust at thee within with a Secunde, then thrust with the Tertz or Quarte close to his Secunde or weakest part of the Rapier at the outside of his weapon over his left arm at his left breast, and when thou dost thrust then go low with thy Hilt."

This technique is similar to the previous except that you lower your hilt a little to make sure that his point is carried down away from you.

> "How to thrust the Quarte within at thy left-handed adversary.
>
> "Let thy left-handed adversary stringere thee at the inside of thy Rapier, and upon a sudden thrust at him within with a Secunde close to the Secunde or weakest part of his Rapier, near his point, if he doth strive to parere thy Secunde with a Quarte towards his right side, then change thy Secunde into a Quarte and Voltere him at the inside of his weapon at his right breast: But if he doth parere too far towards his right side, that thou canst not hit his breast, then let thy Quarte sink in under his left arm and Voltere him with thy Quarte at his left side."[xx]

Here you let your opponent take the inside line. Again engage him while thrusting quickly in Second making sure to enage his *foible* with your *forte*. If he manages to start to parry you then turn your hand to Fourth and while doing a *volte* you will continue the thrust to his chest. If he parries you far enough that you cannot hit directly you will make a small quarter disengagement below his arm and continue on with the thrust.

Capo Ferro devotes only a single small chapter and plate to the topic of fencing a left-hander:

> "Figure that wounds with a *stamazzone riverso* to the face of a left hand fencer and the ability to wound secondly to the chest... Finding your adversary who is left handed in fourth with the arm extended you will commence to stringere on the inside in terza with the dagger higher than the sword. He disengaging to wound you in the face, you will be able to wound him in three ways. First, below with the dagger parrying his sword you will wound him with a stamazzone roverso to the face, or second to the chest. But I warn you because in his disengage it is best to attack in fourth with the single sword to the outside."

So Capo Ferro gives only one type of counter to one single attack that is made by the opponent. He is mute on doing anything else.

The biggest advantage a left-handed fencer has over a right is experience. Left-handed fencers typically fight right-handed fencers but the opposite is not true. As a right-handed fencer you should seek out left-handed fencers to practice with.

I would suggest that when you first fence with a left-handed fencer that you initially work with single sword. This provides a simpler framework to learn the different strong and weak lines of attack found when facing an opponent whose strong side is mirrored to your own. I suggest that you start in the First or Second guard on the left-handed fencers inside line (to the right of their sword). As you move the left-handed fencer may try and take the inside line. Disengage to continue moving into the inside line. When the opportunity presents itself, you should use tempo to disengage and attack with opposition, thrusting over their sword in their outside line while maintaining opposition to their blade or wait for their disengage to take the inside line and do the same action in counter-time.

The simplest way to understand how to fence a left-hander is to simply think of the rapier's thrust as coming in on a straight line. Then it does not matter if the fencer is left or right-handed. Simply make an angle so that their point is off-line, and your point is towards them.

Ridolfo Capo Ferro's depiction of a right-hander fencing a left-hander. Note the wounds with a stamazzone riverso *to the left-hander's face.*

Drill for fencing against a left-hander

The master comes on guard, left-handed, in Fourth. The student will come on guard in Third on the inside of the master's blade. The master will extend in Fourth and the student will disengage in Third, moving their hand to the Fourth position and engage the incoming sword on the outside. The student will then immediately engage the sword on the outside with the dagger (or the hand if a dagger is not being used) and give a reverse cut to the master's face. The cut will be a *stramazzone* made from the wrist and not the elbow or shoulder.

William takes his guard in Fourth--on the outside *of Gary's sword which is in Third.*

William now extends, still in Fourth, while Gary disengages to the outside while turning his own hand to Fourth, stringering the blade, and starts to lunge.

Gary finishes the counter by completing the lunge with the attack going over William's blade and striking him in the chest.

Drill

Both the master and the student will come on guard in Third with the master on the outside of the student's sword. The master will disengage to the inside moving their hand to the Second position and lunge. The student will take a slope pace to the right while moving their hand to Fourth and will thrust the master in the face. The student may use their off-hand (if no dagger is being used) or a dagger to help parry.

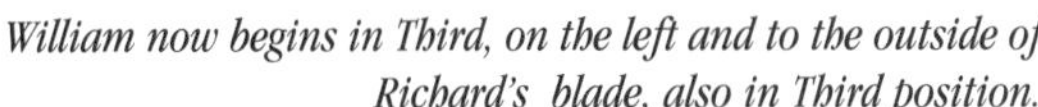

William now begins in Third, on the left and to the outside of Richard's blade, also in Third position.

William disengages to the inside and prepares to lunge while stringering Richard's blade in Second.

William attempts to complete the lunge, but is thwarted as Richard simply turns his hand to Fourth, stepping off-line and thrusting all in single-time.

Advanced Techniques

There are a number of different advanced techniques that may be employed in rapier combat. These include feints and disarms.

Feints

The feint in historic texts is called "falsing"or "deceit." Fabris indicates:

> "When you feign to hit in one line, and while the adversary is defending himself, hit in another, you are said to make a feint."[67]

The following is my expanded definition of a feint:

> "The feint is a simulated attack that is so real in its appearance that your opponent is forced to defend, thus giving you an opportunity to strike them in a different line."

Basically the feint is used to provoke a patterned response that you will be able to capitalize upon in some fashion. Examples of feints might be something like the following:

> *Each time your opponent attempts a thrust along the high line, you simply execute a retreating step to void the distance. Noticing that he always responds the same way, on another occasion you notice that your opponent over-extends in parrying high outside attacks, you begin to feed him more and more attacks there, drawing his hand further out. Finally, beginning another thrust to this line, as he moves to parry, you* cavatione *and attack his inside line.*

One mistake that many novices make is to physically look at their target before they strike for it. If you're clever, so you can appear to make this mistake, inviting your opponent to notice the "error." Then, looking at one target, you simply strike another, hopefully catching your opponent off-guard as he expected a strike to the place you were looking.

Feints do not have to be comprised of gross movements. A shift of a shoulder, a false step, a twist of the hand, all of these can be suggestive--a deceit--drawing the opponent to make a mistake upon which you can capitalize.

Early masters did not always agree on the use of feints. Masters such as Saviolo and di Grassi thought the feint a risky technique, since you could be struck in the process of making the feint if your opponent isn't deceived. While Capo Ferro did not think that use of the feint was advantageous "... for they cause loss of time and distance..."[68] Typically the feint will start with a thrust or cut at some portion of the body that will evoke a parry with the blade. The follow-up to this feint is an attack in another line. Di Grassi was very clear on this subject.

> "For avoiding of this abuse, the best remedy is, that they exercise themselves in delivering these falses only in sport, and (as I have before said) for their practice and pastime: Resolving themselves for a truth, that when they are to deal with an enemy, & when it is upon danger of their lives, they must suppose the enemy to be equal to themselves as well in knowledge as in strength, & accustom themselves to strike in as little time as possible, and that always being well warded. And as for these falses and slips, they must use them for their exercise and pastimes sake only, and not presume upon them, except it be against such persons, who are much more slow, either know not the true principals of this Arte. For deceit or falsing is no other thing, then a blow or thrust delivered, not to the intent to hurt or hit home, but to cause the enemy to discover himself in some part, by means whereof a man may safely hurt him in the same part. And look how many blows or thrusts there may be given, so many falses or deceits may be used, and a great many more, which shall be declared in their proper place: The defense likewise whereof shall in few words be last of all laid open to you."[69]

Making feints with a rapier are much more dangerous to the attacker than with a lighter modern fencing weapon. However, feints may be employed judiciously in your combat. I would suggest that you think carefully about using feints and that if you do use them, that you do so infrequently.

Drill for the development of feints

The master starts in Third and the student in First, both on the inside line. The student extends in First with a slight slope pace to the right. The master parries in Fourth which the student deceives by turning the hand into Third and making a cut to the forward leg while making a traverse to the left.

William starts in Third while Richard begins in First.

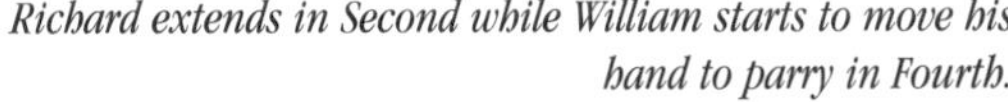

Richard extends in Second while William starts to move his hand to parry in Fourth.

Richard waits until William begins to move his hand, then cuts to the leg.

A drill for the countering of a feint

The master will begin in First and the student in Third. The master will feign a thrust in First only to start the cut as the student remains steady. As the cut falls towards the student's leg they will move the front leg back while extending in Third and thrusting the master in the upper chest or face.

Richard (left) starts in Third with Gary in First. Gary prepares to make a feint...

...Gary now makes an extension in Second without moving his body. Richard remains steady as he sees no threat...

...Gary is now able to make the cut to Richard's leg without fear of a parry from Richard. Richard slips his leg back, however, letting the cut pass while thrusting Gary in the chest.

Grips, Throws, and Disarmament

The historic Masters taught a number of tactics that augmented their fight. Grips, throws and wrestling moves were part of the renaissance swordsman's repertoire of technique. If two fencers came close together they would not try to saw at each other with their swords but would try to disarm or throw their opponent. Marozzo, Lovino, Fabris and other masters show numerous examples of these types of moves.

In Book II Part 3 of *On the Science of Arms* Fabris discusses disarms and throws. However, he states in this chapter that he had not intended to touch on the subject but was convinced to do so by his friends. "Although it was not our intention to treat of the following matters, because it seemed to us that our work could very well stand without them, nevertheless owing to the persuasion of many friends and to gratify them we have been induced to include in our book this treatise on coming to grips, seizing the sword, throwing the cloak and the principles of the dagger, that is the principles of defense against the dagger with bare hands."[70]

He goes on to show two throws and two disarms followed by entangling maneuvers with the cloak and then ends with a section on defending against a dagger with bare hands.

A drill to practice coming to grips

The master and the student are both in Third on the inside. The student attacks in Fourth close to the sword of the master, who defends in Fourth but carries his point out of line. Immediately, the student turns their point upwards and presses the inside of the master's sword, keeping the point out of line and stepping forward First with the left foot and then with the right so that it is behind the master's forward foot. The student then immediately strikes the master with the hilt and throws them to the ground over their leg.

Richard and Margo both come on guard in Third. Margo is on the inside of Richard's sword and has gained an advantage by overlapping it still more.

She now turns her hand to Fourth and begins to engage Richard's sword in an attack...

...in response Richard raises his hand in a high Fourth to parry. As he does this Margo turns her own hand to Third. Richard does not, however, control his point carefully; it drifts dangerously.

Margo now raises her point while maintaining contact with Richard's blade, forcing it still further off-line. She shifts her weight forward, making a sudden step with the left foot. Finally she grabs Richard's hilt and strikes him to the face with her own pommel.

A play from Salvatore Fabris, plate 179, with combatants coming to grips--in this case with a handy pommel-strike to the chin.

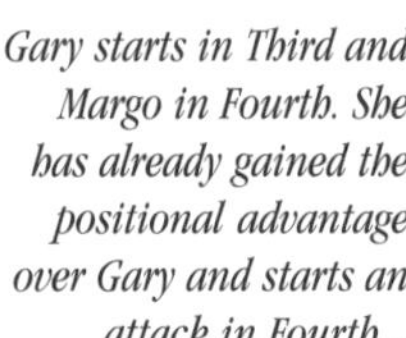

A drill for disarming at the grips

The master starts in Third and the student in Fourth, both on the inside. The student attacks in Fourth. The master retreats slightly and moves the point of his sword to the inside over the student's sword and forces the point down and to the inside with the *forte* of his sword. At the same time he steps forward with the left foot and reaches over his sword with his left hand, gripping the hilt of the student's sword and wresting the sword from the student's grip.

Gary starts in Third and Margo in Fourth. She has already gained the positional advantage over Gary and starts an attack in Fourth...

...but Gary shifts his weight back and moves his point to the left in order to fully engage Margo's sword, starting to regain his own advantage...

As he shifts his weight forward, Gary presses Margo's sword down. He begins here to bring his left hand forward in preparation for some sort of grapple...

Stepping forward with the left foot, Gary reaches out for Margo's pommel, suitably offered under the pressure of his blade...

Gary swiftly grabs her pommel. As Margo's foot has come off the ground (again under strong pressure from Gary's pressing action), it will make it much harder for her to retreat at the critical time.

Now Gary has not one rapier, but two! And for Margo--well, there have been better days.

Fabris illustrates the problem nicely in his plate 181.

Another drill for the development of disarms

The master begins in Fourth and the student in Third. The master extends and attacks in Fourth. The student immediately turns their sword point to the left and forces the master's point down and to the right while stepping forward with the left foot. The student immediately grasps the master's hilt and pulls up, levering the sword out of the master's hand.

Gary (left) begins in Fourth while Rhys starts in a well-formed Third. Gary begins an attack in Fourth by starting his foot movement before moving his blade.

Rhys turns the point of his sword to the left and places strong downward pressure on Gary's sword, forcing Gary's tip down and to the left, safely off-line.

Rhys now steps with his left foot while maintaining strong pressure on Gary's sword. The pressure is critical or there is a possibility that the opponent will simply raise the point where Rhys can run onto it.

Still maintaining pressure, Rhys levers the sword out of Gary's hand, stepping back also to maintain distance--preserving the advantage of the rapier's range and making it hard for Gary to close and grapple.

Fabris shows how effective a disarm can be, combining it with a fatal thrust.

Another drill for the development of disarms

Both the master and the student begin in Third on the inside. The master disengages to the outside while turning his hand to Second. The student turns their hand to Second while stepping forward with the left foot (it should go behind the master's right foot). The student immediately brings their left hand up to the masters throat and throws them over their leg.

William (left) takes his guard in Third out of distance. Gary begins to mvoe into wide measure, also taking Third to the inside of William's sword.

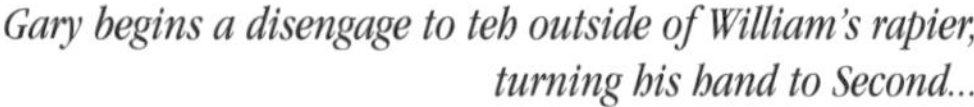

Gary begins a disengage to teh outside of William's rapier, turning his hand to Second...

William also turns his hand to Second, stepping forward boldly with his left foot. William's left hand is kept in a defensive position while he watches to see what his opponent will do next...

As Gary makes the mistake of shifting his weight back, thus denying himself several interesting opportunities, though his hand does remain in Second...but William's hand already has some measure of control; he could at this point grab the blade...

...instead, as Gary 's weight is really too far back, William steps boldly forward, pressing his hand to his opponent's elbow...

Stepping with his foot behind Gary's lead leg, William moves his hand to Gary's unfortunate neck, pitching into a throw onto his back.

Salvatore Fabris shows this same throw, c. 1610 in plate 182.

In the first figure #77 is shown attacking; notice how the left hand maintains a defensive posture as measure of the opponent's intention is made..

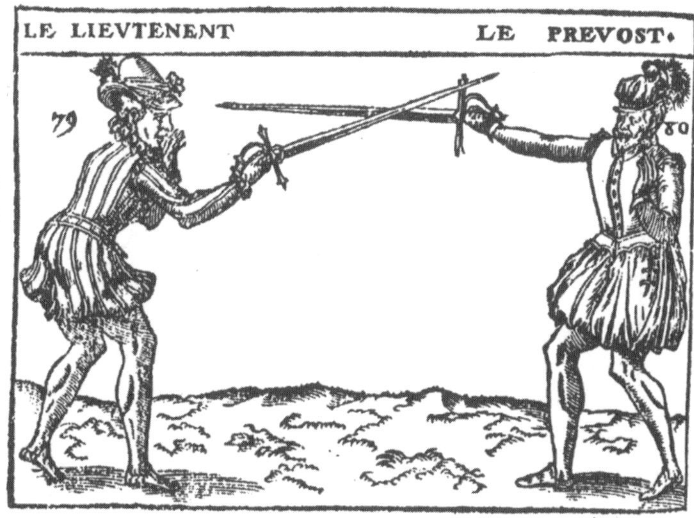

In the second figure #80 (the provost) is parrying the lieutenant's blade. The parry is made to the provost's left side with the edge of the blade and with the palm up.

Sainct Didier shows a typical disarm through both word and woodcut. In the sequence shown in the four woodcuts given here we see the "provost" and "lieutenant" both in the high guard and the lieutenant issuing a thrust. The provost parries the attack with the strong edge of his blade and then grasps the lieutenant's blade near the hilt.

The figures show numbers behind the combatants' heads. These numbers describe the combat sequence, moving from figure 77 through 84 above and on the facing page.

Di Grassi comments extensively on disarms:

> "And each man is to be advertised that when he finds the enemies weapon underneath at the hanging ward, he may safely make a seizure: but it would be done nimbly and with good courage, because he doth then increase towards his enemy in the straight line, that is to say, increase on pace, and therewithal take hold fast of the enemy's sword, near the hilts thereof, yeah though his hand were naked, and under his own sword presently turning his hand outwards, which of force wresteth the sword out of the enemy's hand: neither ought he to fear to make seizure with his naked hand, for it is in such a place, that if he should with his hand encounter a blow, happily it would not cut because the weapon hath there very small force. All the hazard will be, if the enemy should draw back his sword, which causeth it to cut."[71]

Seizures of the blade to disarm your opponent were taught and practicing this technique will help round out your set of tools for use in rapier combat.

In order to wrest the blade from the lieutenant's grasp, the provost steps forward with the left foot and grips the sword near the hilt. It should be noted that this portion of the sword itself (the ricasso) is not sharpened. This makes for safe grasping of the sword. However care must be taken to not be struck when performing this grasp.

In the final figure the provost has wrested the sword from the lieutenant's grasp.

Indeed, the earliest Italian fencing master whose manuscript is known--Fiore de Liberi--was of the opinion that all fighting stemmed from wrestling. His integrated system taught coming to grips with all weapons, a tradition that seems to have remained strong through the 16th and 17th centuries.

Although forbidden in many organizations that practice historical fencing, the tide is perhaps beginning to turn; and the control of both distance and line required to come to grips and disarm will serve the combatant well no matter what the combat conventions are.

A Word About Safety

Grips, throws and disarms have the potential to injure your partner as the original techniques were meant to break bones or throw someone hard to the ground. As in the final plate of the first grappling drill showing the throw over the leg with the strike with the hilt, you should not complete the move or strike forcefully with the hilt. Simply coming into the final position is sufficient. As with all fencing you must have and show control and your first thought must be to the safety of your partner.

Conclusion

Putting it all together

"There are some men, speaking with rashness rather than with knowledge of this art, who have presumed to say that there are some strokes, to which there is no reply, and which cannot be parried. But we are persuaded by sound reasons that every stroke has its reply, except the stroke made at the exact time and at the exact distance; to such a stroke there is no reply and it cannot be parried; whereas the stroke which is deceived in its time or in its distance, has its reply and can easily be parried; so that you can defend yourself against all strokes of the one kind and none of the other, and he who thinks differently is deceived. So are they deceived who think that the same stroke can be used against every opponent. But we say that you can attack all opponents, but must proceed in different ways according to the opportunities offered by the adversary. Let this suffice for the methods of attacking with resolution and without a pause; you must understand how to advance or check yourself, move swiftly or slowly or retire, and to do everything of your own accord and not under the compulsion of the adversary, for that would be a sign that his replies were stronger and that you were trying to save yourself from danger. When you act of your own accord or for some purpose of deceiving, you can return and advance at will. In this consists true judgement and knowledge of arms..."

--Salvatore Fabris

Rapier combat takes years to perfect. Do not become discouraged if you still think that you are learning after a few years. Mastery of the rapier can take a lifetime. The early masters wrote their books when they were in the primes of their lives, and after many years of teaching. The main thing to remember is that in order to be proficient with a rapier you must practice regularly. Once every few months, a month, or even a week is not enough. Being well practiced will help you to be a safe and proficient fencer.

I have chosen quotes from a number of historic masters (including Di Grassi, the semi-anonymous *Pallas Armata*, Capo Ferro and Fabris) to illustrate specific points. Today, we have many more manuscripts being translated into English and have much easier access to historic sources. At the time of the writing of this book, we have di Grassi, Saviolo, Swetnam and *Pallas Armata* in their original English editions. Parts of Thibault, and sections of Caranza have already been translated into English and translations of Capo Ferro, Fabris, Agrippa and Marozzo are in process. As these works become available in readable editions, new students will be able to work directly from the old masters works. This workbook is meant to serve as a gateway to these old texts. Work diligently, patiently, and carefully through all of the drills contained herein, until you have internalized them, and can execute them time and again. Then you will be ready to search out these manuals and study them to not only refine and enhance these lessons, but to gain a true appreciation of the martial expertise of these early masters of the Arte of Defence.

Final Drill for Single rapier

The master and the student will come on guard in Third, out of distance. The student steps into wide distance and engages the master's sword on the inside in Third. The master disengages and turns his hand to Second and thrusts at the student's chest while running along the blade. The master attacks with a half lunge. The student leans back while lowering their hand, the sword going into low Third so that the thrust does not touch their chest. The student's weight should be fully on the back leg. The master recovers from the half lunge and the student at the same timesteps forward with the left foot, turns their hand to Second and attacks the master on the outside. The master traverses left and turns the hand to Second to parry the incoming attack. The student disengages and turns their hand to Fourth on the inside while making a compass step to the left and thrusting for the master's chest. The master makes an incartata and counter-thrusts in Fourth at the student's face. Using the left hand the student forces the point out past their left shoulder, turning their hand to Third and thrusting the Master in the belly.

Final Drill

Out of Distance

Combatants close to wide distance

Attack in Second, defender leans back.

Both recover, recentering their balance...

...defender engages in Second...

A step with the attack in Second...

...now a traverse step....

Followed by a traverse step that changes the line of attack...

...the defender now disengages and attacks in Fourth...

...the atackher thrusts to the face...

..defender parries with the hand and moves her sword to Third....

..and finally, an attack in Third.

[1] The terms *guard* and *ward* are interchangeable. A guard is a positioning of your body and sword so as to guard a specific area of the body.
[2] Salvator Fabris, *De Lo Schermo*, in *the Science of Arms,* A. F. Johnson, translator.. p 30.
[3] Ridolfo Capo ferro. *Gran Simulacrum.* p 14. Translation by the author.
[4] Paraphrasing from the original Italian by the author. Ridolfo Capoferro. *Gran Simulacro.* pp 30-31.
[5] Vincento Saviolo. *His Practice*. p 9.
[6] Giacomo di Grassi has been called one of the three prominent Italian rapier masters. However his book was originally written in 1570 and the type of sword he employed was a sidesword of the time period. Although he is not an actual "rapier" master his techniques are forwards looking and lend themselves well for rapier combat.
[7] Giacomo di Grassi. *His True Arte of Defense.* p.16.
[8] Giacomo di Grassi. *His True Arte of Defense*. p 17.
[9] The distance or proper measure you should keep from your opponent will be discussed later.
[10] Giacomo di Grassi. *His True Arte of Defence.* http://www.cs.unc.edu/~hudson/digrassi/sword.html
[11] Vincentio Saviolo. *His Practice. First Book.* p 9.
[12] Giacomo di Grassi. *His True Arte of Defense.* http://www.cs.unc.edu/~hudson/digrassi/sword.html
[13] *Pallas Armata*. Chap II paragraph 10.
[14] Salvatore Fabris, *De Lo Schermo*, in *On the Science of Arms,* A. F. Johnson, translator p 64, plate 19.
[15] Giacomo di Grassi. *His True Arte of Defense*. p 18
[17] Salvatore Fabris, *De Lo Schermo*, in *On the Science of Arms,* A. F. Johnson, translator p 5.
[16] I use Fabris' explanations of the guards because they are clear and concise.
[18] I use the work of Salvator Fabris as he synthesizes the prevalent techniques for fencing with a rapier at the time. His descriptions are clear and I believe his techniques to be sound.
[19] Ridolfo Capo Ferro. *Gran Simulacrum.* pp 32-33.
[20] *Wards* are also called *guards*.
[21] Salvatore Fabris, *De Lo Schermo*, in *On the Science of Arms,* A. F. Johnson, translator p 5.
[22] Ibid., p 5.
[23] Ibid., p 5.
[24] You may view Lovino on the world wide web at http://jan.ucc.nau.edu/~wew/fencing/lovino.html
[25] Salvatore Fabris, *De Lo Schermo*, in *On the Science of Arms,* A. F. Johnson, translator p 5.
[26] Laura Angotti of Arlington, MA is the first to have translated St. Didier into English to the author's knowledge. The author would like to thank her for this momentous work.
[27] Henry Sainct Didier. "*Tract Containing Secrets of the First Book on the Single Sword...*," Laura Angotti, translator p 4-5.
[28] Ridolfo Capo Ferro. *Gran Simalucrum.* p 7.
[29] To parry is to put aside an attack. A riposte is an attack that immediately follows a parry. So in stesso tempo instead of the riposte following the parry it occurs at the same time.
[30] Egerton Castle. *Schools and Masters of Fence.* (London) p. 144.
[31] Salvatore Fabris, *De Lo Schermo*, in *On the Science of Arms,* A. F. Johnson, translator p 10.
[32] Ibid. p 74.
[33] Giacomo di Grassi. *His True Arte of Defense*. p 11.
[34] Vincento Saviolo. *His Practice.* p 17.
[35] Giacomo di Grassi. *His True Art.* p 27.
[36] Giacomo di Grassi. *His True Art.* p 28.
[37] Original reads "*La misura si prende una certa distanza...*" Translation by the author.
[38] Original reads "*La misura è una giusta distanza, dalla punta della mia spada, all vita dell' aversario, nella quale lo posso ferire...*" Translation by the author.
[40] Original reads *"La misura larga é, quando con l' accrscimento del piede dritto, posso ferire l' aversario..."* Paraphasing by the author.
[41] William Gaugler is a well-respected fencing Master working in the Italian tradition. His *History of Fencing* is a seminal and important work in the field; students should also strongly consider *A Dictionary of Fencing Terminology* by Laureate Press.
[42] William Gaugler. *History of Fencing*. p. 40.
[43] From *Gran Simulcro* by Capo Fero. Translation by William Gaugler. *History of Fencing* p. 42.
[44] From Salvator Fabris, *De Lo Schermo*, translation by Maestra Jeanette Acosta-Martinez, chapter 10.

[45] Ridolfo Capo Ferro. *Gran Simulacrum.* p 27.
[46] Ridolfo Capo Ferro. *Gran Simulacrum*, p.27. *Original reads la spada sola è la regina, e fondamento di tutte l'altre armi.*
[47] Giacomo di Grassi. *His True Art.* p 9.
[48] Author's translation from Page 10 of Manciolino's *Opera Nova.*
[49] Author's translation of the pertinent section from Page 9 of dall'Agocchie's manual.
[50] Giacomo di Grassi. *His True Arte of Defense.* p 21.
[51] Knight, Bernard, *Some Medicological Aspects of Stab Wounds*, Legal Medicine Annual, 1976, p. 95-105.
[52] Lurz, Frank. American Fencing, Fall 1999, p. 14. Saviolo in particular taught against making straight linear attacks.
[53] Translation from Capo Ferro by William Gaugler, *History of Fencing*, p. 37.
[54] Ridolfo Capo Ferro. *Gran Simulacro.* p 22.
[55] Giacomo di Grassi. *His True Arte of Defense.* p 11.
[56] Care must be taken when looking at cut diagrams from the various historical manuals. Some of the authors labeled the diagram from the perspective of the target and some from the perspective of the attacker. The diagram from Fabris is shown from the perspective of the target. So, the *mandritta* attacks will hit the target on the target's left side as labeled in the diagram.
[57] Giacomo di Grassi. *His True Arte of Defense.* p 76.
[58] *è venuto scorrendo il filo* This comes from page 187 of the Johnson translation of Fabris' manual, Book II plate 110.
[59] *Pallas Armata.* Chapter II, Paragraph I.
[60] Weak part of the blade. The part of the blade closest to the point.
[61] A unit of measure. Approximately 8 inches.
[62] Translation provided by Maestra Jeanette Acosta-Martinez.
[63] Author's translation.
[64] A.F. Johnson Translation modified by the author. *On the Science of Arms.* p. 18.
[65] *Pallas Armata* is a very important book to scholars of Elizabethan fencing in that it defines a number of Italian terms and techniques that were not previously defined in English.
[66] *Pallas Armata.* LIB. II. Pars Prior
[67] Salvator Fabris. A.F. Johnson Translation. *On the Science of Arms.* p 22.
[68] Ridolfo Capo Fero. *Gran Simulcrum.* p .29.
[69] Giacomo di Grassi. *His True Arte of Defense.* p. 74.
[70] Shakespeare even used some of these tactics in his plays. For example, in *Hamlet* the use of the disarm was employed. While modern movies generally just show the two actor-combatants coming together with their swords in the air and then wresting each other's blades from hand, many people have wondered over the years how this was actually done in period. Shakespeare was quite aware of the martial arts of his day, and as discussed before, the debate over the new "Italianate" rapier even found its way into *Romeo and Juliet.* Where the techniques shown on the Globe stage derived from the repertoires of Saviolo, di Grassi and the like? The question remains unanswerable, but intriguing.
[71] Giacomo di Grassi. *His True Arte of Defense.* p .76.

Fighting Double

Dagger, Cloak, Buckler
Case of Rapiers

Early *spada da lato* masters, coming from a military sword background, focused their attention on fighting double (with two weapons), particularly the sword and buckler. Antonio Manciolino's treatise devotes fifty-four pages to sword and buckler fencing, and only two to the use of the spada solo. With Agrippa's innovations and simplifications, aimed at a purely civilian context, the focus began to change. As mentioned before, to rapier masters the single sword was the queen of weapons – the foundation upon which all other weapon training was based. The foot soldier's buckler and shield gave way to the civilian gentleman's dagger and cape.[1]

By the early 17th century, fencing masters were increasingly asserting the preeminence of the single rapier, even against the rapier and dagger.

> "In opening our promised work we shall begin with the sword alone, for on the knowledge of the sword depend the principles of all other arms. "[2]

…Even so, rapier and dagger remained an established, even dominant, part of Italian rapier fencing throughout most of the 17th century.

Following in the tradition of the late 16th century, this manual focuses on the single rapier as the key that unlocks the Arte of Defence. Once the previous lessons have been thoroughly internalized, this brief chapter will give you an introduction to fencing double.

Rapier and dagger

The most common weapon combination after the single sword was the sword and dagger. The buckler rapidly lost its preeminence as the sword's companion arm, in favor of the dagger. The dagger was an universal sidearm in civilian dress, was able to easily turn and bind against thrusts, yet was still stout enough to turn cuts in the new style of swordplay.[3]

> "Having as briefly as I might possibly finished all that which might be said, of true knowledge of single Rapier: it seems convenient, that coming from the simple to the compound, I handle these weapons first, which from the Rapier forwards are either most simple or least compound: And especially those which now adays are most used, and in the which men are most exercised, the which weapons are the Rapier and Dagger accompanied together, and are a great increase and furtherance both in striking and defending.
>
> "Wherefore, it is to be first considered, that which these and the like weapons, a man may practice that most desired and renowned manner of skirmishing, which is said to strike and defend both in one time, which is thought to be impossible to be done with the single Rapier, and yet in truth is not so: For there are some kind of blows in the defense of which one may also strike (as in the blows of the edge, down right and reversed) both high and low, and other high blows which here are not spoken of.

> "Wherefore seeing with these weapons a man may very commodiously, both strike and defend, for that the one is a great help to the other, it is to be remembered, that because these weapons are two, and the one of lesser quantity than the other, to each one be allotted that part both of defending and striking, which it is best able to support. So that to the Dagger, by reason of his shortness, is assigned the left side to defend down to the knee: and to the sword all the right side, and the right and left side jointly downwards from the knee. Neither may it seem strange that the only Dagger ought to defend all blows of the left side: for it does most easily sustain every edgeblow, when it encounters the sword in the first and second part thereof."[4]

Because the dagger is shorter than the rapier it is used primarily as a defensive weapon. As di Grassi states, the dagger should be used primarily to defend the left side down to the knee. Thrusts are turned aside to the left with the dagger and less powerful cuts will be able to be parried with the dagger alone.

There are two basic stances to use with rapier and dagger. The first is the same as when a single sword is employed. The second is where you lead with the left foot (see illustration next page).

The benefit of leading with the left foot is that it is a stronger position for defending with the dagger, allowing you to void the body more easily on a concerted attack. It also allows you to more easily attack on the pass; meaning passing the right foot in front of the left. Your attack distance will be much greater. You should practice both stances and determine which works better for your fencing style.

The fencer will still employ *Prima*, *Seconda* and *Terza* with the rapier, *Quarta* is generally not used when employing a dagger in the left hand.

No matter which stance you use, the grip on the dagger is the same. The traditional dagger grip is made by holding the handle of the dagger with the blade pointing up in the hand (dagger hilt just above the thumb and forefinger) and when possible putting the thumb against the back of the flats of the dagger blade. Then, with a simple bending of the wrist the point of the dagger may be aimed directly at your opponent (the author's preferred grip), up, or down. I suggest that you use the left foot forward stance with this dagger grip. With this grip you may easily parry high or low thrusts and light cuts to the left side of the body. The left foot forward stance brings your dagger closer to your opponent and allows you to more quickly beat aside or bind their blade. I also suggest that you hold your dagger in the opposite guard from the rapier. If your rapier is held in the low guard, hold your dagger in high, etc. Almost all attacks from the left foot forward stance with a dagger will be made by performing a passing step to gain distance.

Di Grassi taught that the thrust should mainly be used when defending with the dagger:

> "In the second way, which is framed with the right foot behind, the sword aloft, and the dagger before, & borne as afore said, he ought in like sort discharge a thrust as forcibly as he may, with the increase of a straight pace, staying himself in the low ward. Neither ought any man in the handling of these weapons to assure himself to deliver edgeblows, because he, knoweth that there is an other weapon (and happily the weaker) to defend himself and strike with the stronger. The which stroke is painfully warded by him, who hath already bestowed all his force and power, in delivering the said edgeblow, by means whereof, because there remaineth in him small power to withstand any great encounter, let him provide to thrust only."[5]

The dagger may also be used to prepare an attack. I call this type of maneuver a dagger sweep. The idea is to attack your opponent's blade, not their body, with the dagger, taking their blade out of line. The sweep must be accompanied with a thrust to the opponent's belly or face. After the thrust lands (or in the event that you miss) you must quickly come back on guard, keeping the dagger and sword in front of you in a defensive posture.

Drill

The master comes on guard in Second with the student in First. The master attacks the student and the student parries the thrust to the outside with the dagger, moves the sword hand to Second and thrusts the master in the chest

The master and student are both in Third on the inside. The master disengages and thrusts in Third to the outside. The student turns their sword hand to Second and opposes the attack while stepping with the left foot in a slope pace and thrusting with the dagger to the master's side. (see page following)

The master and the student come on guard in Third on the outside. The master raises the arm to make a cut from the shoulder. The student waits for the cut to start so they will not be deceived. The student parries the cut with the dagger and starts a thrust in Second. As the master moves their dagger to parry the thrust and the student disengages under the dagger and hits with a *stoccata*. (see pages 137 and 138)

William (left) takes First, while Gary assumes Second. Notice how the daggers are kept ready to deflect incoming attacks, or to be used offensively should the opponent close with intent to grapple.

Gary makes a simple thrust for the face in Second; William counters it with the dagger, moving it off line, which draws Gary close enough for his own thrust.

William (left) and Gary both take their guards in Third.

Gary thrusts with a disengagement to the outside. William raises his hand to move the thrust offline, and finishes with a thrust to Gary's side from the outside--by taking this line it is very hard for Gary to counter with his own dagger.

Gary raises an arm to make a cut from the shoulder. William (left) waits in Third.

As Gary strkes with the cut, William parries the blow to his leg with his own dagger.

William makes a half pace with a slight traverse and starts a counter-thrust...

William disengages under the dagger and moves his hand to Third, finishing his thurst to Gary's midsection.

Drill

Coming on guard with a left foot forward stance, the scholar should point the dagger directly at the master. The master will then come on guard in First.(right foot forward) with the sword arm extended out towards the student. The student extends the dagger out and over the master's sword with the point down and pushes the sword down and away from the body. The scholar simultaneously thrusts the master in the face or the belly.

Richard (left) assumes his high guard in First, while Rhys takes his in Third.

Richard extends his sword to prepare for a thrust. Rhys parries the blade to his left and down, counter-thrusting in Fourth.

Rapier and cloak

Another off-hand device that was easily at hand to a Renaissance fencer was the cloak. Di Grassi advocated the use of the cloak for rapier fighting and maintained that it could be a very effective tool. It was still considered a common combination three generations later. However, using a cloak may be a boon or a bane. It can be a boon as it helps to defend against cuts, and it can be a bane if you entangle yourself in your own cloak. A late 16th or early 17th century cape would be appropriate. Full cloaks will weigh down your arm and cause you to fatigue quickly.

Di Grassi maintained that three things must be considered in using the cloak: its length, largeness (size) and flexibility.

> "The use whereof was first found out by chance and after reduced into art. Neither was this for any other cause, then for that nature doth not only delight to invent things, but also to preserve them being invented. And that she may the better do it, she taketh for her help all those things that are commodious for her. Wherefore, as men in diverse accidents have casually proved, that the Cloak helpeth greatly (for as much as they are to wear it daily) they have devised how they may behave themselves in all that, in which the Cloak may serve their turn. . .
>
> "As the Cloak in this Art, hath in it three things to be considered, to wit: length, largeness, and flexibility: so it is to be wayed how far each of these will stretch, to serve the turn."[6]

The cloak's, although not a strong thing in and of itself, lends itself to defense because of its very nature. Being long, it may guard against cuts to the side. Being flexible, it absorbs the strength of the blow. It may also be used to turn a thrust to the side or to entrap the blade.

Typically the cape is held either by the collar, or at one edge close to the hem. In the on guard it should be held out from the body and should drape down from the hand or arm. If you have a long cape or cloak you may fold the cloak once or twice around the hand and forearm. You must ensure that you do not obscure your sight with the cloak. As this can prove to be a deadly mistake.

A point to remember in these cases is that the cloak's flexibility is what protects. If a cut lands on a cloak that is against a solid surface (i.e. your arm, leg or flank) the protection is lost and you will be injured through the cloak.

The cloak may also be used offensively. Holding the cloak by the collar or hem it may be used to entangle a blade or beat it to the side, giving you the time to attack your opponent. It may also be thrown over your opponent's head to blind them temporarily. You may also throw it on your opponent's weapon to weight it down. Throwing the cloak is dangerous in that you may lose it and not accomplish your aims. It may also be twirled or flicked at your opponent to confuse them. They will not know if you are trying to blind them with a throw or are maneuvering to entangle their blade.

DiGrassi's sword and cloak

Drill

Coming on guard with a right foot forward stance, the scholar should hold their rapier in the high guard and holding the cloak by the collar wrap it once about the forearm. Hold the cloak a slight ways out from the body, the arm parallel to the ground and the elbow bent. The master will chest cut the scholar who will absorb the force of the cut with the cloak and will deliver a thrust to the face of the master.

William (left) and Gary both begin in First...

William makes a stramazzone at Gary, while Gary rushes forward, stepping forward with the left foot and engages the hilt with the cloak wapped hand before his own sword begins its thrust.

Gary now thursts between William's sword and cape.

Drill

The scholar will come on guard in the same fashion as previously shown except that the cloak will be firmly gripped at the collar, falling away from the hand. The scholar will use the cloak in an offensive fashion to beat or entangle the master's blade and will thrust to the master's face.

Rhys (left) and William both start in Second...

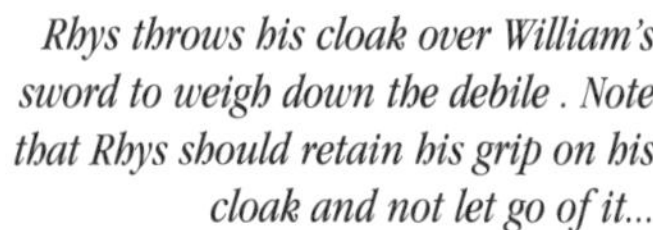

Rhys throws his cloak over William's sword to weigh down the debile . Note that Rhys should retain his grip on his cloak and not let go of it...

Rhys now completes the attack with a lunge.

Rapier and buckler

In Italy, as well as in the rest of Europe, the buckler (*brocchiero*) was one of the types of shields that had been employed for both military and civilian defense, since at least the 12th century. The buckler was a small round shield that was held by a strap or handle in the off-hand.

> "As the form of the Buckler, is round and small, and ought to be a shield & safeguard of the whole body, which is far greater then it: So it is to be understood how it may accomplish the same, being a matter in a manner impossible.
>
> Let every one therefore know, that the little Buckler is not equal in bigness to the body simply, but after a certain sort or manner, from which springeth this commodity, that he which understand it, shall be resolved of the manner how to bear and handle it, and shall know that in it, which shall not only advantage him in the use thereof, but also of many other weapons."[7]

The buckler was a small shield intended to parry or trap an opponent's blade. Bucklers should be round and between twelve and twenty-four inches in diameter. They were constructed of wood or steel, with a sturdy handle or strap attached to the back of the buckler that will allow you to hold the buckler firmly. Make sure that the screws or rivets are tight. Some bucklers had a large cross of banded iron or steel that was placed on the front to help in trapping the point of the opponent's blade.

Effective use of the buckler comes with frequent practice. A savvy duelist is able to out-maneuver the buckler to cause injury. I suggest that you take a left foot forward stance and hold the buckler at chest height out in front of you. Your arm should be extended. The buckler is then used to divert the opponent's blade to the left as you follow up with a thrust or cut.

Traditionally the buckler was also used offensively. Surviving bucklers have spikes set into their face to be used offensively. The small bucklers could be used to punch an opponent, and large bucklers or targets could be swung in such a manner as to strike the opponent with the edge. Care must be taken in practice when using these strategies.

Drill

Taking a left foot forward stance, the student will hold the buckler out in front with the arm extended at chest height and will hold the rapier in the Third ward. The master will thrust or cut at the student who will parry to the inside with the buckler and will return a thrust to the face or belly of the master.

Both William (left) and Richard come on guard in Third, the left leg forward.

William steps forward with the right leg a little off the line and thrusts at Richard over his buckler. Richard moves his buckler just enough to parry the thrust in Fourth.

Richard now steps off the line and thrusts William under his buckler.

Case of rapiers

The case of rapiers is most deservedly considered the deadliest of the rapier forms; both to the defender and to the attacker. Fencing masters reserved its teaching for last with good reason; the handling of two long blades adds a level of complexity over the use of a single sword or sword and dagger. It is all too easy to have your blades cross and become bound, leaving you helpless. Likewise, while the two swords gave great offensive potential at a distance, it lacked the dagger's (or even the buckler's) ability to infight.

The primary thing to remember is that one blade is always used for defense while the other is used for offense. It does not matter which is used for offense and defense; during the course of the fight they will often change roles.

The placement of the feet and body are very important to successful use of a case of rapiers. Your stance should start off with your favored hand forward and in the high guard. (As you become more proficient this may change.) You should hold your "off-hand" in the low ward, thus keeping your tips separated, all the while defending your high and your low lines. As you defend with either the right or the left hand, make your counter attacks with the opposite hand. Also, maintain your upper body square to your adversary, keeping your weight balanced between your legs. "reach" out a bit towards your opponent, keeping him or/her at bay.

When fighting with a case of rapiers there are a number of pitfalls that fencers will fall into. The first is keeping the points too close together. If you allow the tips of your blades to be too close together you are inviting your opponent to sweep both of your blades aside with onc of his. If he follows the sweep with an attack, it will be very hard for you to defend yourself with both of your blades out of line. The second pitfall is in your offense. There is a tendency to flail with the swords. This is when a person blindly attacks either by cuts or thrusts in a continuous fashion. An adept fencer can easily stay out of distance of this type of attack and riposte or counter-attack in time once his or her adversary's "steam" runs out.

The following is the beginning of di Grassi's discourse on the case of rapiers:

> "There are also used now adays, as well in the schools, as in the lists, two swords or rapiers, admitted and approved both of Princes, and of professors of this art, for honorable and knightly weapons, albeit they are not used in wars. Wherefore I shall not vary from my purpose, if I reason also of these, as fair as is agreeable to true art. To him that would handle these weapons, it is necessary that he ca as well manage the left hand as the right, which thing shall be (if not necessary) yet most profitable in every other kind of weapon. But in these principally he is to resolve himself, that he can do no good, without that kind of nimbleness and dexterity. For seeing they are two weapons, & yet of one self same kind, they ought to equally and indifferently to be handled, the one performing that which the other doth, & every of them being apt as well to strike as defend. And therefore a man ought to accustom his body, armes and hands as well to strike as to defend. And he which is not much practiced and excercised therein, ought not to make profession of this Art: for he shall find himself utterly deceived."[8]

Practice different ward and attack combinations to most fully make use of this fighting form.

Drill

The master will bring the student on guard with the right hand in First ward and the left in the Third. The master will then thrust the scholars upper left chest. The scholar will parry with the left sword to the left and will thrust to the face of the master with their right sword.

Tieg (left) starts in First with his left sword and Third for his right. William begins in Second with his right and Third with his left.

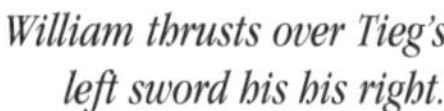

William thrusts over Tieg's left sword his his right.

Tieg turns his hand to Second to parry the William's thrust and turns his right hand to Second to make his own thrust to William's chest. Note that the right knee should be over the instep of the right foot. In this counter he keeps his swords to the center, with William's to the outside.

Drill

The master will bring the scholar on guard as in the prior drill. The master will then come on guard with the tips of his swords too close together. The scholar will sweep the blades out of line with the left sword and will deliver a thrust to the master's stomach with the right sword. Practice the sweep and thrust with both left and right hands.

Gary (left) starts with his right hand in First and his left hand in Third. William starts both blades in Third, the points close together.

Gary disengages and extends his left sword to sweep both of William's points to his left...

Maintaining pressure on both of William's blades, Gary finishes with a quick thrust to his chest.

Conclusion

Fencing is an integration of both the mental and the physical. It is not enough to simply go through mental exercises without physical practice, or to only take part in simple drills without thinking of their potential use in a combat situation. Fencing is like a chess match. You must think ahead and determine the permutations of action based on the techniques employed. In any attack that you might make, what are the possible defenses that your opponent may use and how may you capitalize on them? A person may perform techniques flawlessly yet fail in their execution during an open assault.[9] Drills will help build muscle memory and are indispensable in the study of fencing. Some drills may be performed alone (i.e. footwork and some attack drills) while others must be performed with a partner to fully understand and internalize the techniques.

Within this book are both descriptions of many actual fencing techniques taught by the historical masters and a discussion of the philosophical elements of the duel. In the appendices you will find a twenty week course outline for studying beginning rapier fencing. Learning fencing on one's own is difficult at best. Even with a partner is is difficult to understand proper technique. Not impossible but difficult. If at all possible, I suggest that you locate a capable instructor. Fencing masters and instructors are available that will travel to teach with a pedagogical approach that enables the students to more easily understand and learn the art of fencing. If you have a group but no instructor nearby then fly one in for a weekend seminar to jumpstart your program. Masters and instructors such as Maestro Ramon Martinez (US), Maestra Jeanette Acosta-Martinez (US), Maestro Andrea Lupo Sinclair (Italy), Master Paul Macdonald (Scotland), Stephen Hand (Australia), Stefan Dieke (Germany), myself (US) and others will travel to your area to teach. You may also attend the many Western Martial Arts seminars that are held throughout the year; the *Western Martial Arts Workshop* in the northeast, the *Lansing Swordfighting Symposium*, (Michigan), the *SCA Knowne World Rapier Collegium*, and the *Schola St. George Swordsmanship Symposium* in Livermore, California are just a few held in the US. Today we have a wealth of information available to assist us in our study of Western Martial Arts. Not only for rapier play but also for other medieval and Renaissance weapons as well. In your study of rapier fencing, start with the single sword and after you are comfortable and proficient at fighting single then add in other weapons and defensive devices to fight double. Train as often as you are able and most importantly, make your study of rapier play fun.

[1] Old habits died hard, however. Capo Ferro (1610) still felt a need to devote a brief chapter to use of the rapier with the rotella (round shield), although the brevity and simplicity of his instructions shows how little likely the combination had become.

[2] Salvator Fabris. *De Lo Schermo.* A.F. Johnson translation. p 4.

[3] During the past century or longer it was thought that the dagger was insufficient to ward against the powerful shoulder cuts used with the earlier arming sword. Prior to Manciolino, only Pietro Monte (1509) touches on sword and dagger, and only tangentially. Fifteenth century masters, whether Italian, German or English, make no mention of the form at all. George Silver, who taught an essentially medieval style, taught the use of sword and dagger, but specifically used the sword, not the dagger, to parry cuts: "Observe at these weapons the former rules, defend with your sword & not your dagger," *Brief Instructions Vpo My Paradoxes of Defence* (Cap. 7) and "Sword & Buckler fight, & sword & dagger fight are all one, saving that you may safely defend both blow & thrust, single with your buckler only," (Cap. 9) However Marozzo in *Arte dell'Armi* teaches specifically to parry cuts with the dagger alone.

[4] Giacomo di Grassi. *His True Arte of Defense*. p 29.

[5] Giacomo di Grassi. *His True Arte of Defense*. p 32.

[6] Giacomo di Grassi. *His True Arte of Defense*. p 36-37.

[7] Giacomo di Grassi. *His True Arte of Defense*. p 42.

[8] Giacomo di Grassi. *His True Arte of Defense*. p 54-55.

[9] An "open assault" is open practice where two combatants put into practice the techniques they have practiced in the drills.

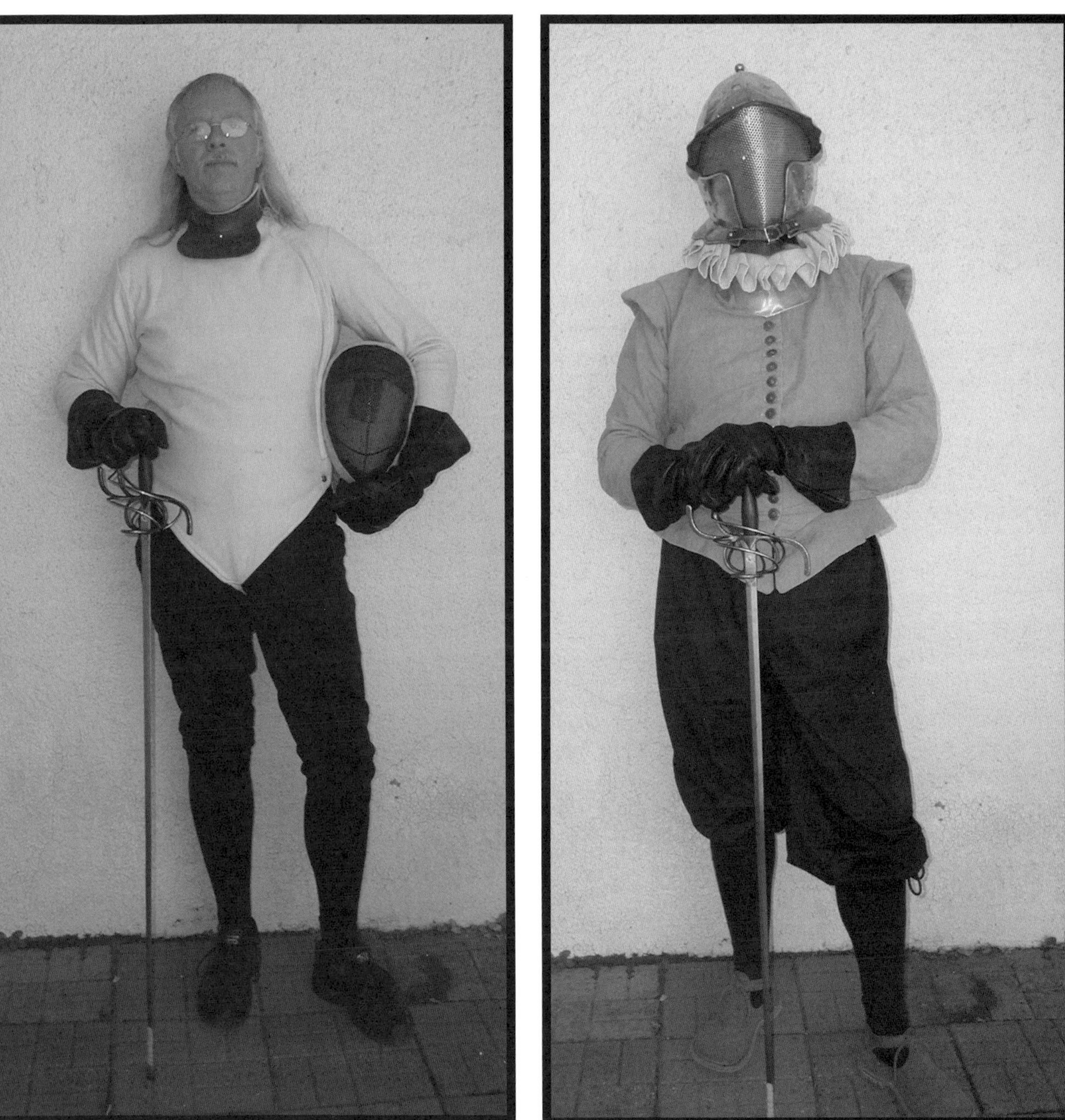

Two sets of equipment as used for the pracice of historical fencing. There are, of course, advantages to each. The modern equipment is in many respects easier to obtain, and does reduce variables for the novice. It consists of a standard set of 3-weapon fencing pants and jacket, a heavy leather gorget, gauntlets and a 3-weapon fencing mask. The sword is by Darkwood Armoury with a practice Del Tin blade. The Renaissance-style clothing confers a greater sense of historically accurate movements and better protection, but is harder to acquire and more expensive. The author here wears a pair of Dutch slops made from fustian, a cotton canvas doublet, leather gauntlets, steel gorget with canvas ruff, and a steel fencing helmet with a perforated facplate.

ARMORING

Your selection of body protection and weapons will affect your experience at rapier combat; either for the positive or the negative. Modern fencing blades are not intended to be used in historical fencing such as rapier. The dimensions and weight of the blades make them very poor choices for this type of fencing activity. Also, the act of performing a correct cut with an epee or foil will stress the blade in ways that were not intended. The use of epee, foil or sabre should be kept for what they are intended; classical and modern fencing.

Today there are a number of companies that provide historically accurate weapons for use in simulating and practicing rapier combat. One such company is **Del Tin Armi Antiche** out of Italy. They produce two types of blades that are fully adequate for rapier combat. These are their practice rapier blade and the bated rapier blade. Both of these blades are approximately 41" long from the shoulder at the tang to the point. The practice rapier blade is slimmer (not as wide) than the bated rapier blade and has a lighter flex, making it a good starting blade for beginning fencers. The bated rapier blade being stiffer is better suited for more experienced fencers who can control their thrusts and make lighter touches on their opponent's.

Darkwood Armoury out of Florida crafts historically accurate hilts for the Del Tin blades and is the author's supplier of choice for rapier simulators (as well as other types of swords). Other suppliers of high quality and combat grade weapons include **Arms & Armour**, **Dennis Graves**, **Triplett Arms**, **American Fencing Supply** and other fencing supply houses.

A number of years ago the historical fencing community began using schlager blades from Germany to simulate rapiers. These first came into the US through American Fencing Supply and were better than what was previously being used. However, schlagers are a poor imitation of a period rapier blade and should be close to the last choice, after classical or modern fencing weapons. A new supplier on the scene is **CAS Iberia**. They are providing a new line of rapiers and other swords intended for practice. At the time of the writing of this book they sell a rapier simulator with two different blade lengths, 37" and 43". The blades look like sword blades in that they have a ricasso and the the blade tapers to the point with a flattened diamond cross section. The blades are very flexible (too flexible for any real cutting play) and so are suited for beginners. Also, the low costs for these swords make them a good choice for a beginner.

No matter what style of weapon you use for your rapier study, you must wear a certain minimum level of protection to protect yourself from broken blades and from concussive injuries. You must wear a protective jacket (doublet) that has enough padding to protect from bruising. Triplette and other companies sell padded doublets that may be used for historical fencing. A normal fencing jacket will not suffice for most rapier simulators. Rapiers are stiffer than modern fencing weapons and more padding is a must.

All combatants must wear 12-kilo or better three-weapon fencing masks to protect the face (or a helm specifically made for historical fencing), some covering to protect the back of the head and a heavy leather or metal gorget to protect the throat. Men must wear a cup and women should wear breast protectors and padded groin protection (breast protectors are available through fencing supply houses).

Heavy leather gauntlets are also to be worn on both hands. Sturdy abrasion resistant pants and sturdy shoes or boots must also be worn. No bare skin should be visible.

You will notice that the fencers in the pictures in this book are wearing a variety of clothing from simple renaissance pants and shirts to wearing doublets. It is my contention that when trying to learn rapier fencing that it is also important to study the clothing of the period in question. The cut of the clothing and the shoes that you wear will alter how you fence. For example, shoes can make a large difference. The first time I wore historically accurate shoes to fence rapier I had to alter the way I stepped. There is a great difference between wearing modern cross training shoes with a good sole that will grips the ground well and a pair of leather soled Elizabethan brogans. I would suggest that you try and fence not only in normal modern practice gear but also in as historically accurate clothing as possible to get a feel for the differences.

As noted previously a number of different organizations study historical fencing. You should work with one of these groups and they will help you with your protective gear and other equipment.

It must be stated: Taking part in combat with bated rapiers can be dangerous. The student takes all responsibility for injuries sustained in this study.

William (center back) places the students at wide measure to practice a lunge in Fourth in opposition.

When William makes the call to attack the students lunge in Fourth.

Teaching Historical Fencing

Teaching fencing is an art that not all may be able to do. There is a certain mind set that must be reached before a person may teach effectively. The fencing instructor must lose the competitive mindset. Teachers are not there to just beat the students. They are there to teach. This means that the instructor gets hit or in fencing terms "touched". Also, it does not mean that when running open practice you do not push the students. They must be pushed.

It does not take a world class fencer to teach fencing. In fact, it is my opinion that one must not have the "winner's" mentality to be able to teach effectively. If the primary interest in fencing is to win, it is very difficult to allow people to make effective attacks against. It is imperative to take on a nurturing philosophy and thus allow the students to grow. Yes, it is hard to admit when a student now has an edge over the teacher in competition, but the true master should still be able to take the student and hone them even further. At 46 years old, the author does not have the speed or endurance of the younger fencers but he can still point out their mistakes and help them to overcome their errors.

A Pedagogical Approach

Learning to fence properly is not just being shown a few moves and then putting a sword in one's hand. To fence properly you must train the body to react in specific ways. This is done through instruction and drills. You may find a sample course outline in the appendices.

In a nutshell the following should be taught:

1. Proper footwork
2. A knowledge of timing and distance
3. Good Defense
4. Good Offense

It is my opinion that without a grounding in proper footwork, a person will not be able to master timing, distance, defense or offense. Footwork is integral to good fencing. I suggest that a person work on footwork for three to four weeks before picking up a sword (except to look at it and heft the weight). Once a grounding in the footwork has been started, then the student should start to practice footwork with a weapon in hand. All the while, instruction on timing and distance is given. Follow with the other topics in the course outline and use this book as a guide.

For the classes themselves I would suggest the following format:

1. Warmup exercises (i.e. footwork drills). This should last no more than10 minutes.

2. Lecture. Introduce new topics or re-cover old topics. This part should last no more than 10 or 15 minutes.

3. Drills. Line or individual drills. This should be as long as necessary or until people are getting bored. Make it fun!

4. Play. This is the part that everyone wants to do. Have the students put the new techniques to work.

There are two basic formats for teaching fencing, the individual lesson and the group lesson. The well-rounded instructor should be able to work in both formats. The instructor may also use more advanced students to work on specific topics with those students that require a little extra one-on-one instruction.

The individual lesson may be considered the mainstay of instruction. It must be stressed that the individual lesson be an uplifting experience for the student. It may be a rigorous exercise but it should not leave the student with a negative feeling. After running a student through a number of drills, the instructor may opt to free fence with the student. This is a *practicum* and the instructor should make openings that the student should try to exploit. During this practicum the instructor may fine tune the student, making suggestions for improvement and giving praise when a move is done in proper time and execution.

Group lessons may also be employed, especially if the school has many students. This procedure allows the instructor to teach a large number of students at the same time and also allows the instructor to gain a general feel for how the group is doing as a whole. This type of lesson should not be confused with open bouting. It is structured and intended to cover a single topic during the course of the lesson. For example, if the instructor desires to teach an attack followed by a parry with the offhand and a counterattack, he would have the students form two lines facing each other, called A and B. He would explain exactly what is to be performed by the students and would indicate that at first he would call all movements. He then would call the attack by A, followed by the offhand parry by B. He then would call the counter attack by B, etc. Once the students seem to be handling the slow drill the instructor would simply call the attack and the students would execute at progressively faster speed until they are using standard attack speed. As the students perform the drill the instructor (and her/his assistants) may walk about correcting mistakes.

There are a number of resources available that may help you in your quest to become a fencing instructor. I would suggest the book "Fencing and the Master" by Szabo. It is a good guide to teaching fencing; although it is geared more for classical and modern fencing it still is applicable to historical fencing. Teaching fencing can be a very rewarding experience for the instructor.

Groups That Study Historical Combat

Today there are a number of different organizations that study historical combat. The following is a short list of these organizations with a brief description of what they teach. The url for their web page is also given. You should visit their websites for up-to-date information as well as contact information.

Association of Historical Fencing

The AHF exists to encourage and preserve the arts of classical and historical fencing. To these ends, the AHF is organizing seminars, lectures, workshops and similar programs, and disseminating knowledge and basic factual material to its membership. To raise public awareness we are hosting exhibitions and demonstrations. The AHF, to the extent practicable, will ensure the availability of qualified masters and instructors in order to teach workshops, etc. We hope to promote the growth of schools and academies both nationally and internationally, but most importantly, we are providing a venue where practitioners andinterested parties can unite to foment the growth of the classical andhistorical fencing community.

http://www.ahfi.org

Chicago Swordplay Guild

Based in Chicago, this group has been teaching and practicing historical swordplay for some time now. They span the 14th - 16th centuries; founders Greg Mele and Mark Rector are both active in the Western Martial Arts / Historical Fencing community.

http://www.chicagoswordplayguild.com

Die Freifechter

Wir praktizieren die Kampftechniken des Mittelalters und der Renaissanceals Kampfsport.

http://www.freifechter.org/cgi-bin/FFshwcls.pl/start

Martinez Academy of Arms

Ramon Martinez & Jeanette Acosta-Ramirez teach Spanish & Italian Rapier and various form of classical fencing. Based in New York City, the Ramirez's are also key figures in the Association for Historical Fencing and in the Western Martial Arts community generally.

http://www.martinez-destreza.com

FISAS

The Italian Ancient and Historical Fencing Federation, (FISAS) was found in order to preserve the traditional teachings of the Art and the Science of True Fencing. FISAS has been active in Italy since 1995. Maestro Andrea Lupo Sinclair has been teaching the main groups of styles: Ancient Fencing, Historical Fencing and Classical Fencing.

http://www.scherma-antica.org/

Macdonald Academy of Arms

European martial arts and historical fencing can be accurately interpreted from the earliest surviving texts of the late 13th century right through to 19th century treatises, all detailing martial principles and techniques for over forty different weapons forms, six centuries of development, characteristic national styles, and multitudinous accepted academic and social combative customs. Training in these arts is exciting and intense, working the body, focusing the mind, and balancing the spirit in reviving a true living tradition which develops the self to a higher level. The Academy is open to all, with no previous fencing or martial arts experience required in any form. Tuition is taught progressively according to the individual students' abilities and aptitude.

http://www.historicalfencing.org/Macdonaldacademy/aboutus.htm

Schola Saint George

Based in the Bay Area, California, the Schola focuses on medieval swordsmanship of the 14th and 15th centuries, basing their curriculum on the Italian Fiore dei Liberi and on combat wthin the lists, chiefly with the medieval longsword and poleaxe.

http://www.scholasaintgeorge.org

Stoccata School of Defense

The Stoccata School of Defence is based in Sydney, Australia, and is dedicated to the study of European swordsmanship using replicas of historic weapons, and techniques drawn from manuals of the period. We conduct regular classes in rapier and sword, including the use of companion weapons.

http://mgw.com.au/ab/stoccata.nsf/

Tattershall School of Defense

The Tattershall School of Defense is a nonprofit corporation founded to meet the needs of the historical-oriented fencing community. The TSD exists to teach, preserve and support the art of the historical fencing (15th, 16th & 17th Centuries) as well as the classical period.

http://www.tattershall.org

This lesson plan is adapted from the author's own curriculum at the Tattershall School of Defence. This lesson plan assumes the students will meet for at least one formal lesson per week with additional practice on their own to hone their skills. Optimally these lessons may be done on a weekly basis with additional practice in between. However, if a technique in a lesson seems difficult or the student is not internalizing the technique, you should continue the lesson for an additional week to make sure the student is able to do it correctly before moving on. If you are able to follow this curriculum a student should be able to learn the basics of single rapier in 20 weeks. As with any athletic endeavor, always begin a lesson with stretching and basic warm-ups.

INTRODUCTION

Introduction to the History of Fencing

FOOTWORK

Advance and Retreat

The Pass

Slope Paces, Traverses and Circular Paces

BASIC WARDS/GUARDS

Prima | Seconda | Terza | Quarta

ATTACKS

Thrusts

Imbrocatta | Stocatta | Punta Riversa

Cuts

Mandritti | Riversi

DEFENCE

Voltes | Incartata |

Dui Tempi Defence

Stesso Tempo Defence

Section One

FIRST LESSON

The student shall learn how to advance and retreat.

1. Introduction

Talk about history. Go over the weapons and weapon combinations. Give an overview of the historic masters. Show onguard, advance, retreat, lunge

2. On Guard Position

Introduce the Terza guardia as the standard on guard and show the advance and retreat. Discuss the placement of the feet. Woodcuts from Marozzo, Agrippa or Capo Ferro may be used to illustrate (or other master's works)

3. Teach the advance and retreat
4. Have students practice the advance and retreat.

SECOND LESSON

The students should be able to successfully advance and retreat. The passing step is introduced. Care must be taken to indicate that the pass must be used sparingly to begin with for safety.

1. Teach the pass forward and pass back.
2. Practice

THIRD LESSON

The student practices the topics from the first & second lesson. New topics to be introduced include the traverse, circular movement and the four primary guard positions.

1. Introduction

Discuss the benefits of the four primary guards. Introduce the traverse and circular movement.

2. Practice the four primary guards

The students take each guard position and move in that position with straight, slope, traverse and passing paces.

FOURTH LESSON

The student is introduced to the sword.

1. Introduction

The students are introduced to sword. Define the parts of the sword. Allow the students to handle the weapons to check weight & balance.

2. Practice foot movement and guards from lessons one through three.

FIFTH LESSON

The students review everything from the first four lessons and the extension is introduced.

1. Introduction

The students are introduced to the extension (preparation for attack).

2. Practice movement. Work on extending the arm in preparation for attacks.

Section 2

SIXTH LESSON

The students start to work with sword in hand.

1. Introduction

The students practice the extension with sword in hand. The four positions of the hand are discussed. The imbrocata and stoccata are taught.

2. Practice

SEVENTH LESSON

The student practices the first two thrusts and is introduced to the punta riversa.

1. Introduction

The punta riversa is added to the student's repertoire of simple attacks.

2. Practice. The students will attack target by simple extension, extension with a step and with a pass.

EIGHTH LESSON

The students are introduced to the lunge. The history of the lunge is given.

1. Introduction

Proper lunge technique is covered. The topic of distance is discussed.

2. Practice

NINTH LESSON

The students are introduced to dui tempi defense.

1. Introduction.

The use of the blade and off-hand for defense is discussed. The protective equipment is shown and explained to the students. All further practice between students or student and instructor will be with protective equipment worn. Introduce the salute and proper fencing etiquette.

2. Practice the use of the sword for parrying thrusts.

TENTH LESSON

Reinforce defense by further practice of dui tempi maneuvers.

1. Practice movement, attacks and defense. Use line drills and individual lessons to illustrate the points.

2. Have the more advanced students attack the beginning students so they may practice their defense.

Section 3

ELEVENTH LESSON

This lesson is for general review.

1. Have the students take part in line drills. Watch for proper execution of attacks and defense. Correct any deficiencies in the students' technique.

2. General practice.

TWELFTH LESSON

Introduce the cuts with the true edge. Use Marozzo's techniques and terminology.

1. Instruct in the use of the tondo, fendente, montante, ridoppio and sgualembrato. Use line drills for the practice.

2. Practice the cuts.

THIRTEENTH LESSON

Introduce the parrying of cuts with the blade.

1. Introduce parries with the right edge of the sword. Give emphasis to parrying with the strong part of the blade and not the guard itself.

2. Use line drills and individual instruction to practice parrying the various cuts.

FOURTEENTH LESSON

Introduce body voids.

1. Talk about the incartata, the volte, slips, etc. Have the students practice these foot movements.

2. Practice using these movements while defending from thrusts and cuts.

FIFTEENTH LESSON

Introduce cuts with the false edge. Use Marozzo's techniques and terminology.

1. Use line drills and individual instruction to teach the use of false edge cuts.

2. Practice.

Section 4

SIXTEENTH LESSON

Introduce stramazone.

1. Show how these cuts may be used to cut the face, wrist and knee.
2. Practice.

SEVENTEENTH LESSON

Have the students practice the various cuts.

1. Review and practice the mandritti, roversi and stramazone.
2. Open practice.

EIGHTEENTH LESSON

Introduce bouting.

1. Discuss the topic of bouting. Go over general rules and why bouting is important.
2. Pair the beginning students with more experienced students and have them practice open combat.

NINETEENTH LESSON

Introduce stesso tempo defense.

1. Teach the counter-attack.
2. Practice.

TWENTIETH LESSON

Review lessons one through nineteen.

1. Review.
2. Practice.

Sample Quiz

Section 1

Name a fencing master who taught before 1550. What style of fencing did he teach?

Name the three types of thrusts.

What are the four primary Italian guards? Describe each.

What is the pass?

What is the importance of the extension?

Explain distance.

What are the parts of the sword?

What is the difference between the true and false edge?

What is the difference between a slope and a traverse pace?

What is the lunge?

Section 2

What early Italian master taught the use of the lunge?

What is the punta riversa and how may it be used?

What are the four principal positions of the hand?

What is dui tempi defense?

Why would the imbrocatta or stocatta be used?

Section 3

Name the cuts delivered from the right side.

What are roversi?

What is an incartata and when might it be used?

What is a traverse?

Describe the volte.

Section 4

What is stesso tempo defense?

What is the stramazone?

What are the five primary rapier weapon combinations?

What are the primary three different types of shields used in the Italian Schools?

What is a bout?

An Article on the Rapier from Patri Pugliese

Dr. Patri Pugliese is a researcher in historical fencing and has been a source for copies of historical manuals for many years. A list of the manuals that he has to offer may be found at: http://www.latourdulac.com/fencing/patri.html

Dr. Pugliese's early fencing training came from his mother's Julia Jones Pugliese, first women's intercollegiate fencing champion in 1929, professional fencing coach until 1994.

RESEARCH STRATEGIES FOR THE STUDY OF EARLY RAPIER PRACTICE — Patri J. Pugliese

The following is intended as a brief description of what I perceive to be two lines of research (or research strategies) currently being carried out by a variety of individuals (including, I suspect, many of whom I am unaware) seriously interested in reconstructing the activity of rapier combat or fencing as it was practiced in the late sixteenth and early seventeenth centuries. The two research strategies I have in mind may be referred to as "textual research" and "physical research." I do not by any means claim to be expert in either of these two areas, but merely present them in an attempt to codify what is being done and to suggest directions for further work.

By "textual research" I mean research based on the careful reading of instruction manuals (and to a lesser extent other written accounts) composed in the sixteenth and early seventeenth centuries. The first step here is to acquire such a manual. A number of manuals (Didier, di Grassi, Saviolo, Silver) were reprinted in facsimile during the past century; but even these reprints are to be found only in select libraries. Most of the key manuals have never been reprinted, and are therefore available only from a few libraries with extensive rare book collections. Having these manuals microfilmed is usually quite expensive and time consuming. There is an obvious advantage here to sharing manuals once a single copy has been obtained, and for some time I have tried to act as a clearinghouse for such manuals. Recently, others (such as Stephen Hick) have supplied me with additional manuals, which I can now make available. I am, of course, interested in any others which readers may have obtained and are willing to have disseminated.

My suggestion is to work in detail through one manual at a time, rather than reading several at once and then trying to produce an integrated combination. The main reason for this is that different manuals were composed at different times, and are describing an art that was evolving, that is to say, changing over time. In addition to changes that were occurring over time, there were also distinct national styles, which introduces major differences in contemporary manuals. Thus, the manuals are most emphatically not alternate descriptions of the same activity and movements. Indeed, it is only by detailed study of the individual works that we will be able to establish the specific characteristics of each national style at various times of its development.

Since we are concerned with the reconstruction of a physical activity, I believe that this careful reading of a specific source should be at least in part performed with weapon in hand. It is one thing to read a description of a complex movement that sounds plausible enough. If you are especially good at visualizing such moves, you may even be able to form a mental image of the process being described. It is doubtful, however, that this move can be appreciated in its details without actually going through it — first slowly to insure that you are actually doing what is being described, and then gradually working up to speed to assess the practicality and effectiveness of the move.

This activity brings me to the second research strategy mentioned above, physical research. By this I mean the process of engaging with weapons in hand and, in effect, seeing what works. In its pure form, this strategy does not refer to historical sources at all, but rather relies on the principle that whatever works best would have been done, especially by those whose well being depended on the efficacy of their activity. The major caveat here for rapier work is that what works with modern foil or epee may have little to do with what would work with a sixteenth or early seventeenth century rapier. In order to see what would have worked with a period weapon, one would, according to this strategy, need to obtain a pair of weapons having the same handling characteristics. I propose that the following are necessary and sufficient to this goal: the hilt length (including the pommel and guard around the ricasso), the blade length (not including the ricasso), the overall length (not actually a separate factor, being the sum of the first two), the position of the center of gravity (that is, at what point along the blade does the weapon balance), the overall weight or mass, the moment of inertia about the center of gravity.

The significance of the last of these may require some explanation. The moment of inertia is a measure of the way in which the mass of a body is distributed along its length, and is a direct indicator of the ease or difficulty of imparting a rotation (as in initiating a cut) to the weapon. Imagine, for instance, a meter long uniform rod o with a pair of kilogram masses fixed at each end. The length, position of the center of gravity, and the total mass of the two bodies are identical, but the handling characteristics if you were to swing each of them would be very different. This example rather exaggerates the problem, for the mere fact of its being shaped like a rapier means that a simulated weapon which matches a period rapier in the other characteristics will not be very different in moment of inertia. Those familiar with using a sword like implement (or for that matter a baseball bat) will be aware of another measurement of interest, the location of the center of percussion or "sweet point." For a given axis of rotation, determined by the way the implement is being gripped and swung, the center of percussion is the point along the length of the sword (or bat) which will deliver the maximum impact for a given swing (and thereby produce the minimum vibration in the hand). No separate determination is needed for this point, however, as its position for a given axis of rotation can be calculated from the moment of inertia. Indeed, the moment of inertia can be calculated if one determines the center of percussion for a given axis, but this requires one to subject the weapon to impacts, which few museums would permit with their original rapiers. There are other means of determining the moment of inertia, but these involve specialized apparatus. A friend is building such an apparatus for me, but until it is completed this last measurement cannot be made.

Measurements of other factors mentioned have been made for a limited number of period weapons located at the Metropolitan Museum of Art in New York. Matthew Larson and myself did this last year with the kind permission of the museum staff, including the late Leonid Tarassuk. Presented below is the data collected for eight of those weapons, which I judge by the design of the guard to be of late sixteenth century manufacture:

Blade	oc(cm)	cd(cm)	od(cm)	cg(cm)	w(kg)
m1	20.0	101.3	121.3	6.4	.800
m2	21.2	105.2	126.4	6.3	1.290
m3	22.3	96.3	118.6	6.2	1.610
m16	20.8	111.9	132.7	7.0	1.360
m17	20.0	105.2	125.2	7.8	1.260
m18	17.6	98.7	116.3	7.9	1.170
AVE	20.7	101.6	123.5	6.8	1.239
MED	21.0	103.3	123.9	6.7	1.275

(o is the point at the end of the pommel, c at the front of the guard, g is the point of the center of gravity and d the tip of the sword)

The numbers at left are our form number, which was filled out for each weapon. These forms include a listing of the museum accession number as well as a number of additional measurements (e.g. blade width at base and near the tip, diameter of the bar stock used in the guard) of lesser importance than the above. The penultimate row gives the averages of the values for the individual weapons. The last row gives the average of the median values. That is, for each characteristic, the highest and lowest three values are ignored, and the remaining two are averaged. This last procedure is intended to discount any single weapon which may be far out of line with the others and possibly irrelevant (say for instance a child's weapon). Indeed, there is one weapon (m1) which is far lighter than the others, but this is offset by another (m6) which is inordinately heavy. Actually, I'd like information on far more rapiers before coming to any firm conclusions, but the above values may serve as a guideline in the interim. By way of contrast, I weighed a few examples of modern practice weapons that were at hand: two Italian foils with weights (masses) of .304 and .344 kg, barely a quarter of the above average; a standard modern epee of .438 kg; a practice rapier with small cup hilt and crossguard and with an epee blade of .563 kg; a practice rapier with large cup hilt and crossguard and with a double wide blade of .717 kg. These weapons are also rather shorter than the 48" (122 cm) typical of the above.

The relative lightness of these practice weapons renders them inappropriate for the process of physical research, since it is clearly possible, and common in modern fencing technique, to perform maneuvers with these lighter weapons which would be very different if not impossible with the heavier period rapier. This does not rule out using lighter practice weapons for the process described above as textual research, since one is primarily relying there on the written instructions in determining what movement to make. A great deal about the practice of rapier combat in the late sixteenth and early seventeenth could, I believe, be learned by such activity. Nevertheless, how a given movement feels and its ease of execution will not be well represented by the lighter practice weapon. At the level of engaging an opponent full out, this difference would, I suspect, prove critical. It is clearly impractical to attempt by regulation to specify the myriad movements which, since they could not be performed well with a period rapier, ought to be deliberately avoided using practice weapons. Indeed, until research is carried out with practice weapons of period design and weight, we can only speculate on precisely which movements are affected and to what degree.

It seems to me that research combining the two strategies outlined above would be the best way to gain insight into period rapier practice. Textual research with weapons in hand of appropriate length, weight and balance would give a real feel for the maneuvers being described in the manuals. The major problem arises as speed is increased in maneuvers where one is facing an opponent — and here I am still talking about the limited context of practicing a set maneuver as specified in some manual. The lack of flexibility of any blade heavy enough to approximate a period one, combined with the inherent inertia of the heavier weapon presents an extremely dangerous prospect. At the very least, modern fencing masks and jackets cannot be regarded as offering sufficient protection. Should such practice ever reach the point of engaging in actual practice combat, and this should not even be contemplated until a good measure of experience with the heavy weapons was acquired in practice work, the armor requirements for even a minimal level of safety would be considerable.

Note from the William Wilson

Since the writing of this article, a number of advances have been made in rapier simulators. Today we have reasonable approximations of daggers and very good approximations of rapiers. The new equipment is much safer and is made to flex thus taking care of some of the problems address by Mr. Pugliese at the end of his article.

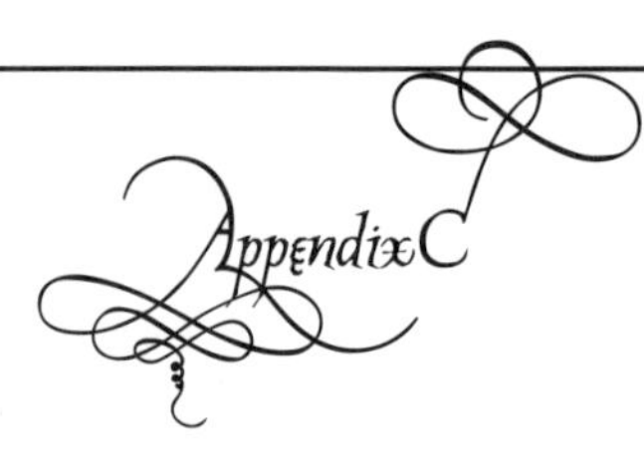

Appendix C

American Fencers Supply
1180 Folsom Street,
San Francisco, CA 94103
415-863-7911

Arms & Armour
1101 Stinson Blvd. NE
Minneapolis, MN 55413
800-745-7345
http://www.armor.com/

Chivalry Sports
8677 E Golf Links Rd
Tucson, AZ 85734
800-730-5464
http://www.renstore.com

Darkwood Armory
5514 Frank Hough Road
Panama City, FL 32404
850-872-1873
http://www.darkwoodarmory.com

Dennis Graves, Sword Cutler
Boulder, CO
303-494-4685

Macdonald Armouries
At the Sign of the Cross and Sword
Brunswick St. Lane
Edinburgh, Scotland EH7 5JA
44 (0)131 5571510
http://www.historicalfencing.org/Macdonaldarmory/aboutus.htm

Museum Replicas, Ltd.
POB 840
Atlanta, GA 30012
800-883-8838
http://www.museumreplicas.com/

Tattershall Arms
Box 1215
Flagstaff, AZ 86002
http://www.infomagic.com/~gwylym/ta

Triplett Competition Arms
411 S Main Street
Mt. Airy, NC 27030
919-786-5294

Manuals

Chivalry Bookshelf
4226 Cambridge Way
Union City, CA, 94587
866-268-1495 toll free (USA)
510.471.2944 (worldwide)
http://www.chivalrybookshelf.com/

Patri Pugliese
39 Capen St
Medford, MA 02155

Tattershall Arms
Box 1215
Flagstaff, AZ 86001

Laura Angotti
76 Westmoreland Ave
Arlington, MA 02174
(English Translation of St. Didier)

Fir Mountain Press
P.O. Box 95674
Seattle, Washington 98145, USA
http://www.angelfire.com/wa/firmountain/

Glossary

The terms used in modern fencing had their origins in the fencing schools of France of the late 17th and early 18th centuries. The terms from the 16th and early 17th centuries are based primarily on those defined and described by the Italian masters of the period. Those that study in the classical Italian tradition will recognize many of the terms used by the historical masters.

Advance: *To move forward.*
Assault: *Engage in a fencing bout in a fencing school.*
Battare: *To beat aside your adversary's blade with rapier, foot, hand or dagger.*
Brocchiero: *A buckler*
Buckler: *A small, typically round, shield held in the hand.*
Campo chiuso: *"closed field"*
Cappa: *cape/cloak*
Causa di honore: *"Cause of Honor"*
Cavatione or Cavare: *Turning your point under your adversary's blade when being bound or thrust. A disengagement. This was spelled* cavere *in* Pallas Armata.
Contratempo: *This is a timed thrust used offensively or defensively.*
Counterattack: *An attack during the opponent's attack that is performed in stesso tempo.*
Cut: *An attack made with the edge of the sword.*
Dagger: *A short bladed weapon used in conjunction with a rapier as a defensive and offensive weapon.*
Debile/debole: *Weak part of the blade.*
Duel: *To settle a point of honor through sword combat.*
Dui tempi (Two times): *Used in conjunction with parry-riposte actions.*
Feint: *A simulated attack that is used to make an opening for the true attack.*
Fendente: *A vertical attack in a downward direction.*
Fermata: *"Stop" May be interpreted as a guard.*
Fermó: *Firm, steady*
Finda: *A feint.*
Forte: *Strong part of the blade.*
Grappling: *Wrestling moves used in swordplay.*
Guard: *A defensive posture.*
Guardia: *Italian for guard or ward.*
Guardia alta: *High guard*
Guardia di chiamata a basso: *Low, downward guard*
Guardia di dentro: *Inside guard*
Guardia di fuori: *Outside guard*
Imbroccata: *This attack is made over the adversary's blade, hand or dagger. The blade travels in a downward direction and the hand is held with the knuckles up (as in a modern prime or high tierce). In the classical Italian school the hand will be in first or first in second position.*
Incartata: *A foot movement where a quarter turn is made. Also spelled inquartata.*
La gamba dritta inanzi: *Right leg forward*
La gamba stanca inanzi: *Left leg forward*
Lunge: *A quick and forceful body movement that takes an attack to the opponent.*
Mandritta or Mandritti: *Cuts from the right side.*
Master: *An instructor of high quality who has taken boards similar to a PhD candidate.*
Measure/misura: *The distance between you and your adversary.*
Montante: *A vertical attack made in an upwards direction.*
Parry or Parare: *To decline, put by, or turn a thrust or blow. To defend with the sword to prevent a cut or thrust from arriving.*
Pass or Passare: *To pass by your adversary while you thrust at him. A walking maneuver as opposed to the lunge. In Italian this verb indicates to step.*
Per batter la spada: *To beat aside the sword*
Prima First: *The first guard position.*
Pugnale: *A dagger*
Punta: *A thrust.*
Punta della spada: *The point of the sword*
Punta Riversa: *This attack is delivered from the left side to any part of your adversary's body, high or low. (The modern term for this attack would be an attack from quarte) In the classical Italian school the hand is held in the fourth position.*
Quarta, Fourth: *The fourth guard position.*
Rapier: *A sword used for civilian combat that strongly emphasizes the point, dating from the 16th - 17th centuries.*
Retreat: *To move backwards.*
Riposte: *An attack after a parry performed in dui tempi.*
Roversi or roverso: *These attacks are the same as the mandritti except they are made from the left side instead of the right.*
Seconda, Second: *The second guard position.*
Sgualembrato: *An oblique downwards motion attack.*
Sidesword: *A type of sword used for civilain combat in the 16th century. The name of this type of sword is spada da lato in Italin and is synonymous with the spada da filo.*
Slope Pace: *An angular step forward to the right or the left.*
Spada: *A sword*
Stance: *How one stands when preparing for sword combat.*
Stesso Tempo: *Single time. Term used in conjunction with counterattacks where the defense and offense are done at the same time.*
Stoccata: *This attack is made under the blade, hand or dagger. The hand is typically held in half pronation, although it may be held in other positions. This attack is normally made to the belly. In the classical Italian school the hand will be in second or second in third or third position.*
Stramazzone: *This is a slicing or cutting blow made with the point/tip of the sword. Called a* tramazzone *by Marozzo.*
Stringering: *Keeping contact with your adversary's blade with your own blade.*
Tempo: *Time or timing.*
Terza, Third: *The third guard position.*
Thrust: *A thrust is an attack made with the point of the weapon.*
Tondo: *A circular cut delivered horizontally.*
Training: *Formalized instruction used to teach specific technique.*
Tramazzone: *See stramazzone.*
Traverse: *A step to the side.*
Void: *To dodge your opponent's blade. A type of void is the volte which is a specialized foot movement to avoid a thrust. The movement is performed by counter thrusting at your opponent with your right foot foremost and while thrusting to step behind and forward of your right foot with your left. This move will turn your chest away to the left from your opponent and if performed correctly will show your back to them.*
Volte: *See* incartata.
Ward: *See guard.*

Bibliography

Primary Sources

Agrippa, Camillo
Trattato do scientia d'arme, con un dialogo di filosofia, di Camillo Agrippa, Milanese. 1553.

Capo Ferro, Ridolfo
Gran Similacro dell'arte e dell uso Scherma di Ridolfo Capo Ferro du Cagli, Maestro dell ecclesa natione Alemanna, nell enclita citta si Siena. 1610.

dall'Agocchie, Giovanni
Dell'arte di Scrimia. 1572.

De Caranza, Jeronimo
De la filosofia de las armas, de su destreza y de la agresion y defension Christiana. Lucifero Fano, 1569.

Didier, Henry de Saint
Tract Containing Secrets of the First Book on the Single Sword... 1573

Di Grassi, Giacomo
Giacomo di Grassi, his true arte of defence... 1594.

Fabris, Salvator
Della vera practica e scientia d'armi. 1624.

Fabris, Salvator
Fencing: On the Science of Arms. A translation of De Lo Schermo, *by A.F. Johnson, Edited by Joshua Pendragon. In Progress.*

Froissart, Jean
Chronicles, Book III, Translated by Geoffrey Brereton.

G.A.
Pallas Armata. London. 1639.

Lovino, G.A.
Traite d'Escrime, 1580

Manciolino, Di Antonio
Bolognese, opera nova dove sono tutti li documti e vantaggi che si ponno havere ne mestier de l'armi d'agni sorte, novemente correcta et stampata. 1531.

Marozzo, Achille
Opera nova di achille Marozzo, Bolognese, Maestro Generale de l'arte de l'armi. 1536.

Saviolo, Vincento
His practise, in two books; the first intreating the use of the rapier and dagger, the second of honour and honourable quarrels. 1595.

Silver, George
Paradoxes of Defence. 1599.

Swetnam, Joseph
The Schoole of the Noble and Worthy Science of Defence. 1617.

Secondary Sources

Anglo, Sydney
The Martial Arts of Renaissance Europe. Yale University Press. 2000.

Aylward, J.D.
The English Master of Arms. Routeledge & Paul Kegan, London, 1956.

Baldick, Robert
The Duel. 1965. C. N. Porter.

Barbasetti, Luigi
The Art of the Foil. E.P. Dutton & Co, Inc. 1960.

Berry, Herbert
The Noble Science: A study and transcription of Sloane Ms. 2530, papers of the Masters of Defence of London, Temp. Henry VIII to 1590. Associated University Presses, Inc. 1991

Billacois, Francois (Edited and Translated by Trista Selous)
The Duel: Its Rise and Fall in Early Modern France. Yale University Press, 1990.

Bryson, Frederick R.
The Sixteenth-Century Italian Duel, A Study in Renaissance Social History. The University of Chicago Press.

Castle, Egerton
Schools and Masters of Fence. George Bull & Sons, 1892.

Clephan, R. Coltman
The Medieval Tournament, Methuen & Co, Ltd., 1919. Reprinted by Dover, 1995

Gaugler, William M.
The History of Fencing: Foundations of Modern European Swordplay. Laureate Press. 1998,

Gaugler, William
The Science of Fencing. Laureate Press, 1997.

Gelli, Jacopo
L'Arte Dell'Armi in Italia. Istituto Italiano D'Arte Grafiche. 1906.

Greer, John Michael
Academy of the Sword: A Renaissance Manual of Hermetic Swordsmanship by Gerard Thibault d'Anvers. Part One: Philosophy and Practice. Fir Mountain Press 1988.

Hutton, Alfred
The Sword and the Centuries. C. E. Tuttle Co, 1973.
Old Sword Play. B. Westermann, 1893.

Kiernan, V. G.
The Duel in European History. Oxford University Press. 1988.

Knight, Bernard
Some Medicolegal Aspects of Stab Wounds. Legal Medicine Annual. 1976.
Morton, E.D.
A-Z of Fencing. MacDonald Queen Anne Press, London.

Norman, A.V.B.
The Rapier and the small-sword, 1460-1820. 1980. Arno Press.

Rapisardi, Giovanni
The Teachings of Marozzo.
http://jan.ucc.nau.edu/~wew/other/gr/. April 1999.

Sabine, Lorenzo
Notes on Duels and Duelling. 1855. Cosby, Nichols & Co.

Szabo, Lorenzo
Fencing and the Master. Franklin Printing House, Budapest. 1977.

Turner, Craig and Tony Soper
Methods and Practice of Elizabethan Swordplay. 1990

Wise, Arthur
The History and Art of Personal Combat. Hugh Evelyn Ltd. 1971

Index

I.33, Royal Armouries Manuscript, 20, 22
Advancing step, 55-6, 155, 161
Agrippa, Camillo, 3, 35, 49-50, 126, 133
Altoni, Francesco, 41
American Fencing Supply (CA), 151, 160
Anglo, Sydney, 2
Angotti, Laura, 160
Armour, 19-20, 22
Arms & Armor (MN), 22, 31-2, 34-6, 38, 160
Assault, 161
Association for Historical Fencing, 53, 154
Attacks, 155-6
With a buckler, 142
With a cape, 140
With case of rapiers, 145-149
With opposition, 100-1
Single Rapier, 85-132
Authenticity, 151
Axioms, William Wilson's, 54, 79, 85, 95
Balance, weapon, 26, 158
Bardi, Nepo, 3, 41
Beat, 105
With dagger, 134
With cloak, 140
Bind, 74, 92, 96, 99-101, 105
With case of rapiers, 147
With cloak, 140
With dagger, 134
Blades, reproduction weapons, 151
Blades, changing of (historical), 21
Blades, development of, 22, 25, 29
Blair, Claude, 19-20
Bonetti, Rocco, 4, 13
Bouting, 157
Buckler, 44-48, 133, 143-4, 161
Button, 28-9
Caizo, fencing master, 10-11
Cape, used as a blocking device, 12, 133, 140-142
Capo Ferro, Ridolfo, 4, 53-6, 63, 66-9, 82, 83, 84-7, 89, 94, 102, 108-9, 112
Caranza, Hieronimo de, 3
Cartel, 11
CAS Iberia, 151
Case of swords, 145-149
Castle, Edgerton, 2-3
Cavatione or Cavare, 102-103, 161
Chabot, Guy de, 10-11
Chastaigneraye, duel of, 10-11
Chicago Swordplay Guild, 154
Chivalry Bookshelf, 160
Chivalry Sports (AZ), 160
Christian I, 32
Circular paces, 155
Civilian swordsmanship, 1, 3, 10-12, 19-21, 133
Claymore, 25
Cleveland Museum of Art, 24
Cloak (see *cape*)
Code Duello, 12
Compass Pace, 55, 61
Corogne, Sir John de, 9-10
Counter attack, 73, 91-2, 161
With dagger, in Fourth, 139
Countra tempo, 161
Crooked Pace, 89
Cross, 21, 25, 28-9
Cup hilt, 21, 37
Cutting, 49, 79-81, 95-99, 135, 156-7, 161
Defense using a cloak, 140
Dagger, 12, 30, 41, 53, 75, 133-139, 161
Parrying with, 134, 137
Dagger sweep, 134
Dall'Agocchie, Giovanni, 3, 41, 49, 86
Darkwood Armoury (FL), 24, 26, 28, 31, 33, 37, 150-1, 160
Debile / Debole (see *Foible*)
De lo Schermo, (see *Fabris*)
Defense, 72-82, 153, 155-6
(see also *fencing double*, *dagger*, *cape*, *buckler*, *case of swords*, .xxx)
Deflecting
With buckler, 72, 144
With a dagger, 72, 135
With the hand, 72, 76-8, 88, 96, 156
Del Tin Armi Antiche (Italy), 21, 36, 151
Di Grassi, Giacomo, 4, 49, 56, 58, 60-1, 64, 72-3, 75, 79, 85, 89, 95, 112, 124, 134, 140, 142, 145, 149, 158
Illustrations, 4, 58, 73, 140
Didier, Henry Sainct, 4, 71, 124-125, 158
Disarms, 117-124
Disengage, 90, 102-3
With a dagger, 136, 138
Distance, 83-4, 153
Double time, 72, 102, 155-6
Doublet, 53, 150-1
Drill, 127-129, 148, 153, 156
Attacks in Opposition, 100-1
Beat, 105-106
Disengage, 103-104
Feints, 113-114
Footwork, 59, 62-3, 71
Grappling, 116-124
Hand parries, 76
Integration, 126-129
Left-Handed opponent, 110
Parries, 80
Developing the Thrust, 89
Developing the Cut, 96-99
With buckler, 144
With case of rapiers, 146-8
With cloak, 141-2
With dagger, 135-9
Duel, 1, 7-17, 148, 161
Def. 7
Dui tempi (see *double time*)
Dusak, 4
Enarmes, 24, 27-9
Epee, blades from, 151
Equipment, 25-6, 31, 53, 150, 156
Espada robera, 19, 25
Espee (see *sword* or *rapier*)
Estoc (see *tuck*)
Etiquette, 156
Etrangues, Sieur de, 11-12
Fabris, Salvatore. 53-4, 65-70, 72, 75, 79, 82, 84, 85, 87, 97, 102, 115, 126, 133
False edge, 11, 27, 29, 42, 156
False distance, 85
Feint, 95, 112-114, 161
Fencing, Historical, 1-4
Fencing mask, 150-1

Fencing, Modern, 1, 55
Fendente, 42-3, 86, 97, 156, 161
Fighting Double (two handed), 53, 72, 133-144
Finda (see *feint*)
Finger rings, 23
Fir Mountain Press (WA), 160
First Position (see also *guards*), 50, 65-6, 70, 77, 80-1, 87, 91, 107-8, 114, 155, 161
With case of rapiers, 146, 147
With dagger, 135, 139
FISAS, 154
Foible, 27, 29, 72-3, 99, 102, 108, 142
Foil, blades from, 151
Footwear, 150-1
Footwork, 44, 55-63, 153, 155, 157
(see also advancing step, slope pace, traversing step, circular pace, compass step, pass)
Forte, 27, 29, 72-3, 80, 108
Fourth position (see also *guards*), 50, 65, 69-70, 73, 75, 81, 87, 92, 103, 105-6, 107-8, 154
Freifechter, die, 154
Froissart, Jean de. 9-10
Fuller, 25, 27
Gaining the sword, 74
Gaugler, William, 41
Gauntlets, 25, 150-1
Giganti, Nicoletto, 87
Glossary, 161
Gorget, 150-1
Gran Simulacrum (see *Capo Ferro*)
Grappling, 115-124, 135, 161
Graves, Dennis, 73, 160
Grip, 27, 29
Gripping the weapon, 64, 134
Grips (see *grappling*)
Gris, James le, 9-10
Guards, 45-8, 50, 53, 66-9, 161
With the dagger, 134
Guardia alta, 47, 161
Guardia di Becca Casa, 44
Guardia di chiamata a basso, 161
Guardia di dentro, 161
Guardia di fuori, 161
Guardia di faccia, 46
Guardia di testi, 47
Half pace, 58, 138
Hamlet, 15-17
Hand, deflecting with, 76-8, 80, 88, 96, 129, 156
Hand, Stephen, 148, 154
Handle (see *grip*)
Helmet, fencing, 150-1
Henri II, (of France), 10-11
Henri III, (of France), 11-12
Henri IV, (of France), 12
Hick, Steve, 158
Hilt, development of, 23-25, 27
Hilt, striking with
His Practice... (see *Saviolo*)
His True Arte of Defence (see *di Grassi*)
Honor, as a reason for a duel, 7, 12-13, 53
Imbroccata, 49, 76, 86, 94, 101, 155-6, 161
Incartata, 63, 101155-6, 161
Inside line (for the thrust), 72
Instructor, 148, 153-4
Italian School, 1
Jacket, fencing, 150-1
Judicial Duels, 7-17
Knuckle bow, 28
Left-Hander, 107,
Length, (of weapons), 20, 25, 31, 37, 41, 158-9
Lessons, group or individual, 152, 155-7
Liberi, Fiore dei, 3
Liechtenauer, Johannes, 4
Longsword, 21-2
Lovino, 115
Luca, Guido Antonio di, 41
Lunge, 89, 92, 101, 105, 142, 152, 156, 161
Lupo-Sinclair, Maestro Andrea, 41, 148
Macdonald, Maestro Paul, 148, 154, 160
Manciolino, Antonio, 3-4, 41, 86, 133
Mandritta or *Mandritti*, 42, 80, 86, 106, 155, 157, 161
Manuals, Fencing, 3
Marozzo, Achille, 2-4, 12, 14, 24, 35, 40—50, 107, 115, 126, 149
Martinez, Maestro Jeanette Acosta-Martinez, 148, 154
Martinez, Maestro Ramon, 3, 148, 154
Marxbrüder, 2
Marziale, Marco, 23
Masters, Fencing, 1, 12, 161
(see Cappo Ferro, di Grassi, Mancialino, Silver, Saviolo, Agrippa)
Measure, 74, 77, 83-4, 161
Mele, Greg, 154
Mental aspects of the fight, 83-4, 126, 148
Mezzo, 27, 29, 73-4,
Metropolitan Museum of Art, NY, 159
Meyer, Joachim, 4
Middle (see *mezzo*)
Military swordsmanship, 1, 19-20, 23, 133
Misura (see *measure*)
Montante, 42-3, 97, 156, 161
Monte, Pietro. 149
Muscle memory, 148
Museum Replicas, Ltd. (GA), 160
Navarez, Pacheco de, 3
Norman, A.V.B, 19-20, 23
Oakshott, Ewart, 19-23
Offhand (see *fighting double*)
Open Assault, 148, 149
Opera Nova (see *Manciolino*)
Outside line (for the thrust), 72
Pallas Armata, *104, 107, 126, 161*
Parry or Parare, 72-76, 79, 95, 161
With case of rapiers, 146-7
With a dagger, 134, 137, 139
Pass or passing step, 55, 57, 155, 161
With a dagger, 134
Per batter la spada (see *beat*)
Philip IV, 8-9, 12
Play, as a training tool, 2, 153
Poldi Pezzoli, Italy, 18, 35
Polearms, 3, 40
Pommel, 28-9, 117
Port, 28-9
Porta di Ferro, 44-5
Practice, 148, 155-6
Prima first (see *First Position*)
Prize playing, 3
Pugliese, Patri, 158-9, 160
Pugn9ale (see *dagger*)
Punta Riversa, 49, 86, 155-6, 161
Quarta (see *Fourth Position*)
Quélus, 11-12
Quillion (see *Cross*)
Rapier
Definitions, 19, 25, 161
Development of, 1,
Properties of, 158-9
Rector, Mark, 154

Reproductions, quality of, 25, 31, 53, 159
Research, techniques, 158-9
Retreat (step), 55-6, 155, 161
Reverse, 42, 86, 155, 157, 161
Ricasso, 28-9, 158
Ridoppo, 42-3, 86, 156, 161
Riposte, 79
Royal Armouries, Leeds, 21, 22, 23
Roversi or *roverso* (see *reverse*)
Safety, stress on, 26, 125, 151, 159
Salute, 156
Saviolo, Vincentio, 1, 7-8, 12, 14, 61, 76, 126, 133-4, 158
SCA, 148
Schlager, blades from, 151
Schola Saint George, 148, 154
Schools and Masters of Defence (see *Castle, Edgerton*)
Schools, Fencing, 2-3, 160
Second Position (see also *guards*), 50, 65, 67, 70, 75, 77, 81, 87, 91-2, 96, 98, 106, 107-8, 112, 155, 161
  With cloak, 142
  With dagger, 135
Sgualembrato, 42-3, 80, 86, 97-98, 156, 161
Shakespeare, William, 13, 15-17
Shoes, period, 150-1
"Short" sword, 13, 19
Silver, George, 13, 19, 22, 158
Sidesword, 20-1, 24-5, 40-50, 133, 161
Single rapier, attacks with
Single rapier, defenses with
Single time, 72, 90, 155, 157, 161
Slips, 156
Slope pace, 55, 60, 88, 155, 161
Smallsword, 20
Society for Creative Anachronism (See *SCA*)
Spada da filo, 41
Spada da latta (see *sidesword*)
Spada solo (see also *single rapier*), 133
Stance, 54-56
  With buckler, 143
  With case of rapiers, 145
  With a dagger, 134
Steps (see *footwork*)
Stesso tempo (see *Single time*)
Stoccata, 41, 49, 76, 86, 92, 155-6, 161
Stoccata School of Defence, 154
Stramazzone, 42, 86, 95, 141, 157, 161
Strewton, Walter de, 2
Strong (see *forte*)
Swept hilt, 19, 21, 31
Swetnam, Joseph, 126
Sword
  development of, 4, 19-24
  medieval, 20-1
Talhoffer, Hans. 8, 20
Tang, 27
Targets, thrusting, 72
Tattershall Arms (AZ), 160
Tattershall School of Defense, 53, 154
Teaching, 53, 153-4
Technique, as a concept, 20, 148, 153,
Tempo (see *timing*)
Terza (see *Third Position*)
Third Position, 50, 56, 65, 68, 70, 78, 80, 87-8, 90-3, 96, 98-9, 103, 105, 107-8, 112, 155, 161
  With buckler, 144
  With case of rapiers, 146, 147
  With the dagger, 136, 139
Thrust, against a buckler, 144
Thrust, dagger, 134, 137, 138
Thrust, sword, 41, 49, 87-93, 141, 155-7
  Faster than the cut, 85-6
  Depth needed to kill, 87
Timing, 84, 153, 161
Tondo, 42-3, 80, 86, 97, 156, 161
Training, 153-7, 161
Tramazzone (see *Stramazzone*)
Trial by Combat, 2, 8
Triplette Competition Arms (NC), 160
True Edge, 27, 29, 41, 86, 156
Traversing step, 55, 61, 155, 161
  With a dagger, 138
Triplette Arms, 151
True distance, 85
Tuck, 20, 24
Two-sword (see *Case of swords*)
Vadi, Filipo, 12
Valentine, Eric, 19
Vasa, Gustav, 34
Vigianni, xxx, 4
Vivionne, Francois de, 10-1
Voiding, 54, 82, 156, 161
Volte (see *Incartata*)
Wallace Collection, London, 24, 36, 37
Ward (see *guard*)
Warm-up exercises, 153
Weak (see *foible*)
Weights, 25, 32, 37, 159
"Winning" in training, 153
Worke for Cutlers (anonymous), 24, 30
Wrestling (see *guard*)